"This world has beauty and delight as well as brokenness and pain. As joy and sorrow mingle together, we long for words to express both our cries for deliverance and our songs of rejoicing. Dane Ortlund's new devotional, *In the Lord I Take Refuge*, invites us to commune with God through the words of the Psalms. These encouraging daily reflections will guide your prayers, refresh your heart, and strengthen your soul as you walk with God in the ups and downs of life."

Melissa Kruger, Director of Women's Initiatives, The Gospel Coalition; author, *Growing Together*

"This devotional book beautifully reminds us that we need no better devotional material than the Psalms themselves. Dane Ortlund is pointing the way, serving as a wise and restrained guide to help us enter and join the prayers and praises of the psalter. He never fails to point us to Christ, the Savior who shines through the Psalms from beginning to end."

Kathleen Nielson, author; speaker; Senior Adviser, The Gospel Coalition

"This is a book to keep by your bed, to begin or end each day feeding on these words God has given to us to pray and sing back to him. Dane's brief insights into each psalm help us to bridge the gap between the psalmist's time and our own, between his battles, questions, joys, desires, and laments and our own, leading us to love and worship."

Nancy Guthrie, Bible teacher; author, *Even Better than Eden*

"Here it is! A devotional book based on the Bible's own devotional book. It is an idea so obvious we may have missed it because—unlike our spiritual forefathers, who often read through the book of Psalms every week—we have allowed ourselves to be obsessed with the short term and the quick fix and to become devoted to the latest thing. But now the author whose *Gentle and Lowly* has helped so many to see Christ more clearly takes us gently by the hand to Jesus's own devotional manual, the prayer book he loved, and the blueprint for his own life and ministry, and leads us to him all over again, day after day. Thank you, Dane Ortlund, for more treasure!"

Sinclair B. Ferguson, Chancellor's Professor of Systematic Theology, Reformed Theological Seminary; Teaching Fellow, Ligonier Ministries

"A book like this is hard to find: not a commentary on the Psalms but a brief model, from a trusted voice, on how to meditate on them. Come to be fed by Dane's meditations and learn how to meditate for yourself; to take a word or phrase in context and linger over it to obtain food, in Christ, for your soul; and to enrich and deepen your own communion with Christ in the Bible's songbook. Take up and feed."

David Mathis, Executive Editor and Senior Teacher, Desiring God; Pastor, Cities Church, Saint Paul, Minnesota; author, *Habits of Grace*

IN THE
LORD
I TAKE
REFUGE

IN THE
LORD
I TAKE
REFUGE

150 Daily Devotions through the Psalms

Dane Ortlund

WHEATON, ILLINOIS

INTRODUCTION

The Psalms are unlike any other portion of Scripture. This is the one book of the Bible written to God. We are taught in many other places in Scripture how to pray. Jesus gave us the Lord's Prayer (Matt. 6:5–15). Paul tells us to "pray without ceasing" (1 Thess. 5:17). But the Psalms are themselves prayers.

In this way the Psalms are uniquely suited to foster communion with God. The Psalms give voice to our hearts. The wide range of human feeling is here given concrete expression. We are given language to address God with thanks and praise, but also with our feelings of desolation or despair or overwhelming guilt because of our sin.

And through it all we see the Savior walking through the Psalms. He is the one who embodies and fulfills all that we find in this book. He gives us supreme reason to give thanks and praise to God (Ps. 107:1). He is the one who experienced true desolation and despair, enduring separation from God so that his people never will (Ps. 22:1–2). Jesus rinses us clean through his atoning work and assures us that he has wiped away all the guilt of our sin.

These profound and precious truths have led to the creation of *In the Lord I Take Refuge*. The purpose of this book is to foster communion with God amid all the ups and downs of daily life in this fallen world. The devotional content is meant to facilitate fellowship with God in the words of the Psalms. The devotionals are therefore intended not to replace deep engagement with the Psalms but rather to help the reader move deeply into this book of the Bible—and thereby to move deeply into communion with the triune God. Whether one reads through this volume straight through, day by day, or instead opens it in a less programmatic manner, the devotionals will consistently draw the reader's eye back to the words of the Psalms themselves, leading to reflection and prayer.

May you find consolation and comfort, assurance and grace, and indeed the very Savior himself as you ponder God and his presence in your life through *In the Lord I Take Refuge*.

BOOK ONE

PSALM 1

1   Blessed is the man
        who walks not in the counsel of the wicked,
    nor stands in the way of sinners,
        nor sits in the seat of scoffers;
2   but his delight is in the law of the LORD,
        and on his law he meditates day and night.

3   He is like a tree
        planted by streams of water
    that yields its fruit in its season,
        and its leaf does not wither.
    In all that he does, he prospers.
4   The wicked are not so,
        but are like chaff that the wind drives away.

5   Therefore the wicked will not stand in the judgment,
        nor sinners in the congregation of the righteous;
6   for the LORD knows the way of the righteous,
        but the way of the wicked will perish.

∽

The first psalm serves as the gateway to the entire book of Psalms, stressing that those who would worship God genuinely must embrace his Law (or Torah)—that is, his covenant instruction founded on his redeeming grace. This psalm addresses topics found also in the Bible's wisdom literature and makes them the subject of song. When we joyfully sing this psalm, its values become ours. We are changed.

In a sustained contrast, Psalm 1 reminds us that in the end there are only two ways to live. And whatever else happens in our lives today, the crucial, bottom-line question is: which of the two ways described in this psalm will we embrace? Beneath the never-ending list of "to do's" clamoring for our attention lies the fundamental choice to receive instruction and influence either from God or from fools. Will we listen to the voice of life or to the voices of death? Will we breathe in God's life-giving instruction, sinking deep roots (v. 3), or will we breathe in the empty instruction of those who "will not stand in the judgment" (v. 5)? Will the trials still to come in our lives prove us to be deep-rooted trees, incapable of being blown over, or will they show us to be chaff, blown away by the slightest breeze?

Happily, this psalm and its two ways to live are not a choice between stoic obedience or gleeful disobedience. The first word of the psalm makes clear that true, solid happiness—what the Bible calls "blessedness"—is found in God and his Word. Verse 2 reiterates—"His *delight* is in the law of the LORD." Nothing can compare with the blessedness—the fruitfulness, the flourishing, the prospering, the delightfulness, of a life saturated with the Word of God.

Walk with God. Soak in his Word. Take his yoke upon you (cf. Matt. 11:29). You will be blessed—truly happy, with a happiness the winds of trial cannot blow away.

PSALM 2

1   Why do the nations rage
        and the peoples plot in vain?
2   The kings of the earth set themselves,
        and the rulers take counsel together,
        against the LORD and against his Anointed, saying,
3   "Let us burst their bonds apart
        and cast away their cords from us."

4   He who sits in the heavens laughs;
        the Lord holds them in derision.
5   Then he will speak to them in his wrath,
        and terrify them in his fury, saying,
6   "As for me, I have set my King
        on Zion, my holy hill."

7   I will tell of the decree:
    The LORD said to me, "You are my Son;
        today I have begotten you.
8   Ask of me, and I will make the nations your heritage,
        and the ends of the earth your possession.
9   You shall break them with a rod of iron
        and dash them in pieces like a potter's vessel."

10 Now therefore, O kings, be wise;
        be warned, O rulers of the earth.
11 Serve the LORD with fear,
        and rejoice with trembling.

12   Kiss the Son,
            lest he be angry, and you perish in the way,
            for his wrath is quickly kindled.
        Blessed are all who take refuge in him.

$\wp$

When we as the people of God sing Psalm 2, we remind ourselves of how God made David and his descendants to be kings, tasked with carrying out God's redemptive purposes in the world. In the face of overwhelming opposition, this psalm exults in the promises made to the Davidic king at his coronation. With its prospect of a worldwide rule for the house of David, this psalm also looks to the future, when David's ultimate heir, the Messiah, would indeed accomplish this.

With the coming of the Messiah, this psalm's triumphant portrait of the Davidic throne takes on heightened significance and finds its ultimate meaning. Believers today are the heirs of this psalm, and its promises come to rest on the worldwide church and its faith in the true and final Davidic heir, Jesus. Those who take refuge in him have found the only truly safe place in this broken world. Those who persist in resisting God and his rule, even if they are powerful "rulers of the earth," will be finally defied and justly destroyed.

Despite whatever tumults rock our lives today, David's greatest son, Jesus himself, has been installed as the ruler of the world. One day this kingship will break open in universal acknowledgment and the universal execution of perfect justice. For now, we can go forth in the glad assurance that in Jesus we will one day leave behind forever the futility of the present. Every injustice in our lives will be undone.

Take heart. We are on the right side.

PSALM 3

A Psalm of David, when he fled from Absalom his son.

1 O LORD, how many are my foes!
  Many are rising against me;
2 many are saying of my soul,
  "There is no salvation for him in God."   *Selah*

3 But you, O LORD, are a shield about me,
  my glory, and the lifter of my head.
4 I cried aloud to the LORD,
  and he answered me from his holy hill.   *Selah*

5 I lay down and slept;
  I woke again, for the LORD sustained me.
6 I will not be afraid of many thousands of people
  who have set themselves against me all around.

7 Arise, O LORD!
  Save me, O my God!
For you strike all my enemies on the cheek;
  you break the teeth of the wicked.

8 Salvation belongs to the LORD;
  your blessing be on your people!   *Selah*

This is the first psalm with a title. David wrote this psalm, we are told, as a response to the heart-wrenching experience of being violently pursued by his own son, Absalom (see 2 Samuel 15–16). We see in this psalm how a man of God models genuine faith in the midst of dire circumstances. What must it have been like to be murderously hunted by his own child?

David felt utterly overwhelmed by the sheer weight of opposition: "Many are rising against me" (Ps. 3:1); "many thousands of people . . . have set themselves against me" (v. 6).

What strengthens David, however, is not strength mustered up from within. What stabilizes him is not self-generated optimism. David knows that earthly help is worthless when the tidal waves of life threaten to overwhelm and drown us. Instead he looks to God: "But you, O Lord, are a shield about me" (v. 3). This is the posture of faith. Only in this way does David's internal frenetic anxiety die away so that he can sleep in peace once more (v. 5). Self-divesting trust in God is the channel through which the deliverance and power of God may flow.

What threatens to overwhelm you today? We have an even greater source of calm than David did, for there is one who did not strike God's enemies on the cheek (v. 7) but instead let himself be struck on the cheek. Indeed, he experienced the ultimate rejection, being nailed to a Roman cross. Jesus allowed himself to be truly overwhelmed by his enemies. The result is that believers can be confident that every overwhelming experience they face is from a loving Father to help them.

PSALM 4

To the choirmaster: with stringed instruments. A Psalm of David.

1   Answer me when I call, O God of my righteousness!
        You have given me relief when I was in distress.
        Be gracious to me and hear my prayer!

2   O men, how long shall my honor be turned into shame?
        How long will you love vain words and seek after
            lies?   *Selah*
3   But know that the Lᴏʀᴅ has set apart the godly for
            himself;
        the Lᴏʀᴅ hears when I call to him.

4   Be angry, and do not sin;
        ponder in your own hearts on your beds, and be
            silent.   *Selah*
5   Offer right sacrifices,
        and put your trust in the Lᴏʀᴅ.

6   There are many who say, "Who will show us some
            good?
        Lift up the light of your face upon us, O Lᴏʀᴅ!"
7   You have put more joy in my heart
        than they have when their grain and wine abound.

8   In peace I will both lie down and sleep;
        for you alone, O Lᴏʀᴅ, make me dwell in safety.

This psalm expresses quiet trust amid troubling circumstances, combining the classic psalm categories of "individual lament" and "psalm of confidence." Many take this psalm to be a companion to Psalm 3, because 4:8 seems to echo 3:5. Perhaps the two psalms were meant to be read at the beginning and end of a single day, since the past tense of 3:5 sets Psalm 3 in the morning while the future tense of 4:8 sets Psalm 4 in the evening.

Psalm 4 echoes the feelings of being overwhelmed that are expressed in the previous psalm. Here, however, David is in anguish not simply because of overwhelming opposition but because of the slander and taunting of his enemies. This is the pain not only of fear but of shame as well (v. 2).

David is expressing the battle that rages within our heart at night as we lay our head down on the pillow. On one side is stacked up all of the clamoring accusations and misunderstandings and painful words of the day—of actual people in our lives or of demonic attack or of our own fallen minds. On the other side is the Lord. Both beckon to us; both invite us to listen. In the darkness of that moment, David makes up his mind: he will trust in the Lord (v. 5). The result? A greater joy than any material prosperity could ever provide (v. 7); a peace that supplies contented sleep (v. 8).

Trust in the Lord. He has set you apart for himself (v. 3). You are his. You have been united to his Son, and the sufferings of this present age can only heighten your future glory and joy (Rom. 8:18; 2 Cor. 4:16–18). Tonight, you may go to bed in peace. You could not be more secure.

PSALM 5

To the choirmaster: for the flutes. A Psalm of David.

1 Give ear to my words, O LORD;
    consider my groaning.
2 Give attention to the sound of my cry,
    my King and my God,
    for to you do I pray.
3 O LORD, in the morning you hear my voice;
    in the morning I prepare a sacrifice for you and
        watch.

4 For you are not a God who delights in wickedness;
    evil may not dwell with you.
5 The boastful shall not stand before your eyes;
    you hate all evildoers.
6 You destroy those who speak lies;
    the LORD abhors the bloodthirsty and deceitful man.

7 But I, through the abundance of your steadfast love,
    will enter your house.
I will bow down toward your holy temple
    in the fear of you.
8 Lead me, O LORD, in your righteousness
    because of my enemies;
    make your way straight before me.

9 For there is no truth in their mouth;
    their inmost self is destruction;

their throat is an open grave;
 they flatter with their tongue.
10 Make them bear their guilt, O God;
 let them fall by their own counsels;
 because of the abundance of their transgressions cast
   them out,
 for they have rebelled against you.

11 But let all who take refuge in you rejoice;
 let them ever sing for joy,
 and spread your protection over them,
  that those who love your name may exult in you.
12 For you bless the righteous, O LORD;
 you cover him with favor as with a shield.

∽

This psalm is another individual lament and is the first instance of a psalm that includes prayers for the personal downfall of one's enemies. Such psalms are not expressions of petty annoyances or insults but are cries to God for justice in the face of bloodthirsty and deceitful persecutors.

This psalm is one of many places in the Bible where we can be greatly encouraged by the sheer earthiness of the Bible. Despite being the religious book of billions, the Christian Scriptures are not abstract or ethereal, disconnected from the visceral emotions and experiences of life in a fallen world. The Bible is concrete, tangible, and rooted in gritty reality. David is "groaning" (v. 1). Disgusted by the deceitful schemes of the wicked, he pleads with God for justice, for a righting of wrongs, for the evil of the wicked to be returned on their own head (v. 10). Such language—even more, such prayer—sounds abrasive to modern ears, immersed as we are in a culture of tolerant niceness. Yet David knows that for God to tolerate wickedness would undermine the very character of God and his righteous purposes for the world.

Content to leave the punishment of all evil in God's hands, David directs his heart elsewhere. He does not let thoughts of evildoers fester in his mind but finally rests in God, his refuge (vv. 11–12), who must do what is right.

And so God did. At the climax of all of human history, God showed us just how concrete and tangible he was willing to become, in the ultimate righting of all wrongs. Refusing to remain abstract or ethereal, the second person of the Trinity became one of us, knowing all of our weaknesses except sin.

Are you groaning today? Your reigning Savior knows what that is like. He too groaned, on a cross, so that every groaning you now experience may result in your ultimate strengthening.

PSALM 6

To the choirmaster: with stringed instruments;
according to The Sheminith. A Psalm of David.

1 O Lᴏʀᴅ, rebuke me not in your anger,
     nor discipline me in your wrath.
2 Be gracious to me, O Lᴏʀᴅ, for I am languishing;
     heal me, O Lᴏʀᴅ, for my bones are troubled.
3 My soul also is greatly troubled.
     But you, O Lᴏʀᴅ—how long?

4 Turn, O Lᴏʀᴅ, deliver my life;
     save me for the sake of your steadfast love.
5 For in death there is no remembrance of you;
     in Sheol who will give you praise?

6 I am weary with my moaning;
     every night I flood my bed with tears;
     I drench my couch with my weeping.
7 My eye wastes away because of grief;
     it grows weak because of all my foes.

8 Depart from me, all you workers of evil,
     for the Lᴏʀᴅ has heard the sound of my weeping.
9 The Lᴏʀᴅ has heard my plea;
     the Lᴏʀᴅ accepts my prayer.
10 All my enemies shall be ashamed and greatly troubled;
     they shall turn back and be put to shame in a
       moment.

5

David is in anguish. He is in the valley. Life is suffocating him, apparently because of interpersonal strife (v. 8). His very soul is in agony (v. 3). But this is a suffering that is physical too, affecting him to his very bones (v. 2). We are given a portrait of David alone on his couch, weeping like a baby. His life has gone into meltdown.

Through it all, to make matters worse, he is keenly aware of his own sin and guilt, as evident from his opening words, in which he asks the Lord to withhold his heavenly rebuke and discipline.

Where does David go in such distress?

"The LORD has heard my plea; the LORD accepts my prayer" (v. 9).

Amid the storm of his life, David looks not out, at his circumstances, nor in, at his own internal resources, but up, to the Lord of mercy. Unloading the burdens of his heart to God in prayer, David does not apply a formula to his pain but rather this: God. When we are brought into the dark valleys of life as we journey through this fallen world, we have, and we need, one thing: God. And we can know that we have the Lord with us, moment by moment, because he sent his own Son to walk through this world's sorrows. He was "a man of sorrows, and acquainted with grief" (Isa. 53:3). And why? So that God could withhold his "anger" and "wrath" (Ps. 6:1) from us despite our deserving it. Bringing our complaints and afflictions to God in Jesus' name, we can know for certain that "the LORD has heard my plea; the LORD accepts my prayer."

PSALM 7

A Shiggaion of David, which he sang to the LORD
concerning the words of Cush, a Benjaminite.

1 O LORD my God, in you do I take refuge;
   save me from all my pursuers and deliver me,

2 lest like a lion they tear my soul apart,
   rending it in pieces, with none to deliver.

3 O LORD my God, if I have done this,
   if there is wrong in my hands,

4 if I have repaid my friend with evil
   or plundered my enemy without cause,

5 let the enemy pursue my soul and overtake it,
   and let him trample my life to the ground
   and lay my glory in the dust.   *Selah*

6 Arise, O LORD, in your anger;
   lift yourself up against the fury of my enemies;
   awake for me; you have appointed a judgment.

7 Let the assembly of the peoples be gathered about you;
   over it return on high.

8 The LORD judges the peoples;
   judge me, O LORD, according to my righteousness
   and according to the integrity that is in me.

9 Oh, let the evil of the wicked come to an end,
   and may you establish the righteous—

you who test the minds and hearts,
O righteous God!
10 My shield is with God,
who saves the upright in heart.
11 God is a righteous judge,
and a God who feels indignation every day.

12 If a man does not repent, God will whet his sword;
he has bent and readied his bow;
13 he has prepared for him his deadly weapons,
making his arrows fiery shafts.
14 Behold, the wicked man conceives evil
and is pregnant with mischief
and gives birth to lies.
15 He makes a pit, digging it out,
and falls into the hole that he has made.
16 His mischief returns upon his own head,
and on his own skull his violence descends.

17 I will give to the LORD the thanks due to his
righteousness,
and I will sing praise to the name of the LORD,
the Most High.

∽

The certainty of a final day of judgment is not meant to be a matter of trembling and anxiety for believers. Instead, it is meant to be a matter of deep consolation. David has been slandered by a man of the tribe of Benjamin—a fellow Israelite is verbally attacking him. Leaders, in particular, know what this feels like, but all believers can testify to times in which they were misunderstood, misrepresented, or otherwise treated unjustly. What does David do?

Note first what he does *not* do. He does not exonerate himself *before others*. He does not explain to others how mistaken this accusation is. Instead, he takes his complaint to God. As he does so, David pleads for divine vindication based on an honest assessment of matters: "The LORD judges the peoples" (v. 8). Liberated from his own need to defend himself, David places judgment solely in the hands of God.

It might seem perplexing that David asks God to judge him according to David's own righteousness (v. 8). But we must understand that David makes clear throughout the Psalms that his only hope of being acquitted before God is God's own mercy ("Have mercy on me, O God, according to your steadfast love," 51:1; "Give ear to my pleas for mercy," 143:1). David is also simply pursuing the truth. Note that in verses 3–5 he asks that he would be assessed accordingly if he is indeed in the wrong. David is not putting on blinders to his own sinfulness; rather, he is asking for truth and objective honesty to be pursued.

Are you misunderstood today? Even if you are sure you are in the right, why not be wronged rather than fight back, even in subtle ways (1 Cor. 6:7)? After all, our Lord Jesus himself was right his whole life yet treated as wrongfully as anyone in human history—"yet he opened not his mouth" (Isa. 53:7). And why? So that for all the times we truly are in the wrong, we can be truly exonerated and acquitted, despite what we actually deserve. Reflecting on this gospel freedom, we are freed from insisting on defending ourselves now.

PSALM 8

To the choirmaster: according to The
Gittith. A Psalm of David.

1 O Lord, our Lord,
  how majestic is your name in all the earth!
 You have set your glory above the heavens.
2   Out of the mouth of babies and infants,
 you have established strength because of your foes,
   to still the enemy and the avenger.

3 When I look at your heavens, the work of your fingers,
   the moon and the stars, which you have set in place,
4 what is man that you are mindful of him,
   and the son of man that you care for him?

5 Yet you have made him a little lower than the heavenly
     beings
   and crowned him with glory and honor.
6 You have given him dominion over the works of your
     hands;
   you have put all things under his feet,
7 all sheep and oxen,
   and also the beasts of the field,
8 the birds of the heavens, and the fish of the sea,
   whatever passes along the paths of the seas.

9 O Lord, our Lord,
   how majestic is your name in all the earth!

The Bible restores our human dignity, scarred but not lost in the fall. Alluding to the opening chapters of Genesis, where mankind is called to exercise dominion over the created order, David brings us to praise God for the remarkable care he has entrusted to us. He is the God of the heavens, having placed the stars in their orbits, and yet he has entrusted to humanity the care of the earth. When he speaks of our being crowned "with glory and honor" (v. 5), David speaks of the image of God bestowed upon every human.

The references to "foes," "enemy," and "avenger" in the course of praising God for his creation remind us that there was also a fall (v. 2; Gen. 3:1–24). Yet despite our fall into sin, God still dignifies his people as the stewards of his creation (Ps. 8:5–8; Gen. 1:28–31).

And yet we need a Savior to overcome not only personal sin but also the fallen condition of the creation (Gen. 3:15, 18–19). By quoting this psalm, the writer of the book of Hebrews later clarifies that Christ, our Savior, is the perfect representation of the humanity described in this psalm (Heb. 2:6–8).

The One through whom the world was created (John 1:3; Heb. 1:2) came to restore the image marred at the fall. Verses 1 and 9 of Psalm 8 not only serve as bookends for the psalm; they also anticipate the end of all things, when Christ's enemies will be made a footstool for his feet and his name will be majestic through all the earth (Eph. 1:22).

PSALM 9

*To the choirmaster: according to
Muth-labben. A Psalm of David.*

1 I will give thanks to the LORD with my whole heart;
    I will recount all of your wonderful deeds.
2 I will be glad and exult in you;
    I will sing praise to your name, O Most High.

3 When my enemies turn back,
    they stumble and perish before your presence.
4 For you have maintained my just cause;
    you have sat on the throne, giving righteous
        judgment.

5 You have rebuked the nations; you have made the
        wicked perish;
    you have blotted out their name forever and ever.
6 The enemy came to an end in everlasting ruins;
    their cities you rooted out;
    the very memory of them has perished.

7 But the LORD sits enthroned forever;
    he has established his throne for justice,
8 and he judges the world with righteousness;
    he judges the peoples with uprightness.

9 The LORD is a stronghold for the oppressed,
    a stronghold in times of trouble.

10 And those who know your name put their trust in you,
    for you, O Lord, have not forsaken those who seek
        you.

11 Sing praises to the Lord, who sits enthroned in Zion!
    Tell among the peoples his deeds!
12 For he who avenges blood is mindful of them;
    he does not forget the cry of the afflicted.

13 Be gracious to me, O Lord!
    See my affliction from those who hate me,
    O you who lift me up from the gates of death,
14 that I may recount all your praises,
        that in the gates of the daughter of Zion
        I may rejoice in your salvation.

15 The nations have sunk in the pit that they made;
    in the net that they hid, their own foot has been
        caught.
16 The Lord has made himself known; he has executed
        judgment;
    the wicked are snared in the work of their own
        hands. *Higgaion. Selah*

17 The wicked shall return to Sheol,
    all the nations that forget God.

18 For the needy shall not always be forgotten,
    and the hope of the poor shall not perish forever.

19 Arise, O Lord! Let not man prevail;
    let the nations be judged before you!

20   Put them in fear, O LORD!

     Let the nations know that they are but men!   *Selah*

∽

David writes this psalm in the midst of international strife and tumult—not unlike our own days in the twenty-first century. While many believers around the world today live in relative political stability, many others, like those in Israel in David's time, do not. The news headlines each morning remind us of the unrest of the world and of the anxiety that accompanies such unrest.

"But the LORD sits enthroned forever; he has established his throne for justice, and he judges the world with righteousness" (vv. 7–8). God is never caught by surprise amid global upheaval and strife. He is never perplexed or left groping for solutions. He reigns. And one day, all that is done in this stormy world will be brought into the light and into judgment.

Our part is to trust him. David does not take a posture of haughty superiority when he considers the godlessness of the nations. Rather, he remembers his own need: "Be gracious to me, O LORD!" (v. 13). David does not deserve God's help; it is a matter of God being "gracious." David lifts his eyes, and ours, beyond the walls of this life into the unending world of the next life—"The needy shall not always be forgotten, and the hope of the poor shall not perish forever" (v. 18). Indeed, it is only the needy who cry out for God's help. Our need is all we bring. As he delivers us in times of adversity and in our ultimate need— the need for saving mercy from him, which has been granted to us in Christ—we sing with David and rejoice in God's saving mercy (v. 14).

PSALM 10

1   Why, O Lord, do you stand far away?
     Why do you hide yourself in times of trouble?

2   In arrogance the wicked hotly pursue the poor;
     let them be caught in the schemes that they have
       devised.
3   For the wicked boasts of the desires of his soul,
     and the one greedy for gain curses and renounces
       the Lord.
4   In the pride of his face the wicked does not seek him;
     all his thoughts are, "There is no God."
5   His ways prosper at all times;
     your judgments are on high, out of his sight;
     as for all his foes, he puffs at them.
6   He says in his heart, "I shall not be moved;
     throughout all generations I shall not meet adversity."
7   His mouth is filled with cursing and deceit and
       oppression;
     under his tongue are mischief and iniquity.
8   He sits in ambush in the villages;
     in hiding places he murders the innocent.
    His eyes stealthily watch for the helpless;
9   he lurks in ambush like a lion in his thicket;
   he lurks that he may seize the poor;
     he seizes the poor when he draws him into his net.
10 The helpless are crushed, sink down,
     and fall by his might.

11 He says in his heart, "God has forgotten,
        he has hidden his face, he will never see it."

12 Arise, O LORD; O God, lift up your hand;
        forget not the afflicted.
13 Why does the wicked renounce God
        and say in his heart, "You will not call to account"?
14 But you do see, for you note mischief and vexation,
        that you may take it into your hands;
    to you the helpless commits himself;
        you have been the helper of the fatherless.
15 Break the arm of the wicked and evildoer;
        call his wickedness to account till you find none.

16 The LORD is king forever and ever;
        the nations perish from his land.
17 O LORD, you hear the desire of the afflicted;
        you will strengthen their heart; you will incline your
            ear
18 to do justice to the fatherless and the oppressed,
        so that man who is of the earth may strike terror no
            more.

༄

The tone of Psalm 10 turns sharply from the psalms that have
come just before. Here we find the psalmist distraught at
the victimization of the helpless. And this cruelty seems to come
not at the hand of foreign nations but at the hands of fellow
Israelites—fellow members of the people of God.

The sight of such evil carried out against fellow humans—fellow members of God's people—can easily cause deep cynicism

33

and emotional fatigue. How does one persevere in the face of horrors done to others, especially horrors perpetrated by those who ought to have been the kindest? Everything in us screams out for justice.

David feels the same way, but he realizes that "you [the Lord] do see, for you note mischief and vexation, that you may take it into your hands" (v. 14). The Lord will "do justice to the fatherless and the oppressed" (v. 18). God will, one day, right all wrongs, straighten out all that is bent, and rinse this world clean of all injustice.

And how do we know this? Because in the middle of human history God proved the lengths to which he was willing to go to undo injustice. He sent his own Son, the one man who was ever truly just, to go to a cross and swallow all of the injustice of all of those who would simply trust in him. Does this mean we can overlook injustices committed against the helpless today? On the contrary—it means that we are freshly empowered and motivated to fight the horrors of this world, knowing that the horror of our own sin has been justly wiped away, by sheer grace, in the work of Christ, received by faith.

PSALM 11

To the choirmaster. Of David.

1 In the LORD I take refuge;
how can you say to my soul,
  "Flee like a bird to your mountain,
2 for behold, the wicked bend the bow;
    they have fitted their arrow to the string
    to shoot in the dark at the upright in heart;
3 if the foundations are destroyed,
  what can the righteous do?"

4 The LORD is in his holy temple;
  the LORD's throne is in heaven;
  his eyes see, his eyelids test the children of man.
5 The LORD tests the righteous,
  but his soul hates the wicked and the one who loves
    violence.
6 Let him rain coals on the wicked;
  fire and sulfur and a scorching wind shall be the
    portion of their cup.
7 For the LORD is righteous;
he loves righteous deeds;
  the upright shall behold his face.

5

Those who walk with God experience a range of trials, a few of which are mentioned in this psalm. They are told to flee to a mountain (v. 1), implying that they are vulnerable and unprotected. They are shot at (v. 2), implying that they are the target of attacks, such as verbal ostracism. But God "is in his holy temple," and "his eyes see" (v. 4). Nothing goes unnoticed by the Lord of heaven. He will bring justice one day. And on that day, "the upright shall behold his face" (v. 7). Have you considered this promise? Have you taken it down deep into your soul?

What does this promise mean? The term "upright" refers not to the sinlessly perfect but to those who operate out of a basic trust in God, knowing their imperfections; those who, like God, love righteousness and hate wickedness (v. 7). What does it mean that believers will see the face of God?

It means we will become ourselves, finally. It means dawn will rise on the dark gray of this fallen world. It means final rest will be ours. It means we will be with the One of whom even the best earthly friendships are only a faint glimpse and to whom the most sublime earthly joys are finally pointing. As the very end of the Bible puts it: "They will see his face" (Rev. 22:4).

PSALM 12

To the choirmaster: according to The Sheminith. A Psalm of David.

1   Save, O LORD, for the godly one is gone;
      for the faithful have vanished from among the
         children of man.
2   Everyone utters lies to his neighbor;
      with flattering lips and a double heart they speak.

3   May the LORD cut off all flattering lips,
      the tongue that makes great boasts,
4   those who say, "With our tongue we will prevail,
      our lips are with us; who is master over us?"

5   "Because the poor are plundered, because the needy
         groan,
      I will now arise," says the LORD;
      "I will place him in the safety for which he longs."
6   The words of the LORD are pure words,
      like silver refined in a furnace on the ground,
      purified seven times.

7   You, O LORD, will keep them;
      you will guard us from this generation forever.
8   On every side the wicked prowl,
      as vileness is exalted among the children of man.

This psalm is a community lament, suited to occasions when the people of God are under the authority of liars in positions of leadership. Note the repeated theme throughout the psalm: dishonesty with the lips.

What is the pain of dishonesty? Why does being lied to, or lied about, hurt so deeply? Is it not because we are being misrepresented such that others think more poorly of us than they ought? In other words, who we really are, and what others think we are, become separate realities instead of corresponding. Being lied *to* is also a barbed pain. We are being manipulated or taken advantage of; we become a victim of another's deceiving words.

God comes to us in that darkness and says: "Because the needy groan, I will now arise. . . . I will place him in the safety for which he longs" (v. 5). And note what the psalmist then says: "The words of the Lord are pure words" (v. 6). That is to say, God, unlike the liars in leadership, is not being deceptive when he promises this.

And what does he promise? Safety. Deliverance. Calmness. God delights to rescue us in our need. How do we know this? Because in Christ he's already achieved the greatest deliverance and accomplished our greatest safety—deliverance from hell and condemnation, safety from Satan and eternal death. Jesus groaned on the cross in this life so that you and I need never groan in the next one.

PSALM 13

To the choirmaster. A Psalm of David.

1 How long, O LORD? Will you forget me forever?
    How long will you hide your face from me?
2 How long must I take counsel in my soul
    and have sorrow in my heart all the day?
How long shall my enemy be exalted over me?

3 Consider and answer me, O LORD my God;
    light up my eyes, lest I sleep the sleep of death,
4 lest my enemy say, "I have prevailed over him,"
    lest my foes rejoice because I am shaken.

5 But I have trusted in your steadfast love;
    my heart shall rejoice in your salvation.
6 I will sing to the LORD,
    because he has dealt bountifully with me.

S

David is on the verge of despair. His emotional resources are spent. He sees no way forward. Darkness closes in. He feels as if God has forgotten him.

This is not an isolated experience, shared by merely some of us. It is an experience that all of God's children walk through, in ways and times and seasons unique to our own journey and walk with the Lord.

Where does this psalm lead us? As is the pattern of the Christian life, David begins in darkness but fights toward light; he begins in feelings of death (v. 3) but moves toward life; he begins, in a sense, in crucifixion but moves to resurrection. For David knows he can trust in God's "steadfast love," his covenantal insistence on delivering his people (v. 5).

But if David can bank everything on God, even when on the brink of despair, how much more can we today? For David saw God's steadfast love only in fairly abstract terms, in past acts of deliverance through events such as the exodus. We see God's steadfast love in concrete terms, in the great climactic act of deliverance in the person of his own Son. Jesus Christ was steadfast love embodied not merely in an event but in a person.

PSALM 14

To the choirmaster. Of David.

1   The fool says in his heart, "There is no God."
          They are corrupt, they do abominable deeds;
          there is none who does good.

2   The LORD looks down from heaven on the children
               of man,
          to see if there are any who understand,
          who seek after God.

3   They have all turned aside; together they have become
          corrupt;
      there is none who does good,
      not even one.

4   Have they no knowledge, all the evildoers
      who eat up my people as they eat bread
      and do not call upon the LORD?

5   There they are in great terror,
      for God is with the generation of the righteous.
6   You would shame the plans of the poor,
      but the LORD is his refuge.

7   Oh, that salvation for Israel would come out of Zion!
      When the LORD restores the fortunes of his people,
      let Jacob rejoice, let Israel be glad.

∽

The apostle Paul quotes Psalm 14 in Romans 3, the greatest passage in the New Testament describing universal human sinfulness. We can see why Paul does so when we read this sobering lament. David emphasizes that not a single person acts justly throughout his life. We live in a world that does not operate the way it was meant to. Sickness, disease, strife, dishonesty, theft, backbiting, bitterness, selfishness—a world that was created beautiful has become ugly in many ways, brought into ruin through mankind's sin.

Especially painful are the ways in which God's own people are afflicted by evildoers (v. 5). "Oh, that salvation for Israel would come out of Zion!" laments David (v. 7). What David saw dimly we see clearly. Salvation would come out of Zion—but not salvation for Israel alone. For Israel was not merely victimized by human sinfulness; they themselves were part of the problem. They were not exempt from human evil. Salvation would come out of Israel, but it would be for all the world.

Sin is universal. No one is exempt. But grace is universally available. No one need be exempt. All that is required is a trusting faith in Jesus Christ, the living embodiment of the salvation that came out of Israel.

PSALM 15

A Psalm of David.

1   O LORD, who shall sojourn in your tent?
      Who shall dwell on your holy hill?

2   He who walks blamelessly and does what is right
      and speaks truth in his heart;
3   who does not slander with his tongue
      and does no evil to his neighbor,
      nor takes up a reproach against his friend;
4   in whose eyes a vile person is despised,
      but who honors those who fear the LORD;
      who swears to his own hurt and does not change;
5   who does not put out his money at interest
      and does not take a bribe against the innocent.
      He who does these things shall never be moved.

The psalm speaks of one who is truthful "in his heart" (v. 2), one "in whose eyes a vile person is despised" (v. 4). Such a person has a certain moral internal compass or perspective. This is someone who "honors those who fear the LORD" (v. 4)—that is, he lives in reverent devotion to the Lord, inside and out.

To such a life we are called. But who can claim to live such a life perfectly?

Verse 1 speaks of dwelling on God's holy mountain. Strikingly, this exact phrase is used earlier in the Psalter in what is, according to the New Testament, one of the most christologically charged psalms: Psalm 2. In Psalm 2:6, Yahweh says: "As for me, I have set my King on Zion, my holy hill" (same Hebrew phrase as in 15:1). In Psalm 2, though, God is not asking who will dwell on this holy mountain. He is declaring whom he himself has set there—a man whom the New Testament identifies as Christ himself (Heb. 1:2; 5:5).

Who shall dwell on God's holy hill? Jesus.

To dwell on God's holy mountain means to pass into and abide in the temple. But Jesus did not come simply *to* the temple; he came *as* the temple. Jesus dwells on God's holy hill not by entering a humanly made building in order to meet with God but by entering a divinely made body to meet with us. The Word "tabernacled" among us (cf. John 1:14). He himself does what the temple was meant to do—to restore man to God, to rejoin earth to heaven, to bring the "walking together in the cool of the day" of Eden (cf. Gen. 3:8) back to reality once more.

PSALM 16

A Miktam of David.

1   Preserve me, O God, for in you I take refuge.
2   I say to the Lord, "You are my Lord;
        I have no good apart from you."

3   As for the saints in the land, they are the excellent ones,
        in whom is all my delight.

4   The sorrows of those who run after another god shall
            multiply;
        their drink offerings of blood I will not pour out
        or take their names on my lips.

5   The Lord is my chosen portion and my cup;
        you hold my lot.
6   The lines have fallen for me in pleasant places;
        indeed, I have a beautiful inheritance.

7   I bless the Lord who gives me counsel;
        in the night also my heart instructs me.
8   I have set the Lord always before me;
        because he is at my right hand, I shall not be shaken.

9   Therefore my heart is glad, and my whole being rejoices;
        my flesh also dwells secure.
10   For you will not abandon my soul to Sheol,
        or let your holy one see corruption.

11   You make known to me the path of life;
            in your presence there is fullness of joy;
            at your right hand are pleasures forevermore.

∾

This psalm ushers believers into a renewed confidence and contentment in the care of the Lord. The ringing note on which the psalm ends has been deeply calming encouragement to saints down through the ages. "In your presence there is fullness of joy; at your right hand are pleasures forevermore" (v. 11). Nothing else is needed. "The Lord is my chosen portion" (v. 5).

Have you tasted this? Have you been freed from the endless quest to secure stability and joy in the things of this world? Have you been ushered into the invincibility of knowing that no matter what you lose in terms of your health, finances, marriage, children, job, emotional sanity, the Lord is your ever-present refuge and life?

Three hundred years ago the pastor and theologian Jonathan Edwards captured the glad contentment of this psalm when he said in one sermon:

> The heart of a godly man doth freely choose God and Christ for his portion. Take away all torment and set hell aside and he could and might have his choice and he would choose God rather than anything else. If the godly man might have his choice either to live always in this world in the enjoyment of all manner of worldly prosperity or else in God's time die and go to heaven to dwell forever there in the enjoyment of God and Jesus Christ, he would choose the latter.

PSALM 17

A Prayer of David.

1   Hear a just cause, O LORD; attend to my cry!
         Give ear to my prayer from lips free of deceit!
2   From your presence let my vindication come!
         Let your eyes behold the right!

3   You have tried my heart, you have visited me by night,
         you have tested me, and you will find nothing;
         I have purposed that my mouth will not transgress.
4   With regard to the works of man, by the word of your
                 lips
         I have avoided the ways of the violent.
5   My steps have held fast to your paths;
         my feet have not slipped.

6   I call upon you, for you will answer me, O God;
         incline your ear to me; hear my words.
7   Wondrously show your steadfast love,
         O Savior of those who seek refuge
         from their adversaries at your right hand.

8   Keep me as the apple of your eye;
         hide me in the shadow of your wings,
9   from the wicked who do me violence,
         my deadly enemies who surround me.

10   They close their hearts to pity;
          with their mouths they speak arrogantly.
11   They have now surrounded our steps;
          they set their eyes to cast us to the ground.
12   He is like a lion eager to tear,
          as a young lion lurking in ambush.

13   Arise, O LORD! Confront him, subdue him!
          Deliver my soul from the wicked by your sword,
14   from men by your hand, O LORD,
          from men of the world whose portion is in this life.
      You fill their womb with treasure;
          they are satisfied with children,
          and they leave their abundance to their infants.

15   As for me, I shall behold your face in righteousness;
          when I awake, I shall be satisfied with your likeness.

∽

David in Psalm 17 is afflicted by unjust accusation and hostility from his enemies. In both words (v. 10) and actions (v. 11), his accusers seek to bring him down.

The anxiety, pain, and resentment that arise in the midst of such attacks can feel overwhelming. Everything in us longs to defend ourselves, to fight back, to vindicate our name. But what does David do? He rests his heart in God and in God's final justice. He appeals to heaven for vindication rather than seeking to execute it on earth. David knows deep down that God is the "Savior of those who seek refuge from their adversaries at your right hand" (v. 7).

Yet it is painfully clear that while God promises to be with us, he does not promise to relieve in this life every earthly pain and injustice. Thus the note on which David ends: "As for me, I shall behold your face in righteousness; when I awake, I shall be satisfied with your likeness" (v. 15). Whatever unfolds in this life, David knows that one day he will be at rest in the presence of the Lord.

If David knew this, how much more ought we—we who see the length to which God would ultimately go, at the height of human history, in "the fullness of time" (Gal. 4:4), to send his Son through death and out the other side: Jesus Christ, the God-man, whom we will indeed see one day soon face to face (Rev. 22:3–4).

PSALM 18

To the choirmaster. A Psalm of David, the servant of the Lord, who addressed the words of this song to the Lord on the day when the Lord delivered him from the hand of all his enemies, and from the hand of Saul. He said:

1   I love you, O LORD, my strength.
2   The LORD is my rock and my fortress and my deliverer,
        my God, my rock, in whom I take refuge,
        my shield, and the horn of my salvation, my
            stronghold.
3   I call upon the LORD, who is worthy to be praised,
        and I am saved from my enemies.

4 The cords of death encompassed me;
   the torrents of destruction assailed me;
5 the cords of Sheol entangled me;
   the snares of death confronted me.

6 In my distress I called upon the Lord;
   to my God I cried for help.
   From his temple he heard my voice,
   and my cry to him reached his ears.

7 Then the earth reeled and rocked;
   the foundations also of the mountains trembled
   and quaked, because he was angry.
8 Smoke went up from his nostrils,
   and devouring fire from his mouth;
   glowing coals flamed forth from him.
9 He bowed the heavens and came down;
   thick darkness was under his feet.
10 He rode on a cherub and flew;
   he came swiftly on the wings of the wind.
11 He made darkness his covering, his canopy around him,
   thick clouds dark with water.
12 Out of the brightness before him
   hailstones and coals of fire broke through his clouds.

13 The Lord also thundered in the heavens,
   and the Most High uttered his voice,
   hailstones and coals of fire.
14 And he sent out his arrows and scattered them;
   he flashed forth lightnings and routed them.
15 Then the channels of the sea were seen,
   and the foundations of the world were laid bare

at your rebuke, O LORD,
  at the blast of the breath of your nostrils.

16   He sent from on high, he took me;
        he drew me out of many waters.
17   He rescued me from my strong enemy
        and from those who hated me,
          for they were too mighty for me.
18   They confronted me in the day of my calamity,
        but the LORD was my support.
19   He brought me out into a broad place;
        he rescued me, because he delighted in me.

20   The LORD dealt with me according to my righteousness;
        according to the cleanness of my hands he rewarded
          me.
21   For I have kept the ways of the LORD,
        and have not wickedly departed from my God.
22   For all his rules were before me,
        and his statutes I did not put away from me.
23   I was blameless before him,
        and I kept myself from my guilt.
24   So the LORD has rewarded me according to my
          righteousness,
        according to the cleanness of my hands in his sight.

25   With the merciful you show yourself merciful;
        with the blameless man you show yourself blameless;
26   with the purified you show yourself pure;
        and with the crooked you make yourself seem
          tortuous.

27 For you save a humble people,
    but the haughty eyes you bring down.
28 For it is you who light my lamp;
    the LORD my God lightens my darkness.
29 For by you I can run against a troop,
    and by my God I can leap over a wall.
30 This God—his way is perfect;
    the word of the LORD proves true;
    he is a shield for all those who take refuge in him.

31 For who is God, but the LORD?
    And who is a rock, except our God?—
32 the God who equipped me with strength
    and made my way blameless.
33 He made my feet like the feet of a deer
    and set me secure on the heights.
34 He trains my hands for war,
    so that my arms can bend a bow of bronze.
35 You have given me the shield of your salvation,
    and your right hand supported me,
    and your gentleness made me great.
36 You gave a wide place for my steps under me,
    and my feet did not slip.
37 I pursued my enemies and overtook them,
    and did not turn back till they were consumed.
38 I thrust them through, so that they were not able to rise;
    they fell under my feet.
39 For you equipped me with strength for the battle;
    you made those who rise against me sink under me.
40 You made my enemies turn their backs to me,
    and those who hated me I destroyed.

41   They cried for help, but there was none to save;
        they cried to the LORD, but he did not answer them.
42   I beat them fine as dust before the wind;
        I cast them out like the mire of the streets.

43   You delivered me from strife with the people;
        you made me the head of the nations;
        people whom I had not known served me.
44   As soon as they heard of me they obeyed me;
        foreigners came cringing to me.
45   Foreigners lost heart
        and came trembling out of their fortresses.

46   The LORD lives, and blessed be my rock,
        and exalted be the God of my salvation—
47   the God who gave me vengeance
        and subdued peoples under me,
48   who rescued me from my enemies;
        yes, you exalted me above those who rose against me;
        you delivered me from the man of violence.

49   For this I will praise you, O LORD, among the nations,
        and sing to your name.
50   Great salvation he brings to his king,
        and shows steadfast love to his anointed,
        to David and his offspring forever.

The Lord's strong deliverance of David from Saul elicits from David a song of love (v. 1). The Lord has delivered David from deadly peril at the hands of an aggressive and hostile enemy. David recognizes that it is only by God's mercy and provision that he has been spared.

While David does appeal to his own uprightness, we should remember two things. First, the events of this psalm are described in 2 Samuel, the book in which David's greatest sins are narrated. Second, David is not claiming sinless perfection but is merely acknowledging that Saul has been aggressive toward him in a way far out of proportion to what David deserved. David is being treated unjustly. But God has delivered him.

But the psalm is not merely biographical of David, nor is it simply pietistic words for the worshiper. When David speaks similar words elsewhere, it is apparent that the purpose of the preservation of his line is to provide a Redeemer for the world (2 Sam. 7:4–17; 22:1–51). Indeed, the note on which he ends this psalm is of God's covenant commitment "to David and his offspring forever" (Ps. 18:50). It is only in Jesus that this commitment finds its pinnacle and truest fulfillment. God's gracious character and care find their ultimate revelation in Christ Jesus. When we look at our Savior, we are seeing the flesh-and-blood embodiment of the care and provision that God showed to David.

We can trust God, no matter how dire the circumstance. For in the gospel the direst of circumstances—our deserved condemnation and an eternity in hell—have already been emptied of their threat and power.

PSALM 19

To the choirmaster. A Psalm of David.

1   The heavens declare the glory of God,
    and the sky above proclaims his handiwork.
2   Day to day pours out speech,
    and night to night reveals knowledge.
3   There is no speech, nor are there words,
    whose voice is not heard.
4   Their voice goes out through all the earth,
    and their words to the end of the world.
    In them he has set a tent for the sun,
5   which comes out like a bridegroom leaving his
        chamber,
    and, like a strong man, runs its course with joy.
6   Its rising is from the end of the heavens,
    and its circuit to the end of them,
    and there is nothing hidden from its heat.

7   The law of the LORD is perfect,
    reviving the soul;
    the testimony of the LORD is sure,
    making wise the simple;
8   the precepts of the LORD are right,
    rejoicing the heart;
    the commandment of the LORD is pure,
    enlightening the eyes;
9   the fear of the LORD is clean,
    enduring forever;

54

the rules of the LORD are true,
and righteous altogether.
10 More to be desired are they than gold,
even much fine gold;
sweeter also than honey
and drippings of the honeycomb.
11 Moreover, by them is your servant warned;
in keeping them there is great reward.

12 Who can discern his errors?
Declare me innocent from hidden faults.
13 Keep back your servant also from presumptuous sins;
let them not have dominion over me!
Then I shall be blameless,
and innocent of great transgression.

14 Let the words of my mouth and the meditation of my
heart
be acceptable in your sight,
O LORD, my rock and my redeemer.

∽

God does not want to stay hidden from us. He wants us to know him. We know him through his creation (vv. 1–6) and also through his law, the Torah, God's revelation to Moses now found in the first five books of the Bible.

David exults in the preciousness of this Word. Is this how you feel about the revelation God has given of himself in his Word? How do you approach Scripture? Do you see it as fuel to revive your soul (v. 7)—"rejoicing the heart" (v. 8)? Do you desire the

Word of God more than a ten million dollar inheritance and all that it could purchase (v. 10)?

And yet the Word of God not only reveals who God is; it also reveals who we are, in all our sin and need. The lofty call of Scripture is worthy of all pursuit, yet frustratingly beyond our reach in light of our weakness and inadequacy. David knows this—thus his concluding remarks in the psalm, beginning with "Who can discern his errors?" (v. 12). He closes by praying for his words and thoughts to be acceptable in the sight of God. And he knows that by grace they will be, for in the final words of the psalm he calls God "my redeemer" (v. 14). But how, in light of his sin? Only, ultimately, through the redeeming work of God's only Son, Jesus Christ—who, though perfectly "acceptable" (v. 14) was punished as one unacceptable so that we, unacceptable through sin, might be accepted eternally into God's presence.

PSALM 20

To the choirmaster. A Psalm of David.

1   May the LORD answer you in the day of trouble!
     May the name of the God of Jacob protect you!
2   May he send you help from the sanctuary
     and give you support from Zion!
3   May he remember all your offerings
     and regard with favor your burnt sacrifices!   *Selah*

4   May he grant you your heart's desire
          and fulfill all your plans!
5   May we shout for joy over your salvation,
          and in the name of our God set up our banners!
      May the LORD fulfill all your petitions!

6   Now I know that the LORD saves his anointed;
          he will answer him from his holy heaven
          with the saving might of his right hand.
7   Some trust in chariots and some in horses,
          but we trust in the name of the LORD our God.
8   They collapse and fall,
          but we rise and stand upright.

9   O LORD, save the king!
          May he answer us when we call.

∽

In David's day, how did nations win battles? Through superior military strength. Horses. Chariots. Yet David saw beyond surface realities to the deeper meaning of all that happens—the sovereign governance of God, caring for his people, protecting them, giving them what they most need. For this reason David writes, "Some trust in chariots and some in horses, but we trust in the name of the LORD our God" (v. 7). It is one thing to use chariots and horses in battle. It is another thing to trust in them.

What about your own life? Consider your finances, for example. It is one thing to use money. It is another thing to trust in money. God calls us to use money shrewdly, yet not to entrust ourselves to it as our final security. God alone is able to bear the weight of our deepest trust. And God alone will never let us down when we place the full weight of our trust on him. In Christ he proved it.

PSALM 21

To the choirmaster. A Psalm of David.

1   O LORD, in your strength the king rejoices,
        and in your salvation how greatly he exults!
2   You have given him his heart's desire
        and have not withheld the request of his lips.   *Selah*
3   For you meet him with rich blessings;
        you set a crown of fine gold upon his head.
4   He asked life of you; you gave it to him,
        length of days forever and ever.
5   His glory is great through your salvation;
        splendor and majesty you bestow on him.
6   For you make him most blessed forever;
        you make him glad with the joy of your presence.
7   For the king trusts in the LORD,
        and through the steadfast love of the Most High he
            shall not be moved.

8   Your hand will find out all your enemies;
        your right hand will find out those who hate you.
9   You will make them as a blazing oven
        when you appear.

The LORD will swallow them up in his wrath,
>   and fire will consume them.
10   You will destroy their descendants from the earth,
>   and their offspring from among the children of man.
11   Though they plan evil against you,
>   though they devise mischief, they will not succeed.
12   For you will put them to flight;
>   you will aim at their faces with your bows.

13   Be exalted, O LORD, in your strength!
>   We will sing and praise your power.

∽

This psalm is a hymn of exultation in the Lord's abundant provision for and protection of the king, David. His deepest desires have been met (v. 2). He has been granted long life (v. 4). He is blessed (v. 6).

Does this sound irrelevant? Do you read these lines and have difficulty appreciating them? After all, it seems so ancient and foreign. It is nice that David's life turned out so well, you might think. But what about me and my seemingly insignificant life, so fraught with challenges and weakness?

The glory of the Bible is that there is no such thing as an irrelevant passage, because the entire Scripture is a web of texts that work together to tell us of God's great plan to save the weak through Jesus Christ. Here in Psalm 21, for example, we find David rejoicing in God's goodness to him as the anointed king. But his own rule would quickly fade from history. A greater King, however, would one day come. Unlike David's temporary "crown of fine gold" (v. 3), this King's reign would last forever.

In contrast to David's "length of days" (v. 4), which came to an end in death, this King would defeat death and truly live forever.

This final King, Jesus Christ, came at the height of human history to dignify your small human existence and to promise you, as you trust in him, an eternal crown, co-reigning with him forever and ever (Rev. 22:5). Your significance and destiny are everlasting and invincible.

PSALM 22

To the choirmaster: according to The Doe
of the Dawn. A Psalm of David.

1   My God, my God, why have you forsaken me?
         Why are you so far from saving me, from the words
             of my groaning?
2   O my God, I cry by day, but you do not answer,
         and by night, but I find no rest.

3   Yet you are holy,
         enthroned on the praises of Israel.
4   In you our fathers trusted;
         they trusted, and you delivered them.
5   To you they cried and were rescued;
         in you they trusted and were not put to shame.

6   But I am a worm and not a man,
         scorned by mankind and despised by the people.

7 　All who see me mock me;
　　　　they make mouths at me; they wag their heads;
8 　"He trusts in the LORD; let him deliver him;
　　　　let him rescue him, for he delights in him!"

9 　Yet you are he who took me from the womb;
　　　　you made me trust you at my mother's breasts.
10 　On you was I cast from my birth,
　　　　and from my mother's womb you have been my God.
11 　Be not far from me,
　　　　for trouble is near,
　　　　and there is none to help.

12 　Many bulls encompass me;
　　　　strong bulls of Bashan surround me;
13 　they open wide their mouths at me,
　　　　like a ravening and roaring lion.

14 　I am poured out like water,
　　　　and all my bones are out of joint;
　　　my heart is like wax;
　　　　it is melted within my breast;
15 　my strength is dried up like a potsherd,
　　　　and my tongue sticks to my jaws;
　　　　you lay me in the dust of death.

16 　For dogs encompass me;
　　　　a company of evildoers encircles me;
　　　they have pierced my hands and feet—
17 　I can count all my bones—
　　　　they stare and gloat over me;

18   they divide my garments among them,
         and for my clothing they cast lots.

19   But you, O Lord, do not be far off!
         O you my help, come quickly to my aid!
20   Deliver my soul from the sword,
         my precious life from the power of the dog!
21   Save me from the mouth of the lion!
     You have rescued me from the horns of the wild oxen!

22   I will tell of your name to my brothers;
         in the midst of the congregation I will praise you:
23   You who fear the Lord, praise him!
         All you offspring of Jacob, glorify him,
         and stand in awe of him, all you offspring of Israel!
24   For he has not despised or abhorred
         the affliction of the afflicted,
     and he has not hidden his face from him,
         but has heard, when he cried to him.

25   From you comes my praise in the great congregation;
         my vows I will perform before those who fear him.
26   The afflicted shall eat and be satisfied;
         those who seek him shall praise the Lord!
         May your hearts live forever!

27   All the ends of the earth shall remember
         and turn to the Lord,
     and all the families of the nations
         shall worship before you.
28   For kingship belongs to the Lord,
         and he rules over the nations.

29 All the prosperous of the earth eat and worship;
    before him shall bow all who go down to the dust,
    even the one who could not keep himself alive.
30 Posterity shall serve him;
    it shall be told of the Lord to the coming generation;
31 they shall come and proclaim his righteousness to a
        people yet unborn,
    that he has done it.

∽

The pain of feeling forsaken is not a rarity among the people of God. As life unfolds before us as we walk with God, we will often battle feelings of wondering where God is. "If God were really with me," we may ask, "would this be happening?" Where is his fatherly care in this loss, in this sickness, in this depression, in this pain?

These feelings and thoughts do not take God by surprise. He has given us many texts in Scripture to care for us in these times of darkness. Psalm 22 is one of these. "My God, my God, why have you forsaken me?" (v. 1), we cry out. Perhaps the pain is too raw even to tell another person about it. We are suffering alone, the pain of solitude amplifying the agony.

Notice that David assumes God has forsaken him. He does not ask God if he has forsaken him. He asks why, assuming God already has. Yet in light of the promises made to David in Scripture (see, for example, 2 Sam. 7:4–17), David ought to have known that God would never have finally forsaken him.

We can hardly blame David, though, since we often harbor the same suspicion that God has left us—that we are alone. Yet we have even more reason to be free of such thoughts, to know that God has not left us. For we know there was only one member of God's people who was ever truly forsaken by God. For that reason, as he was hanging on a Roman cross, he spoke David's own words: "My God, my God, why have you forsaken me?" (Mark 15:34). For God had indeed forsaken him. And why? So that we never are forsaken, despite our deserving to be.

PSALM 23

A Psalm of David.

1 The LORD is my shepherd; I shall not want.
2 He makes me lie down in green pastures.
 He leads me beside still waters.
3 He restores my soul.
 He leads me in paths of righteousness
  for his name's sake.

4 Even though I walk through the valley of the shadow
   of death,
  I will fear no evil,
 for you are with me;
  your rod and your staff,
  they comfort me.

5 You prepare a table before me
  in the presence of my enemies;
 you anoint my head with oil;
  my cup overflows.

6   Surely goodness and mercy shall follow me
          all the days of my life,
        and I shall dwell in the house of the Lord
          forever.

$\backsim$

This is perhaps the most famous poem in the history of the world. And justly so. It is deep consolation for the people of God.

This psalm tells us that life with God means we have no lack (v. 1). A life walking with him is like "green pastures" and "still waters" (v. 2). But notice that David does not claim this about God when life is easy. This is how God cares for us when we "walk through the valley of the shadow of death" (v. 4). How can this be? How can life be green pastures and still waters in the enveloping fog of deep fears or bitter disappointment? In a sadness that refuses to lift, a habitual sin in which you feel trapped, a rejection by one you loved, or a deep sense that you keep disappointing God? The psalm tells us: "You are with me" (v. 4). Period.

Would you rather have the mountaintop experience without God, or the dark valley with him?

How does the presence of God actually help me when I am in darkness? In this way: We know that Jesus Christ walked through the ultimate valley of the shadow of death, the darkness of condemnation and hell—a fate that should have landed on us. The result is that in our temporary dark valleys we can know that despite our sin and failure, God will bring us, in full moral integrity, to be with him forever—where we will dwell in the house of the Lord forever, where all the mess and darkness of our little lives will be found to have worked backward to make us more resplendent and happy than we otherwise could have been.

PSALM 24

A Psalm of David.

1   The earth is the LORD's and the fullness thereof,
        the world and those who dwell therein,
2   for he has founded it upon the seas
        and established it upon the rivers.

3   Who shall ascend the hill of the LORD?
        And who shall stand in his holy place?
4   He who has clean hands and a pure heart,
        who does not lift up his soul to what is false
        and does not swear deceitfully.
5   He will receive blessing from the LORD
        and righteousness from the God of his salvation.
6   Such is the generation of those who seek him,
        who seek the face of the God of Jacob.   *Selah*

7   Lift up your heads, O gates!
        And be lifted up, O ancient doors,
        that the King of glory may come in.
8   Who is this King of glory?
        The LORD, strong and mighty,
        the LORD, mighty in battle!
9   Lift up your heads, O gates!
        And lift them up, O ancient doors,
        that the King of glory may come in.

10   Who is this King of glory?
          The LORD of hosts,
          he is the King of glory!   *Selah*

⅁

This psalm was likely a song written to celebrate the entrance of the ark into Jerusalem. The ark was where the Ten Commandments and other artifacts of historical import were housed and was a symbol of God's actual presence among his people.

This psalm glories in the fact that the Lord created the cosmos and rules over it (vv. 1–2) and yet comes down to his people and lives among them because of his covenant with them (vv. 3–10). This remarkable paradox—that God is infinitely great and powerful yet delights to stoop to meet needy people—resounds throughout the Bible (see, for example, Isa. 57:15; 66:1–2).

The ultimate proof that this is who God is comes to us in the gospel. For, in the fullness of time, the high and lofty God came near to his people, tangibly near, in flesh and blood. The ark that David brought into Jerusalem was a box containing the presence of God. The Son of David who came to Jerusalem was a man who himself was the presence of God. Although God the Son enjoyed eternal glory in the presence of his Father, he drew near to needy sinners in the person of Jesus Christ. He is the true "King of Glory" who will come at the end of history to establish his eternal kingdom on earth.

PSALM 25

Of David.

1   To you, O Lᴏʀᴅ, I lift up my soul.
2   O my God, in you I trust;
       let me not be put to shame;
       let not my enemies exult over me.
3   Indeed, none who wait for you shall be put to shame;
       they shall be ashamed who are wantonly treacherous.

4   Make me to know your ways, O Lᴏʀᴅ;
       teach me your paths.
5   Lead me in your truth and teach me,
       for you are the God of my salvation;
       for you I wait all the day long.

6   Remember your mercy, O Lᴏʀᴅ, and your steadfast love,
       for they have been from of old.
7   Remember not the sins of my youth or my
          transgressions;
       according to your steadfast love remember me,
       for the sake of your goodness, O Lᴏʀᴅ!

8   Good and upright is the Lᴏʀᴅ;
       therefore he instructs sinners in the way.
9   He leads the humble in what is right,
       and teaches the humble his way.

10   All the paths of the LORD are steadfast love and
                  faithfulness,
          for those who keep his covenant and his testimonies.

11   For your name's sake, O LORD,
          pardon my guilt, for it is great.
12   Who is the man who fears the LORD?
          Him will he instruct in the way that he should
                  choose.
13   His soul shall abide in well-being,
          and his offspring shall inherit the land.
14   The friendship of the LORD is for those who fear him,
          and he makes known to them his covenant.
15   My eyes are ever toward the LORD,
          for he will pluck my feet out of the net.

16   Turn to me and be gracious to me,
          for I am lonely and afflicted.
17   The troubles of my heart are enlarged;
          bring me out of my distresses.
18   Consider my affliction and my trouble,
          and forgive all my sins.

19   Consider how many are my foes,
          and with what violent hatred they hate me.
20   Oh, guard my soul, and deliver me!
          Let me not be put to shame, for I take refuge in you.
21   May integrity and uprightness preserve me,
          for I wait for you.

22   Redeem Israel, O God,
          out of all his troubles.

In verse 13 David says that the soul of the man who fears the Lord "shall abide in well-being." The word "abide" here means literally to spend the night sleeping. It is used, for example, in Genesis 19:2 to speak of Lot's spending the night in Sodom. Here is what this psalm is asking: How do you get to a place where your soul, no matter what storms are raging around you, is as calm as if asleep for the night?

In this psalm David recounts various adversities, such as enemies (Ps. 25:2, 19), need of guidance (vv. 4, 5, 12), loneliness (v. 16), and guilt (vv. 7, 11, 18). David describes our own lives too as he recounts these trials.

What does he do with these difficulties? What is his solution? Notice that he does not apply a different answer to each adversity. He turns to one source of healing for all of these diverse pains: "To you, O LORD, I lift up my soul" (v. 1). "I take refuge in you" (v. 20). He does not address adversity with a prayer for better circumstances. He casts himself on God.

When life overwhelms us, when the bottom is falling out, this is where Scripture takes us: to God. We do not achieve internal calm by securing external calm. We find internal calm by looking to God.

PSALM 26

Of David.

1 Vindicate me, O Lord,
    for I have walked in my integrity,
    and I have trusted in the Lord without wavering.
2 Prove me, O Lord, and try me;
    test my heart and my mind.
3 For your steadfast love is before my eyes,
    and I walk in your faithfulness.

4 I do not sit with men of falsehood,
    nor do I consort with hypocrites.
5 I hate the assembly of evildoers,
    and I will not sit with the wicked.

6 I wash my hands in innocence
    and go around your altar, O Lord,
7 proclaiming thanksgiving aloud,
    and telling all your wondrous deeds.

8 O Lord, I love the habitation of your house
    and the place where your glory dwells.
9 Do not sweep my soul away with sinners,
    nor my life with bloodthirsty men,
10 in whose hands are evil devices,
    and whose right hands are full of bribes.

11   But as for me, I shall walk in my integrity;
         redeem me, and be gracious to me.
12   My foot stands on level ground;
         in the great assembly I will bless the LORD.

§

"Vindicate me, O LORD" (v. 1). David finds himself moving through life amid injustice, false accusations, bribery, and evil. In pleading for vindication and recounting his innocence, David is not pretending he has never sinned. After all, he asks God to be gracious to him (v. 11) and exults in God's "steadfast love" (v. 3). Rather, David is pleading for God to act in a way that accords with reality. He is asking for justice.

David knows that he can count on the Lord to deliver him because this is who God has always been for his people. David gives thanks as he reflects on God's "wondrous deeds" (v. 7). What deeds might these be? Preeminent among these acts of God would be the exodus, the supreme act of deliverance for his people. And David himself has known specific instances of God delivering him, such as from dangerous episodes with Saul (see Psalm 18). Indeed, throughout the Old Testament we see a pattern emerging of God delivering his saints, vindicating them, and bringing them to safety.

This pattern came to fulfillment with the coming of Jesus Christ, whose mission was to provide final vindication for his people. He endured injustice, false accusations, and evildoing. He bore all this and yet, unlike David, did not beg for justice or vindication. Why? Because he was receiving the condemnation we deserved. Jesus did *not* cry out, and so we *can* cry out for justice and vindication from God, despite our sinfulness. As the French reformer John Calvin said, "Jesus remained silent before Pilate so that ever after he might speak for us." Praise God.

PSALM 27

Of David.

1   The LORD is my light and my salvation;
        whom shall I fear?
    The LORD is the stronghold of my life;
        of whom shall I be afraid?

2   When evildoers assail me
        to eat up my flesh,
    my adversaries and foes,
        it is they who stumble and fall.

3   Though an army encamp against me,
        my heart shall not fear;
    though war arise against me,
        yet I will be confident.

4   One thing have I asked of the LORD,
        that will I seek after:
    that I may dwell in the house of the LORD
        all the days of my life,
    to gaze upon the beauty of the LORD
        and to inquire in his temple.

5 For he will hide me in his shelter
   in the day of trouble;
 he will conceal me under the cover of his tent;
   he will lift me high upon a rock.

6 And now my head shall be lifted up
   above my enemies all around me,
 and I will offer in his tent
   sacrifices with shouts of joy;
 I will sing and make melody to the LORD.

7 Hear, O LORD, when I cry aloud;
   be gracious to me and answer me!
8 You have said, "Seek my face."
 My heart says to you,
   "Your face, LORD, do I seek."
9   Hide not your face from me.
 Turn not your servant away in anger,
   O you who have been my help.
 Cast me not off; forsake me not,
   O God of my salvation!
10 For my father and my mother have forsaken me,
   but the LORD will take me in.

11 Teach me your way, O LORD,
   and lead me on a level path
   because of my enemies.
12 Give me not up to the will of my adversaries;
   for false witnesses have risen against me,
   and they breathe out violence.

13   I believe that I shall look upon the goodness of the LORD
          in the land of the living!
14   Wait for the LORD;
          be strong, and let your heart take courage;
          wait for the LORD!

∽

W hat else do you need in life beyond the truths of Psalm 27?
          Fears press in on David (vv. 1, 3). Such is life. Who
among us does not know what it is to wake up in the morning
and, as consciousness slides over us once more, feel clutching at
our hearts the pressing anxieties and fears of the day ahead? This
is normal. This is life.

Consider the words of this psalm. Read them slowly. Drink
them in. If the Lord is your light and salvation, of whom will you
be afraid (v. 1)? Even if your own parents forsake you, the Lord
will take you in (v. 10). And note David's single longing, the "one
thing" he has asked: to dwell in the house of the Lord and gaze
upon the beauty of the Lord (v. 4).

Have you tasted this? Is the Lord beautiful to you? What is
the beauty of God? It is his brilliance, his radiance, his sun-like
shining forth in who he is for sinners. And in Jesus we see the
ultimate embodiment of the beauty of God. Jonathan Edwards
put it this way:

> Christ has infinite loveliness to win and draw our love.
> He is more excellent than the angels of heaven. . . .
> In beholding his beauty, the angels do day and night
> entertain and feast their souls and in celebrating of it
> do they continually employ their praises. Nor yet have
> the songs of angels ever declared all the excellency of

Jesus Christ, for it is beyond their songs and beyond the thoughts of those bright intelligences to reach it.

Our hearts are hungry for beauty. In Jesus Christ, we see the face of God, just as David longed to see the face of God (vv. 8–9). See him in the Gospels, and in all of Scripture. Commune with him. Adore him. He is the deepest longing of our hearts.

PSALM 28

Of David.

1   To you, O LORD, I call;
      my rock, be not deaf to me,
  lest, if you be silent to me,
      I become like those who go down to the pit.
2   Hear the voice of my pleas for mercy,
      when I cry to you for help,
  when I lift up my hands
      toward your most holy sanctuary.

3   Do not drag me off with the wicked,
      with the workers of evil,
  who speak peace with their neighbors
      while evil is in their hearts.
4   Give to them according to their work
      and according to the evil of their deeds;

give to them according to the work of their hands;
>   render them their due reward.
5 Because they do not regard the works of the LORD
>   or the work of his hands,
he will tear them down and build them up no more.

6 Blessed be the LORD!
>   For he has heard the voice of my pleas for mercy.
7 The LORD is my strength and my shield;
>   in him my heart trusts, and I am helped;
my heart exults,
>   and with my song I give thanks to him.

8 The LORD is the strength of his people;
>   he is the saving refuge of his anointed.
9 Oh, save your people and bless your heritage!
>   Be their shepherd and carry them forever.

§

David is desperate. Note the urgency of the first two verses of the psalm. We do not know the exact nature of his plight, but perhaps he is perplexed by not knowing who his true friends are. Perhaps he is discovering that he is on the receiving end of deceitfulness (v. 3).

How does David deal with this bewildering sense of help-lessness and confusion? How do *you* deal with these realities? After all, David is not alone in such struggles. He faces them in ways unique to him and his time and culture, but the words of this psalm are the words of a heart struggle that transcends any particular cultural location.

David responds by turning to God: "The LORD is my strength and my shield; in him my heart trusts, and I am helped" (v. 7). David does not expend his energies engaging his enemies or defending himself or pursuing any other humanly contrived strategy. He receives the horizontal affliction but goes to a vertical solution. And is this a superficial, empty solution? Far from it: "My heart exults, and with my song I give thanks to him" (v. 7).

In David's descendant we see why we too can trust in the Lord, and with far more concrete reason. While David cried for God to "be their shepherd and carry them forever" (v. 9), the Lord Jesus Christ came as the final good shepherd, and he carries his lambs in his arms (John 10:1–18).

PSALM 29

A Psalm of David.

1 Ascribe to the LORD, O heavenly beings,
       ascribe to the LORD glory and strength.
2 Ascribe to the LORD the glory due his name;
       worship the LORD in the splendor of holiness.

3 The voice of the LORD is over the waters;
       the God of glory thunders,
       the LORD, over many waters.
4 The voice of the LORD is powerful;
       the voice of the LORD is full of majesty.

5 The voice of the LORD breaks the cedars;
   the LORD breaks the cedars of Lebanon.
6 He makes Lebanon to skip like a calf,
   and Sirion like a young wild ox.

7 The voice of the LORD flashes forth flames of fire.
8 The voice of the LORD shakes the wilderness;
   the LORD shakes the wilderness of Kadesh.

9 The voice of the LORD makes the deer give birth
   and strips the forests bare,
   and in his temple all cry, "Glory!"

10 The LORD sits enthroned over the flood;
   the LORD sits enthroned as king forever.
11 May the LORD give strength to his people!
   May the LORD bless his people with peace!

∽

The twentieth-century American preacher A. W. Tozer once said: "What comes into our minds when we think about God is the most important thing about us." Who is God, to you?

Ponder this psalm. Has the awe-inspiring greatness of God displayed in unspeakable majesty and strength been pressed into your heart? If not, this psalm helps to do so.

The Bible gives us multiple angles of who God is: he is both transcendent and immanent, both high and low, both great and good, both mighty and merciful. Some of us may tend to emphasize one or the other of these in our thoughts of God, but the Bible insists that we hold both up together. This ought not to surprise us, for greatness without goodness is terrifying, while goodness without greatness is impotent.

The apparent tension between these twin realities was finally resolved in Jesus Christ. In him we see the merciful heart of God, and the unprecedented nearness of God, in our very midst—healing the sick, forgiving the penitent, welcoming the children. Yet for all those who do not bow the knee in contrition to Christ, only fury and wrath await them at his second coming (Rev. 19:11–16). Now is the time to humble ourselves and plead for mercy—which, in accord with his deepest heart, he delights to give.

PSALM 30

A Psalm of David. A song at the dedication of the temple.

1   I will extol you, O LORD, for you have drawn me up
       and have not let my foes rejoice over me.
2   O LORD my God, I cried to you for help,
       and you have healed me.
3   O LORD, you have brought up my soul from Sheol;
       you restored me to life from among those who go
         down to the pit.

4   Sing praises to the LORD, O you his saints,
       and give thanks to his holy name.
5   For his anger is but for a moment,
       and his favor is for a lifetime.

Weeping may tarry for the night,
>   but joy comes with the morning.

6   As for me, I said in my prosperity,
>   "I shall never be moved."
7   By your favor, O LORD,
>   you made my mountain stand strong;
>   you hid your face;
>   I was dismayed.

8   To you, O LORD, I cry,
>   and to the Lord I plead for mercy:
9   "What profit is there in my death,
>   if I go down to the pit?
>   Will the dust praise you?
>   Will it tell of your faithfulness?
10 Hear, O LORD, and be merciful to me!
>   O LORD, be my helper!"

11 You have turned for me my mourning into dancing;
>   you have loosed my sackcloth
>   and clothed me with gladness,
12 that my glory may sing your praise and not be silent.
>   O LORD my God, I will give thanks to you forever!

∽

David wrote this psalm, as the title indicates, for the dedication of the temple, an event that took place after David's lifetime (1 Kings 8:63). We see David calling on his fellow worshipers to sing thanks and praise to God (Ps. 30:4). What did the temple signify?

The temple was supremely significant in the life of the people of Israel because it signified the very presence of God in their midst. In a sense Eden had been the very first temple. There God dwelt with humanity in uninterrupted fellowship. The divine and human, the infinite and the finite, communed. The fall into sin expelled mankind from the garden, however, and God withdrew his presence to heaven. How could their fellowship be restored? The answer that unfolds through the Old Testament is first the tabernacle, which was simply an early portable temple, and then the temple itself. In the tabernacle and the temple, the divine and the human, the sacred and the profane, once more met. They were a tiny, restored Eden.

Yet the temple was not God's final answer of how he would dwell once more among his people, for he gave us abundant reason to join David in singing his praise and giving thanks to him forever (v. 12). We now know just how it is that God's "anger is but for a moment, and his favor is for a lifetime" (v. 5). God drew near to his people through his own Son, Jesus—not in a building made of stones and wood but in a body made of flesh and blood. Through Jesus' death and resurrection, God draws near to sinners and enjoys fellowship with us once more. Let us praise him.

PSALM 31

To the choirmaster. A Psalm of David.

1   In you, O Lᴏʀᴅ, do I take refuge;
      let me never be put to shame;
      in your righteousness deliver me!
2   Incline your ear to me;
      rescue me speedily!
   Be a rock of refuge for me,
      a strong fortress to save me!

3   For you are my rock and my fortress;
      and for your name's sake you lead me and guide me;
4   you take me out of the net they have hidden for me,
      for you are my refuge.
5   Into your hand I commit my spirit;
      you have redeemed me, O Lᴏʀᴅ, faithful God.

6   I hate those who pay regard to worthless idols,
      but I trust in the Lᴏʀᴅ.
7   I will rejoice and be glad in your steadfast love,
      because you have seen my affliction;
      you have known the distress of my soul,
8   and you have not delivered me into the hand of the
         enemy;
      you have set my feet in a broad place.

9   Be gracious to me, O LORD, for I am in distress;
         my eye is wasted from grief;
         my soul and my body also.
10   For my life is spent with sorrow,
         and my years with sighing;
     my strength fails because of my iniquity,
         and my bones waste away.

11   Because of all my adversaries I have become a reproach,
         especially to my neighbors,
     and an object of dread to my acquaintances;
         those who see me in the street flee from me.
12   I have been forgotten like one who is dead;
         I have become like a broken vessel.
13   For I hear the whispering of many—
         terror on every side!—
     as they scheme together against me,
         as they plot to take my life.

14   But I trust in you, O LORD;
         I say, "You are my God."
15   My times are in your hand;
         rescue me from the hand of my enemies and from
             my persecutors!
16   Make your face shine on your servant;
         save me in your steadfast love!
17   O LORD, let me not be put to shame,
         for I call upon you;
     let the wicked be put to shame;
         let them go silently to Sheol.

18 Let the lying lips be mute,
        which speak insolently against the righteous
        in pride and contempt.

19 Oh, how abundant is your goodness,
        which you have stored up for those who fear you
    and worked for those who take refuge in you,
        in the sight of the children of mankind!
20 In the cover of your presence you hide them
        from the plots of men;
    you store them in your shelter
        from the strife of tongues.

21 Blessed be the LORD,
        for he has wondrously shown his steadfast love
            to me
        when I was in a besieged city.
22 I had said in my alarm,
        "I am cut off from your sight."
    But you heard the voice of my pleas for mercy
        when I cried to you for help.

23 Love the LORD, all you his saints!
        The LORD preserves the faithful
        but abundantly repays the one who acts in pride.
24 Be strong, and let your heart take courage,
        all you who wait for the LORD!

Wﾠhat does it mean to "take refuge" in God, as David says numerous times in this psalm (vv. 1, 2, 4)? What does it mean that God is our "fortress" (v. 3)?

At one level, this is quite foreign to us. We live today in modern buildings, not ancient fortresses in which people took refuge from assaulting armies. Most of us do not need to defend our homes with weapons in the same way that David did. Thus we do not need to think of taking refuge in God as David did—right?

Wrong. Consider basketball star Michael Jordan's words when he was inducted into the NBA Hall of Fame, the greatest honor a basketball player could receive. His words are telling. He concluded his speech by saying, "The game of basketball has been everything to me—*my refuge*, my place I've always gone when I needed to find comfort and peace." Without meaning to, Michael Jordan used the language and metaphors of the Psalms to depict his relationship to the game of basketball. What did he mean? He meant that he drew strength and built stability, emotionally and psychologically, on his success in a sport.

For him it was basketball. What is it for you? Have you learned to lift your quest for a stable refuge from all the things of this earth to the one true refuge, the one that will never let you down or disappoint you, the one refuge that will hide you in safety and security even when you have failed it? "Be strong, and let your heart take courage, all you who wait for the LORD!" (v. 24).

PSALM 32

A Maskil of David.

1   Blessed is the one whose transgression is forgiven,
        whose sin is covered.
2   Blessed is the man against whom the LORD counts no
           iniquity,
        and in whose spirit there is no deceit.

3   For when I kept silent, my bones wasted away
        through my groaning all day long.
4   For day and night your hand was heavy upon me;
        my strength was dried up as by the heat of summer.
                                        Selah

5   I acknowledged my sin to you,
        and I did not cover my iniquity;
    I said, "I will confess my transgressions to the LORD,"
        and you forgave the iniquity of my sin.   *Selah*

6   Therefore let everyone who is godly
        offer prayer to you at a time when you may be found;
    surely in the rush of great waters,
        they shall not reach him.
7   You are a hiding place for me;
        you preserve me from trouble;
        you surround me with shouts of deliverance.   *Selah*

8   I will instruct you and teach you in the way you should
         go;
      I will counsel you with my eye upon you.
9   Be not like a horse or a mule, without understanding,
      which must be curbed with bit and bridle,
      or it will not stay near you.

10   Many are the sorrows of the wicked,
      but steadfast love surrounds the one who trusts in
         the LORD.
11   Be glad in the LORD, and rejoice, O righteous,
      and shout for joy, all you upright in heart!

∽

This song exults in the wonder of forgiveness from God. What is forgiveness? It is looking a failure square in the face and wiping it from your slate. But how is forgiveness won? Only through acknowledging it squarely. Forgiveness does not come to the self-justifying. It comes only to the contrite, the honest. Note that David speaks of the one "in whose spirit there is no deceit" (v. 2). This is a picture of the way to be forgiven. "I acknowledged my sin to you," he says later in the psalm (v. 5). One must take off the mask. Stop the pretense. Humble oneself before the Lord with honest transparency.

There is an inner health that is nurtured through open confession of one's sins. When we stuff down our guilt, it festers within us: "When I kept silent, my bones wasted away" (v. 3). It feels like a death to open up in honesty about our failings. But it is actually the pathway to life and sanity.

At one level, forgiveness may seem deeply unjust. How can God simply wipe away true, actual, blatant, wicked thoughts, words, and deeds? In the Old Testament, God promised forgiveness through the sacrificial system. But how could the blood of animals wash away our sins? Only as they pointed forward to the true and final sacrifice, the one to whom all preceding sacrifices pointed. In the fullness of time God sent his own Son to be our sacrificial Lamb (1 Cor. 5:7; Heb. 9:13–14). In him we receive forgiveness because the punishment we deserved was poured out on him. Reflecting on the forgiveness of sin, Martin Luther wrote:

> This fountain is inexhaustible; it never fails no matter how much we draw from it. Even if we all dip from it without stopping, it cannot be emptied, but it remains a perennial fount, an unfathomable well, an eternal fountain.

PSALM 33

1   Shout for joy in the LORD, O you righteous!
       Praise befits the upright.
2   Give thanks to the LORD with the lyre;
       make melody to him with the harp of ten strings!
3   Sing to him a new song;
       play skillfully on the strings, with loud shouts.

4   For the word of the LORD is upright,
       and all his work is done in faithfulness.

5   He loves righteousness and justice;
       the earth is full of the steadfast love of the LORD.

6   By the word of the LORD the heavens were made,
       and by the breath of his mouth all their host.
7   He gathers the waters of the sea as a heap;
       he puts the deeps in storehouses.

8   Let all the earth fear the LORD;
       let all the inhabitants of the world stand in awe of him!
9   For he spoke, and it came to be;
       he commanded, and it stood firm.

10   The LORD brings the counsel of the nations to nothing;
       he frustrates the plans of the peoples.
11   The counsel of the LORD stands forever,
       the plans of his heart to all generations.
12   Blessed is the nation whose God is the LORD,
       the people whom he has chosen as his heritage!

13   The LORD looks down from heaven;
       he sees all the children of man;
14   from where he sits enthroned he looks out
       on all the inhabitants of the earth,
15   he who fashions the hearts of them all
       and observes all their deeds.
16   The king is not saved by his great army;
       a warrior is not delivered by his great strength.
17   The war horse is a false hope for salvation,
       and by its great might it cannot rescue.

18   Behold, the eye of the LORD is on those who fear him,
        on those who hope in his steadfast love,
19   that he may deliver their soul from death
        and keep them alive in famine.

20   Our soul waits for the LORD;
        he is our help and our shield.
21   For our heart is glad in him,
        because we trust in his holy name.
22   Let your steadfast love, O LORD, be upon us,
        even as we hope in you.

∽

The resounding note of Psalm 33 is the endless rule of God in heaven over all that happens on earth. Over all the madness and chaos of this world, all the political conflicts and military endeavors and voting booths and family dysfunctions and physical illnesses and financial meltdowns—God reigns. His sovereign supervision directs all that unfolds here in this life.

For the psalmist this is a cause of great joy, as the psalm begins and ends with expressions of great gladness (vv. 1–3, 21–22). Why? Because when you trust in the Lord as your help and shield (v. 20)—in other words, when you locate your inner calm and security in God instead of in your own management of circumstances—the frenetic anxieties that clutch at your heart lose their viselike grip. At first this trust feels like a dangerous free fall—who knows where I might be swept off to if I hand over the reins of my life to another? But if we can settle in our hearts that the Lord is our Heavenly Father and will guide us only into that which will finally result in our joy and radiance, even if it means passing through pain, we find his sovereign rule freeing rather than threatening.

After all, did he not prove it? How has he shown that he is determined to deliver our soul from death (v. 19)? By sending his Son to die in our place. If the Father was willing to go through *that* for our good, what wouldn't he be willing to do for our final gladness and glory?

PSALM 34

Of David, when he changed his behavior before Abimelech,
so that he drove him out, and he went away.

1   I will bless the LORD at all times;
         his praise shall continually be in my mouth.
2   My soul makes its boast in the LORD;
         let the humble hear and be glad.
3   Oh, magnify the LORD with me,
         and let us exalt his name together!

4   I sought the LORD, and he answered me
         and delivered me from all my fears.
5   Those who look to him are radiant,
         and their faces shall never be ashamed.
6   This poor man cried, and the LORD heard him
         and saved him out of all his troubles.
7   The angel of the LORD encamps
         around those who fear him, and delivers them.

8   Oh, taste and see that the LORD is good!
       Blessed is the man who takes refuge in him!
9   Oh, fear the LORD, you his saints,
       for those who fear him have no lack!
10   The young lions suffer want and hunger;
       but those who seek the LORD lack no good thing.

11   Come, O children, listen to me;
       I will teach you the fear of the LORD.
12   What man is there who desires life
       and loves many days, that he may see good?
13   Keep your tongue from evil
       and your lips from speaking deceit.
14   Turn away from evil and do good;
       seek peace and pursue it.

15   The eyes of the LORD are toward the righteous
       and his ears toward their cry.
16   The face of the LORD is against those who do evil,
       to cut off the memory of them from the earth.
17   When the righteous cry for help, the LORD hears
       and delivers them out of all their troubles.
18   The LORD is near to the brokenhearted
       and saves the crushed in spirit.

19   Many are the afflictions of the righteous,
       but the LORD delivers him out of them all.
20   He keeps all his bones;
       not one of them is broken.
21   Affliction will slay the wicked,
       and those who hate the righteous will be condemned.

22   The LORD redeems the life of his servants;
        none of those who take refuge in him will be
        condemned.

∽

W e have all come across someone who constantly complains. No matter what good things wash into their lives, they focus on the bad. Psalm 34 takes that sinful impulse within all of us and flips it inside out. No matter how many bad things wash into our life, we can be someone who focuses on the good. "I will bless the LORD at all times; his praise shall continually be in my mouth" (v. 1). The rest of the psalm unpacks why and how we can praise God moment by moment as we move through life.

Notice one particular element of rejoicing in God in all of life. "Those who look to him are radiant" (v. 5). Have you ever met a radiant man or woman? Have you seen a countenance of brilliant light on the face of someone else? This is on another plane beyond mere physical attractiveness or health. Have you ever spent time with someone who had a certain glow, a certain magnetic charm, and you knew that it was because that person had lived a life of looking to the Lord?

Consider the ways that the psalmist speaks of the abundant provision and care of the Lord. To look to the Lord and be radiant as a result is to walk through life in happy defiance of any circumstantial adversity sending your emotional life into meltdown. You have God. You are safe. You have everything.

This is true even when you are "brokenhearted" and "crushed in spirit" (v. 18). For God has demonstrated that he is not a stoic God, a distant God removed from our frailties and distresses. In Jesus, God drew near. He entered into our broken-heartedness. The Lord Jesus knows what it is to be crushed in spirit. He endured everything we do, with the sole exception of sin (Heb. 4:15). Enjoy life in Christ. Walk with him. Look to him. Become radiant and glorious (2 Cor. 3:18).

PSALM 35

Of David.

1 Contend, O LORD, with those who contend with me;
    fight against those who fight against me!
2 Take hold of shield and buckler
    and rise for my help!
3 Draw the spear and javelin
    against my pursuers!
  Say to my soul,
    "I am your salvation!"

4 Let them be put to shame and dishonor
    who seek after my life!
  Let them be turned back and disappointed
    who devise evil against me!
5 Let them be like chaff before the wind,
    with the angel of the LORD driving them away!
6 Let their way be dark and slippery,
    with the angel of the LORD pursuing them!

7 For without cause they hid their net for me;
    without cause they dug a pit for my life.

8   Let destruction come upon him when he does not
            know it!
    And let the net that he hid ensnare him;
        let him fall into it—to his destruction!

9   Then my soul will rejoice in the LORD,
        exulting in his salvation.
10 All my bones shall say,
        "O LORD, who is like you,
    delivering the poor
        from him who is too strong for him,
        the poor and needy from him who robs him?"

11 Malicious witnesses rise up;
        they ask me of things that I do not know.
12 They repay me evil for good;
        my soul is bereft.
13 But I, when they were sick—
        I wore sackcloth;
        I afflicted myself with fasting;
    I prayed with head bowed on my chest.
14   I went about as though I grieved for my friend
            or my brother;
    as one who laments his mother,
        I bowed down in mourning.

15 But at my stumbling they rejoiced and gathered;
        they gathered together against me;
    wretches whom I did not know
        tore at me without ceasing;
16 like profane mockers at a feast,
        they gnash at me with their teeth.

17 How long, O Lord, will you look on?
    Rescue me from their destruction,
    my precious life from the lions!
18 I will thank you in the great congregation;
    in the mighty throng I will praise you.

19 Let not those rejoice over me
    who are wrongfully my foes,
and let not those wink the eye
    who hate me without cause.
20 For they do not speak peace,
    but against those who are quiet in the land
    they devise words of deceit.
21 They open wide their mouths against me;
    they say, "Aha, Aha!
    Our eyes have seen it!"

22 You have seen, O Lord; be not silent!
    O Lord, be not far from me!
23 Awake and rouse yourself for my vindication,
    for my cause, my God and my Lord!
24 Vindicate me, O Lord, my God,
    according to your righteousness,
    and let them not rejoice over me!
25 Let them not say in their hearts,
    "Aha, our heart's desire!"
Let them not say, "We have swallowed him up."

26 Let them be put to shame and disappointed altogether
    who rejoice at my calamity!
Let them be clothed with shame and dishonor
    who magnify themselves against me!

27 Let those who delight in my righteousness
   shout for joy and be glad
   and say evermore,
  "Great is the LORD,
   who delights in the welfare of his servant!"
28 Then my tongue shall tell of your righteousness
   and of your praise all the day long.

∽

The taunts and evil devices of David's enemies come through resoundingly in this psalm. David is under assault, and once more he turns to God for deliverance. His own human resources are no match for the adversity he is facing—he must appeal to the only one who has the strength to protect him and overcome his adversaries.

This is often how life feels. Adversaries face us at every turn. Sometimes this comes in the form of human adversaries, as it did for David. This may be especially true for those in leadership. But all Christians can attest to the reality of what the apostle Paul would call, one thousand years after David, "the spiritual forces of evil in the heavenly places" (Eph. 6:12). Immersed in a great spiritual battle as we journey toward heaven, hated by the armies of hell, we too pray with David, "Contend, O LORD, with those who contend with me! . . . Let them be put to shame and dishonor who seek after my life!" (Ps. 35:1, 4).

And we wage this war in Jesus' name. That is, we fight off the temptations and assaults of hell with the weapons of the gospel, in the glad knowledge that God has once and for all emptied hell of its weapons of accusation and condemnation. David prays of his enemies, "Let them be clothed with shame and dishonor" (v. 26). And Paul said of Christ: "He disarmed the rulers and authorities

and put them to open shame, by triumphing over them in him"
(Col. 2:15). Our enemies have been defanged. They are now all
gums and no bite. Christ on the cross absorbed the shame we
deserve to free us from it. Truly, "Great is the LORD, who delights
in the welfare of his servant!" (Ps. 35:27).

PSALM 36

To the choirmaster. Of David, the servant of the LORD.

1 Transgression speaks to the wicked
    deep in his heart;
there is no fear of God
    before his eyes.
2 For he flatters himself in his own eyes
    that his iniquity cannot be found out and hated.
3 The words of his mouth are trouble and deceit;
    he has ceased to act wisely and do good.
4 He plots trouble while on his bed;
    he sets himself in a way that is not good;
    he does not reject evil.

5 Your steadfast love, O LORD, extends to the heavens,
    your faithfulness to the clouds.
6 Your righteousness is like the mountains of God;
    your judgments are like the great deep;
    man and beast you save, O LORD.

7   How precious is your steadfast love, O God!
         The children of mankind take refuge in the shadow
             of your wings.
8   They feast on the abundance of your house,
         and you give them drink from the river of your
             delights.
9   For with you is the fountain of life;
         in your light do we see light.

10   Oh, continue your steadfast love to those who know you,
         and your righteousness to the upright of heart!
11   Let not the foot of arrogance come upon me,
         nor the hand of the wicked drive me away.
12   There the evildoers lie fallen;
         they are thrust down, unable to rise.

ᔕ

This burden of this psalm is to present a stark contrast between
the empty deceitfulness of the wicked on the one hand and
the enduring, solid, soul-satisfying faithfulness of the Lord on
the other.

David's prayer in this psalm, then, is for the Lord's faithfulness,
not the evildoer's treachery, to determine his life and rule (v. 11).
The wicked are set against him. The Lord is set for him. Who will
prevail? With this psalm David brings us with him into a renewed,
settled confidence that it is the Lord who will triumph in our
lives. He will care for us. He will get the last word.

And in the meantime, it is in him that believers find their
deepest satisfaction. Consider the imagery of this song: "The
children of mankind take refuge in the shadow of your wings"
(v. 7)—strong, shaded protection. "They feast on the abundance

of your house, and you give them drink from the river of your delights" (v. 8)—nourishing, overflowing sustenance. "With you is the fountain of life" (v. 9)— endless, inexhaustible vitality. "In your light do we see light" (v. 9)—shining, radiant illumination.

And where do we today discover these benefits? To be sure, as David did—in God himself. Yet for us there is an even deeper, sharper awareness of how to access these benefits in God—we do so in union with Christ. He himself is our protection: "I am the good shepherd" (John 10:11). He is our sustenance: "I am the bread of life" (John 6:35). He is our vitality: "I came that they may have life and have it abundantly" (John 10:10). He is our illumination: "I am the light of the world" (John 8:12).

PSALM 37

Of David.

1   Fret not yourself because of evildoers;
        be not envious of wrongdoers!
2   For they will soon fade like the grass
        and wither like the green herb.

3   Trust in the LORD, and do good;
        dwell in the land and befriend faithfulness.
4   Delight yourself in the LORD,
        and he will give you the desires of your heart.

5   Commit your way to the LORD;
        trust in him, and he will act.
6   He will bring forth your righteousness as the light,
        and your justice as the noonday.

7   Be still before the LORD and wait patiently for him;
        fret not yourself over the one who prospers in his way,
        over the man who carries out evil devices!

8   Refrain from anger, and forsake wrath!
        Fret not yourself; it tends only to evil.
9   For the evildoers shall be cut off,
        but those who wait for the LORD shall inherit the
            land.

10   In just a little while, the wicked will be no more;
        though you look carefully at his place, he will not be
            there.
11   But the meek shall inherit the land
        and delight themselves in abundant peace.

12   The wicked plots against the righteous
        and gnashes his teeth at him,
13   but the Lord laughs at the wicked,
        for he sees that his day is coming.

14   The wicked draw the sword and bend their bows
        to bring down the poor and needy,
        to slay those whose way is upright;
15   their sword shall enter their own heart,
        and their bows shall be broken.

16 Better is the little that the righteous has
   than the abundance of many wicked.
17 For the arms of the wicked shall be broken,
   but the LORD upholds the righteous.

18 The LORD knows the days of the blameless,
   and their heritage will remain forever;
19 they are not put to shame in evil times;
   in the days of famine they have abundance.

20 But the wicked will perish;
   the enemies of the LORD are like the glory of the
       pastures;
   they vanish—like smoke they vanish away.

21 The wicked borrows but does not pay back,
   but the righteous is generous and gives;
22 for those blessed by the LORD shall inherit the land,
   but those cursed by him shall be cut off.

23 The steps of a man are established by the LORD,
   when he delights in his way;
24 though he fall, he shall not be cast headlong,
   for the LORD upholds his hand.

25 I have been young, and now am old,
   yet I have not seen the righteous forsaken
   or his children begging for bread.
26 He is ever lending generously,
   and his children become a blessing.

27 Turn away from evil and do good;
   so shall you dwell forever.
28 For the LORD loves justice;
   he will not forsake his saints.
   They are preserved forever,
   but the children of the wicked shall be cut off.
29 The righteous shall inherit the land
   and dwell upon it forever.

30 The mouth of the righteous utters wisdom,
   and his tongue speaks justice.
31 The law of his God is in his heart;
   his steps do not slip.

32 The wicked watches for the righteous
   and seeks to put him to death.
33 The LORD will not abandon him to his power
   or let him be condemned when he is brought to trial.

34 Wait for the LORD and keep his way,
   and he will exalt you to inherit the land;
   you will look on when the wicked are cut off.

35 I have seen a wicked, ruthless man,
   spreading himself like a green laurel tree.
36 But he passed away, and behold, he was no more;
   though I sought him, he could not be found.

37 Mark the blameless and behold the upright,
   for there is a future for the man of peace.
38 But transgressors shall be altogether destroyed;
   the future of the wicked shall be cut off.

39   The salvation of the righteous is from the LORD;
          he is their stronghold in the time of trouble.
40   The LORD helps them and delivers them;
          he delivers them from the wicked and saves them,
          because they take refuge in him.

၄

This psalm upends our natural impulses of how to live a full
and abundant life. The core message of this psalm is that
true fullness of life comes not as we expect. It is found not in
manipulating our circumstances or controlling those around us
or violently silencing those who threaten our ambitions but in
quietly looking to God and letting him sort out our lives. "Be
still before the LORD and wait patiently for him" (v. 7). There is
a glorious inevitability to the final glory of God's people as they
look to him, trust in him, delight in him (vv. 4–6). When the
wicked, on the other hand, function out of self-trust and seek
to build their lives on their own strength and reliance, enduring
significance becomes elusive (vv. 35–36). They vanish as quickly
as plumes of smoke disappear from a roaring fire (v. 20).

"But the meek shall inherit the land" (v. 11). It is those who
refuse to force their way into worldly control and power that
will, one day, inherit such rule. This deconstructs our motives
and liberates our ambitions once again. We need not scramble
for control. The way up is down. Jesus took this verse (v. 11) and
reiterated it in the beatitudes: "Blessed are the meek, for they shall
inherit the earth" (Matt. 5:5).

And it is in the Lord Jesus himself that we see this counterin-
tuitive truth fully embodied. Jesus, the glorious Son of God, was
condemned and crucified. Yet it was through the horrors of this
anguish that he was brought through death and out the other side

into light and glory and splendor (Phil. 2:6–11). United to this Savior, we follow in his footsteps, knowing that the way to glory is through suffering (Rom. 8:18). We follow this pattern in the glad knowledge that the deepest possible suffering—condemnation and hell—landed on him instead of us.

PSALM 38

A Psalm of David, for the memorial offering.

1   O Lord, rebuke me not in your anger,
        nor discipline me in your wrath!
2   For your arrows have sunk into me,
        and your hand has come down on me.

3   There is no soundness in my flesh
        because of your indignation;
    there is no health in my bones
        because of my sin.
4   For my iniquities have gone over my head;
        like a heavy burden, they are too heavy for me.

5   My wounds stink and fester
        because of my foolishness,
6   I am utterly bowed down and prostrate;
        all the day I go about mourning.
7   For my sides are filled with burning,
        and there is no soundness in my flesh.

8   I am feeble and crushed;
        I groan because of the tumult of my heart.

9   O Lord, all my longing is before you;
        my sighing is not hidden from you.
10   My heart throbs; my strength fails me,
        and the light of my eyes—it also has gone from me.
11   My friends and companions stand aloof from my plague,
        and my nearest kin stand far off.

12   Those who seek my life lay their snares;
        those who seek my hurt speak of ruin
        and meditate treachery all day long.

13   But I am like a deaf man; I do not hear,
        like a mute man who does not open his mouth.
14   I have become like a man who does not hear,
        and in whose mouth are no rebukes.

15   But for you, O Lord, do I wait;
        it is you, O Lord my God, who will answer.
16   For I said, "Only let them not rejoice over me,
        who boast against me when my foot slips!"

17   For I am ready to fall,
        and my pain is ever before me.
18   I confess my iniquity;
        I am sorry for my sin.
19   But my foes are vigorous, they are mighty,
        and many are those who hate me wrongfully.
20   Those who render me evil for good
        accuse me because I follow after good.

21   Do not forsake me, O Lord!
          O my God, be not far from me!
22   Make haste to help me,
          O Lord, my salvation!

∽

It is one thing to endure pain. It is another thing to endure pain that you know has come from your own sin.

David writes this psalm out of the anguish of his heart. He is completely overwhelmed with life, "utterly bowed down and prostrate" (v. 6). But his pain is doubled by the knowledge that this pain is "because of my sin" (v. 3), "because of my foolishness" (v. 5). As a result, he is at wit's end, enduring physical distress (v. 3), emotional pain (v. 8), and relational dysfunction (v. 11).

Every child of God knows something of this pain—to know that various trials in life arise from our own foolishness. This is a double pain, for we are not innocent victims of someone else's folly; it is our own folly. Does God have an answer for this? Is this an anguish that goes beyond the resources of the grace of God? Can true believers sin their way out of the mercy of God?

May it never be. The apostle Paul insists with reassuring clarity that where sin piles up, grace piles up even higher. God's answer for those who squander his grace through folly is: more grace. In Jesus, this unending fountain of inexhaustible grace has been secured. In perfect justice and righteousness God can treat believers not in accord with what they deserve on their own. Praise God.

PSALM 39

To the choirmaster: to Jeduthun. A Psalm of David.

1 I said, "I will guard my ways,
  that I may not sin with my tongue;
  I will guard my mouth with a muzzle,
   so long as the wicked are in my presence."
2 I was mute and silent;
  I held my peace to no avail,
and my distress grew worse.
3   My heart became hot within me.
As I mused, the fire burned;
  then I spoke with my tongue:

4 "O LORD, make me know my end
  and what is the measure of my days;
  let me know how fleeting I am!
5 Behold, you have made my days a few handbreadths,
  and my lifetime is as nothing before you.
Surely all mankind stands as a mere breath!   *Selah*
6   Surely a man goes about as a shadow!
Surely for nothing they are in turmoil;
  man heaps up wealth and does not know who will
   gather!

7 "And now, O Lord, for what do I wait?
  My hope is in you.
8 Deliver me from all my transgressions.
  Do not make me the scorn of the fool!

9   I am mute; I do not open my mouth,
        for it is you who have done it.

10   Remove your stroke from me;
        I am spent by the hostility of your hand.

11   When you discipline a man
        with rebukes for sin,
    you consume like a moth what is dear to him;
        surely all mankind is a mere breath!   *Selah*

12   "Hear my prayer, O LORD,
        and give ear to my cry;
        hold not your peace at my tears!
    For I am a sojourner with you,
        a guest, like all my fathers.

13   Look away from me, that I may smile again,
        before I depart and am no more!"

§

The shortness of life! The frailty of this transient existence! Psalm 39 reminds us of the book of Ecclesiastes in its sober reminder of the frightful brevity of life in this world. From about age thirty on, our bodies are powering down. We are *dying*. As James puts it, "You are a mist that appears for a little time and then vanishes" (James 4:14). This is a key theme of this solemn psalm.

What then? Are we to throw up our hands and give up on life? By no means. Rather, we are to pray, "O LORD, make me know my end and what is the measure of my days" (Ps. 39:4). We are not to give way to cynicism or hopelessness. We are to be sober minded, considering the shortness of life. We are to acknowledge our sinfulness (v. 8) and recognize that when we plant our hopes in the things of this world, God will discipline us and bring bitter disappointment regarding that idolatry. He will "consume like a moth what is dear to him" (v. 11).

Why does the Lord do this? Why is his hand so heavy upon us at times? Because he loves us too much to allow us to follow our natural inclinations to build our joy on the sandy foundation of the things of earth—even good things like health or money or vacations or family or education or work. He insists that our final hope rests on him. Only then will we be spared ultimate disappointment. For God is the one hope of this life who will not, in the end, let us down.

PSALM 40

To the choirmaster. A Psalm of David.

1   I waited patiently for the LORD;
            he inclined to me and heard my cry.
2   He drew me up from the pit of destruction,
            out of the miry bog,
     and set my feet upon a rock,
            making my steps secure.
3   He put a new song in my mouth,
            a song of praise to our God.
     Many will see and fear,
            and put their trust in the LORD.

4   Blessed is the man who makes
            the LORD his trust,

who does not turn to the proud,
    to those who go astray after a lie!
5 You have multiplied, O Lᴏʀᴅ my God,
    your wondrous deeds and your thoughts toward us;
    none can compare with you!
I will proclaim and tell of them,
    yet they are more than can be told.

6 In sacrifice and offering you have not delighted,
    but you have given me an open ear.
Burnt offering and sin offering
    you have not required.
7 Then I said, "Behold, I have come;
    in the scroll of the book it is written of me:
8 I delight to do your will, O my God;
    your law is within my heart."

9 I have told the glad news of deliverance
    in the great congregation;
behold, I have not restrained my lips,
    as you know, O Lᴏʀᴅ.
10 I have not hidden your deliverance within my heart;
    I have spoken of your faithfulness and your salvation;
I have not concealed your steadfast love and your
    faithfulness
from the great congregation.

11 As for you, O Lᴏʀᴅ, you will not restrain
    your mercy from me;
your steadfast love and your faithfulness will
    ever preserve me!

12 For evils have encompassed me
        beyond number;
    my iniquities have overtaken me,
        and I cannot see;
    they are more than the hairs of my head;
        my heart fails me.

13 Be pleased, O LORD, to deliver me!
        O LORD, make haste to help me!
14 Let those be put to shame and disappointed altogether
        who seek to snatch away my life;
    let those be turned back and brought to dishonor
        who delight in my hurt!
15 Let those be appalled because of their shame
        who say to me, "Aha, Aha!"

16 But may all who seek you
        rejoice and be glad in you;
    may those who love your salvation
        say continually, "Great is the LORD!"
17 As for me, I am poor and needy,
        but the Lord takes thought for me.
    You are my help and my deliverer;
        do not delay, O my God!

∽

In this psalm David looks both backward and forward as he
considers his need for God. He looks back to past deliverance
from God: "He drew me up from the pit of destruction . . . and set
my feet upon a rock" (v. 2). And he looks to future deliverance:
"Your steadfast love and your faithfulness will ever preserve me"

(v. 11). And all of this is the context for his present predicament: "O LORD, make haste to help me!" (v. 13). David looks to the past and to the future for help in the present.

How do you process present adversity? Neighbors ridicule you? Colleagues at work reject your ideas? The medical exam comes back with bad news? When life is going into meltdown, it is often extremely difficult to feel the love of God as a present reality. God seems distant. Aloof. Deaf.

The way forward is to consider what God has done for you in the past and what you know he will do in the future. And what can we say that God has done for us in the past? Something far greater than what David articulates when he says, "Behold, I have come . . . I delight to do your will, O my God; your law is within my heart" (vv. 7–8). Such is the posture of a sincere believer. But who can say they have done this perfectly? Only one. The greater Son of David came into this world and never faltered from doing the will of God. He then suffered what our sin deserves and rose triumphant from the grave. Looking back at this supreme act of deliverance, and forward to Christ's second return and our final deliverance, we look to God in confidence, despite our present adversities.

PSALM 41

To the choirmaster. A Psalm of David.

1   Blessed is the one who considers the poor!
       In the day of trouble the Lord delivers him;
2   the Lord protects him and keeps him alive;
       he is called blessed in the land;
       you do not give him up to the will of his enemies.
3   The Lord sustains him on his sickbed;
       in his illness you restore him to full health.

4   As for me, I said, "O Lord, be gracious to me;
       heal me, for I have sinned against you!"
5   My enemies say of me in malice,
       "When will he die, and his name perish?"
6   And when one comes to see me, he utters empty words,
       while his heart gathers iniquity;
       when he goes out, he tells it abroad.
7   All who hate me whisper together about me;
       they imagine the worst for me.

8   They say, "A deadly thing is poured out on him;
       he will not rise again from where he lies."
9   Even my close friend in whom I trusted,
       who ate my bread, has lifted his heel against me.
10   But you, O Lord, be gracious to me,
       and raise me up, that I may repay them!

11   By this I know that you delight in me:
         my enemy will not shout in triumph over me.
12   But you have upheld me because of my integrity,
         and set me in your presence forever.

13   Blessed be the LORD, the God of Israel,
         from everlasting to everlasting!
            Amen and Amen.

ॐ

David feels betrayed. Even those closest to him, those who shared meals with him, have turned against him (v. 9). But David's relational challenges are not his only difficulty. He himself is guilty: "Heal me, for I have sinned against you!" (v. 4).

David's problems are not isolated to him. These are universal adversities. Consider the grace of God in giving us the realism of the Psalms. The Psalms are not trite, superficial answers to life's deepest problems. The Psalms take us deep down into the pain of this life, and then they take us up again into divine renewal and true hope. We see this when verse 10 begins by saying "But . . ." David's pains are not the sum total of his life. The deepest reality of his life is the promises of God: "But you, O LORD, be gracious to me, and raise me up . . ." (v. 10).

David knew only in shadows what we know in full light: even though he would one day die and be buried in the ground, he will indeed be raised up by the mercy of God. He will be finally and invincibly raised, in fully physical form, one day—as will every believer in Jesus Christ, David's great Son. Christ endured all the pains of this world, yet without sin, and was raised as the firstfruits of the one great harvest that will be gathered on the last day (1 Cor. 15:20–22).

BOOK TWO

PSALM 42

To the choirmaster. A Maskil of the Sons of Korah.

1 As a deer pants for flowing streams,
    so pants my soul for you, O God.
2 My soul thirsts for God,
    for the living God.
When shall I come and appear before God?
3 My tears have been my food
    day and night,
while they say to me all the day long,
  "Where is your God?"
4 These things I remember,
    as I pour out my soul:
how I would go with the throng
    and lead them in procession to the house of God
with glad shouts and songs of praise,
    a multitude keeping festival.

5 Why are you cast down, O my soul,
    and why are you in turmoil within me?
Hope in God; for I shall again praise him,
6   my salvation and my God.

My soul is cast down within me;
    therefore I remember you
from the land of Jordan and of Hermon,
    from Mount Mizar.

7 Deep calls to deep
        at the roar of your waterfalls;
   all your breakers and your waves
        have gone over me.
8 By day the LORD commands his steadfast love,
        and at night his song is with me,
        a prayer to the God of my life.
9 I say to God, my rock:
        "Why have you forgotten me?
   Why do I go mourning
        because of the oppression of the enemy?"
10 As with a deadly wound in my bones,
        my adversaries taunt me,
   while they say to me all the day long,
        "Where is your God?"

11 Why are you cast down, O my soul,
        and why are you in turmoil within me?
   Hope in God; for I shall again praise him,
        my salvation and my God.

∽

The psalmist is deeply discouraged. He says to God that it feels as if all "your waves have gone over me" (v. 7). Some adversities are so great that they cannot be handled in the same way as some of the other, more minor disappointments and frustrations of life. This particular type of adversity passes a threshold that the garden-variety trials do not reach. Imagine wading out into the ocean. You begin to feel the waves coming against you. First your ankles, then your knees, and so on. As you continue further into the water, eventually a wave comes that cannot be out-jumped. It washes over you. You are now submerged and completely terrified.

What is someone who professes faith in Christ to do when the waves of life wash over him? Will his faith prove to be genuine? Or will he spurn Christ and rush toward the false harbors of this world?

At such a moment of trial, we are forced into one of two positions: either cynicism and coldness of heart or true depth with God. A spouse betrays. A habitual sin, left unchecked, blows up in our face. We are publicly shamed in some way that will haunt us as long as we live. A malignant, inoperable tumor. Profound disillusionment in some way. It feels like "a deadly wound in my bones" (v. 10).

When that moment comes, sent by the hand of a tender Father, will we believe what we have confessed about God to be true, or will we suspect him of deserting us? The two lines of professed-belief and heart-belief, to this point parallel, are suddenly forced either to overlap completely or to move further apart. We cannot go on as before. And why does this happen? Because God will not let us remain the people we would be as long as the waves reached only our waist.

But above all else, when life implodes, remember that his own dear Son went through the greatest nightmare himself, in our place. The tidal wave of true separation from the Father washed over Another so that it need never wash over us.

PSALM 43

1   Vindicate me, O God, and defend my cause
        against an ungodly people,
    from the deceitful and unjust man
        deliver me!
2   For you are the God in whom I take refuge;
        why have you rejected me?
    Why do I go about mourning
        because of the oppression of the enemy?

3   Send out your light and your truth;
        let them lead me;
    let them bring me to your holy hill
        and to your dwelling!
4   Then I will go to the altar of God,
        to God my exceeding joy,
    and I will praise you with the lyre,
        O God, my God.

5   Why are you cast down, O my soul,
        and why are you in turmoil within me?
    Hope in God; for I shall again praise him,
        my salvation and my God.

5

This psalm, perhaps originally connected to the previous psalm, continues the psalmist's reflection on his deep discouragement. Note how, throughout both of these psalms, the writer *talks to himself*: "Why are you cast down, O my soul, and why are you in turmoil within me? Hope in God" (v. 5; also 42:5, 11). The great twentieth-century preacher Martyn Lloyd-Jones reflected on this passage:

> Have you realized that most of your unhappiness in life is due to the fact that you are listening to yourself instead of talking to yourself? Take those thoughts that come to you the moment you wake up in the morning. You have not originated them, but they start talking to you, they bring back the problem of yesterday, etc. Somebody is talking. Who is talking to you? Your self is talking to you. Now this man's treatment was this; instead of allowing this self to talk to him, he starts talking to himself, 'Why art thou cast down, O my soul?' he asks. His soul had been repressing him, crushing him. So he stands up and says: 'Self, listen for a moment, I will speak to you'.

The Psalms guide us into learning how to talk to ourselves—rebuking the hope-sucking discouragements that tend to torpedo our emotional buoyancy. How? Not through self-help pep talks. Not through recounting all the good in our life, hoping it will outweigh the bad. Rather, through remembering who God is: "Hope in God; for I shall again praise him, my salvation and my God" (43:5).

The Hebrew word for "salvation" here reads literally "the salvation of my face." God does not save me in ethereal abstraction. He draws near to me, so near that the Bible describes it in terms of saving my very face. In Jesus, we see this salvation draw near as God has "shone in our hearts to give the light of the knowledge of the glory of God in the face of Jesus Christ" (2 Cor. 4:6).

PSALM 44

To the choirmaster. A Maskil of the Sons of Korah.

1   O God, we have heard with our ears,
        our fathers have told us,
    what deeds you performed in their days,
        in the days of old:
2   you with your own hand drove out the nations,
        but them you planted;
    you afflicted the peoples,
        but them you set free;
3   for not by their own sword did they win the land,
        nor did their own arm save them,
    but your right hand and your arm,
        and the light of your face,
        for you delighted in them.

4   You are my King, O God;
        ordain salvation for Jacob!

5   Through you we push down our foes;
         through your name we tread down those who rise
              up against us.
6   For not in my bow do I trust,
         nor can my sword save me.
7   But you have saved us from our foes
         and have put to shame those who hate us.
8   In God we have boasted continually,
         and we will give thanks to your name forever.   *Selah*

9   But you have rejected us and disgraced us
         and have not gone out with our armies.
10   You have made us turn back from the foe,
         and those who hate us have gotten spoil.
11   You have made us like sheep for slaughter
         and have scattered us among the nations.
12   You have sold your people for a trifle,
         demanding no high price for them.
13   You have made us the taunt of our neighbors,
         the derision and scorn of those around us.
14   You have made us a byword among the nations,
         a laughingstock among the peoples.
15   All day long my disgrace is before me,
         and shame has covered my face
16   at the sound of the taunter and reviler,
         at the sight of the enemy and the avenger.

17   All this has come upon us,
         though we have not forgotten you,
         and we have not been false to your covenant.
18   Our heart has not turned back,
         nor have our steps departed from your way;

19   yet you have broken us in the place of jackals
        and covered us with the shadow of death.
20   If we had forgotten the name of our God
        or spread out our hands to a foreign god,
21   would not God discover this?
        For he knows the secrets of the heart.
22   Yet for your sake we are killed all the day long;
        we are regarded as sheep to be slaughtered.

23   Awake! Why are you sleeping, O Lord?
        Rouse yourself! Do not reject us forever!
24   Why do you hide your face?
        Why do you forget our affliction and oppression?
25   For our soul is bowed down to the dust;
        our belly clings to the ground.
26   Rise up; come to our help!
        Redeem us for the sake of your steadfast love!

∽

This psalm is a song of corporate lament. Together God's people cry out, wondering why God has left them in such apparent forsakenness. It is deeply bewildering to feel abandoned by God. But this is sometimes our experience.

But note what the people also affirm: they agree that any favor they have received from God has been a gift. Past deliverance has been by sheer mercy: "Not by their own sword did they win the land, nor did their own arm save them, but your right hand and your arm" (v. 3). This is the fundamental message of the Bible. Fallen men and women stand in need of a salvation that comes wholly from outside of them. They contribute nothing but their need. When God's people stand in need of fresh deliverance, therefore, this is all they can plead: "Rise up; come to our help! Redeem us for the sake of your steadfast love!" (v. 26).

Centuries after this psalm was written, God would show just how far he would go *not* to forsake his people. In Jesus Christ, God drew near to sinners to assure them of his undying love, if they would only lay down their arms and humble themselves enough to receive it. When you find yourself feeling forsaken, look to Jesus and his great work of atonement, of restoring us to God.

PSALM 45

To the choirmaster: according to Lilies.
A Maskil of the Sons of Korah; a love song.

1 My heart overflows with a pleasing theme;
    I address my verses to the king;
    my tongue is like the pen of a ready scribe.

2 You are the most handsome of the sons of men;
    grace is poured upon your lips;
    therefore God has blessed you forever.
3 Gird your sword on your thigh, O mighty one,
    in your splendor and majesty!

4 In your majesty ride out victoriously
    for the cause of truth and meekness and righteousness;
    let your right hand teach you awesome deeds!

5   Your arrows are sharp
        in the heart of the king's enemies;
        the peoples fall under you.

6   Your throne, O God, is forever and ever.
        The scepter of your kingdom is a scepter of
            uprightness;
7   you have loved righteousness and hated wickedness.
    Therefore God, your God, has anointed you
        with the oil of gladness beyond your companions;
8   your robes are all fragrant with myrrh and aloes and
            cassia.
    From ivory palaces stringed instruments make you glad;
9   daughters of kings are among your ladies of honor;
        at your right hand stands the queen in gold of Ophir.

10   Hear, O daughter, and consider, and incline your ear:
        forget your people and your father's house,
11   and the king will desire your beauty.
    Since he is your lord, bow to him.
12   The people of Tyre will seek your favor with gifts,
        the richest of the people.

13   All glorious is the princess in her chamber, with robes
           interwoven with gold.
14   In many-colored robes she is led to the king,
        with her virgin companions following behind her.
15   With joy and gladness they are led along
        as they enter the palace of the king.

16   In place of your fathers shall be your sons;
        you will make them princes in all the earth.

17   I will cause your name to be remembered in all
            generations;
      therefore nations will praise you forever and ever.

∽

The theme of this psalm is the magnificence of the king. He is magnificent in speech (v. 2), virtue (v. 4), military conquest (v. 5), and even, at the height of the psalm, romance (vv. 13–15). He will never be forgotten, so glorious is his rule (v. 17).

This is the ideal king. Even today, when most nations are not under the rule of a pure monarchy, this is the king, the ruler, every human heart longs for. A king of justice and of virtue, of might and of beauty. Yet the story of the Old Testament is of the consistent failure of Israel's kings to live up to this ideal. Not only did they fall short of this, many of them went in the other direction, ruling wickedly and encouraging idolatry and faithlessness to the God who had delivered them from Egypt and brought them into the Promised Land.

The book of Hebrews helps us to understand that the ideal king did eventually come—once, and only once. Hebrews 1 applies this psalm to Jesus Christ as God's final heir and king, his true and only Son (Heb. 1:8–9). He is the true and final king in speech, speaking only what is right and good; in virtue, truly walking in "truth and meekness and righteousness" (Ps. 45:4); in military conquest, triumphing over the devil and his forces (Col. 2:14–15); and yes, even in romantic love, for he took a bride to himself in a union of which every romance is but a faint echo (Eph. 5:31–32; Rev. 21:2).

PSALM 46

To the choirmaster. Of the Sons of Korah.
According to Alamoth. A Song.

1   God is our refuge and strength,
       a very present help in trouble.
2   Therefore we will not fear though the earth gives way,
       though the mountains be moved into the heart of
         the sea,
3   though its waters roar and foam,
       though the mountains tremble at its swelling.   *Selah*

4   There is a river whose streams make glad the city of God,
       the holy habitation of the Most High.
5   God is in the midst of her; she shall not be moved;
       God will help her when morning dawns.
6   The nations rage, the kingdoms totter;
       he utters his voice, the earth melts.
7   The Lord of hosts is with us;
       the God of Jacob is our fortress.   *Selah*

8   Come, behold the works of the Lord,
       how he has brought desolations on the earth.
9   He makes wars cease to the end of the earth;
       he breaks the bow and shatters the spear;
       he burns the chariots with fire.
10   "Be still, and know that I am God.
       I will be exalted among the nations,
       I will be exalted in the earth!"

11   The LORD of hosts is with us;
        the God of Jacob is our fortress.   *Selah*

∽

To turn on the television or radio or to drive down a billboard-filled highway is to be bombarded with the message that various products and services are the secret to achieving inner calm. If you can just get the right body, the right education, the right financial structure, the right entertainment system—then you will have achieved that deep "soul-sigh" everyone longs for. Psalm 46 offers an alternative to the world. It says: Be still. Be quiet. Look up. Calm down. God reigns.

This psalm does not offer a Pollyanna view of life. This psalm gives us sober realism. Even though the earth goes haywire (vv. 2–3), even though nations assault each other (v. 6), all of this is under the wise and far-reaching hand of God.

What troubles you today? What is it about which you think, "If I can just get *that* sorted out, life will become manageable"? What worries your heart as you lie awake in bed? God says: I, not any circumstantial solution, am your refuge amid your adversities. I am a very present help in trouble. I am God. Be still.

PSALM 47

To the choirmaster. A Psalm of the Sons of Korah.

1   Clap your hands, all peoples!
      Shout to God with loud songs of joy!
2   For the LORD, the Most High, is to be feared,
      a great king over all the earth.
3   He subdued peoples under us,
      and nations under our feet.
4   He chose our heritage for us,
      the pride of Jacob whom he loves.   *Selah*

5   God has gone up with a shout,
      the LORD with the sound of a trumpet.
6   Sing praises to God, sing praises!
      Sing praises to our King, sing praises!
7   For God is the King of all the earth;
      sing praises with a psalm!

8   God reigns over the nations;
      God sits on his holy throne.
9   The princes of the peoples gather
      as the people of the God of Abraham.
    For the shields of the earth belong to God;
      he is highly exalted!

God rules, but not merely over his own people, or merely over part of the universe. He rules over all. The psalmist here connects God's supreme reign to the specific promises to Abraham, namely, that all peoples would be blessed in him (v. 9; see Gen. 12:1–3). Right from the start, God's plan was to welcome in all the nations of the earth. God called Abraham not simply so that he could bless Abraham's descendants, the Jews, but so that *through* the Jews he could bless the whole world.

What is your family background? Do you have Scandinavian roots? African? Filipino? Dutch? Mexican? Polish? If you are a Christian, you are part of the fulfillment of the promises made to Abraham all the way back near the beginning of the Bible in Genesis 12. This is why the psalmist calls for praise and rejoicing from "all peoples" (Ps. 47:1).

One day, through the salvation wrought in Jesus Christ, the true and final descendant of Abraham (Gal. 3:16), God will welcome into the new heavens and the new earth a beautiful international diversity of ethnicities. As the heavenly throne room says of Jesus, the final Lamb: "Worthy are you to take the scroll and to open its seals, for you were slain, and by your blood you ransomed people for God from every tribe and language and people and nation" (Rev. 5:9).

PSALM 48

A Song. A Psalm of the Sons of Korah.

1 Great is the Lord and greatly to be praised
   in the city of our God!
2 His holy mountain, beautiful in elevation,
   is the joy of all the earth,
  Mount Zion, in the far north,
   the city of the great King.
3 Within her citadels God
   has made himself known as a fortress.

4 For behold, the kings assembled;
   they came on together.
5 As soon as they saw it, they were astounded;
   they were in panic; they took to flight.
6 Trembling took hold of them there,
   anguish as of a woman in labor.
7 By the east wind you shattered
   the ships of Tarshish.
8 As we have heard, so have we seen
   in the city of the Lord of hosts,
  in the city of our God,
   which God will establish forever. *Selah*

9 We have thought on your steadfast love, O God,
   in the midst of your temple.
10 As your name, O God,
   so your praise reaches to the ends of the earth.

Your right hand is filled with righteousness.
11   Let Mount Zion be glad!
Let the daughters of Judah rejoice
      because of your judgments!

12   Walk about Zion, go around her,
      number her towers,
13   consider well her ramparts,
      go through her citadels,
that you may tell the next generation
14   that this is God,
our God forever and ever.
      He will guide us forever.

∽

Psalm 48 celebrates Zion as God's special city, his chosen place; this is where he has chosen to dwell. It is striking to consider the role of cities throughout the Bible. Humanity was first placed in a garden, not a city. The first city, Babel, reflected mankind's pride and arrogance. Yet, at the end of all things, it is not a garden but a city that comes down out of heaven—the new Jerusalem (Rev. 21:1–2). God takes humanity's rebellion and creates something beautiful out of it.

Here in Psalm 48 we find a reflection on the city that God made his own, Zion. Zion is the name of the mountain on which Jerusalem was built. Throughout the Old Testament, Zion comes to represent the promises of God. This is where he lives. Specifically, God lives in the temple, the most important building on Zion. This is why David speaks of reflecting on God's steadfast love while in the temple (v. 9). The temple was where God could be found.

But notice that at the end of Psalm 48, the psalmist equates Zion, the city in which God placed his presence, with *God himself* (vv. 12–13). The buildings of the city, the building of the temple, so represented God's presence that they could virtually be called God. Consider where you and I are now in redemptive history. God came to earth in the person of his Son, who called himself the temple (John 2:19–22) and who said that believing sinners are united to him and become part of this temple (Eph. 2:19–22). Do you live in a city? A town? A village? God does not simply dwell among you, in some special building. He dwells *in* you. He could not be closer. You are never alone.

PSALM 49

To the choirmaster. A Psalm of the Sons of Korah.

1   Hear this, all peoples!
      Give ear, all inhabitants of the world,
2   both low and high,
      rich and poor together!
3   My mouth shall speak wisdom;
      the meditation of my heart shall be understanding.
4   I will incline my ear to a proverb;
      I will solve my riddle to the music of the lyre.

5   Why should I fear in times of trouble,
      when the iniquity of those who cheat me
        surrounds me,

6   those who trust in their wealth
      and boast of the abundance of their riches?

7   Truly no man can ransom another,
      or give to God the price of his life,

8   for the ransom of their life is costly
      and can never suffice,

9   that he should live on forever
      and never see the pit.

10   For he sees that even the wise die;
      the fool and the stupid alike must perish
      and leave their wealth to others.

11   Their graves are their homes forever,
      their dwelling places to all generations,
      though they called lands by their own names.

12   Man in his pomp will not remain;
      he is like the beasts that perish.

13   This is the path of those who have foolish confidence;
      yet after them people approve of their boasts.   *Selah*

14   Like sheep they are appointed for Sheol;
      death shall be their shepherd,
   and the upright shall rule over them in the morning.
      Their form shall be consumed in Sheol, with no
         place to dwell.

15   But God will ransom my soul from the power of Sheol,
      for he will receive me.   *Selah*

16   Be not afraid when a man becomes rich,
      when the glory of his house increases.

17   For when he dies he will carry nothing away;
      his glory will not go down after him.

18	For though, while he lives, he counts himself blessed
	—and though you get praise when you do well for
		yourself—
19	his soul will go to the generation of his fathers,
	who will never again see light.
20	Man in his pomp yet without understanding is like the
	beasts that perish.

∽

Psalm 49 is a wisdom psalm, teaching believers how to walk before God with skill in godliness. The specific burden of this wisdom psalm is to settle us into the knowledge that the security of worldly wealth is a mirage. The poor die; the rich die. A man may amass wealth, but he cannot use it to buy more time: "Truly no man can ransom another, or give to God the price of his life" (v. 7).

How then can the psalmist claim with any confidence that his own life *will* be ransomed? "God will ransom my soul from the power of Sheol, for he will receive me" (v. 15). The psalmist evidently claims that not only will God grant him more life, but God will even extend his life beyond death ("the power of Sheol"). The answer to this question is the great secret at the heart of the universe. For those who trust in anything in themselves, whether riches or anything else, there is no opportunity for a ransom—that is, for a purchase price to be paid to give more life.

But what if someone who deserved endless life willingly allowed it to be cut short? What if someone who should never have had to experience the grave endured it?

Jesus Christ left the beauty of heaven to walk through the brokenness of this fallen world. And he went willingly to a Roman cross to ransom sinners from the clutches of death and hell and condemnation. The price he paid—his own dear life—is costly enough to win back the lives of all of those who repent and trust in him. This is the good news, the gospel. Receive it afresh, today.

PSALM 50

A Psalm of Asaph.

1   The Mighty One, God the LORD,
         speaks and summons the earth
         from the rising of the sun to its setting.
2   Out of Zion, the perfection of beauty,
         God shines forth.

3   Our God comes; he does not keep silence;
         before him is a devouring fire,
         around him a mighty tempest.
4   He calls to the heavens above
         and to the earth, that he may judge his people:
5   "Gather to me my faithful ones,
         who made a covenant with me by sacrifice!"
6   The heavens declare his righteousness,
         for God himself is judge!   *Selah*

7   "Hear, O my people, and I will speak;
         O Israel, I will testify against you.
         I am God, your God.

8   Not for your sacrifices do I rebuke you;
        your burnt offerings are continually before me.
9   I will not accept a bull from your house
        or goats from your folds.
10 For every beast of the forest is mine,
        the cattle on a thousand hills.
11 I know all the birds of the hills,
        and all that moves in the field is mine.

12 "If I were hungry, I would not tell you,
        for the world and its fullness are mine.
13 Do I eat the flesh of bulls
        or drink the blood of goats?
14 Offer to God a sacrifice of thanksgiving,
        and perform your vows to the Most High,
15 and call upon me in the day of trouble;
        I will deliver you, and you shall glorify me."

16 But to the wicked God says:
        "What right have you to recite my statutes
        or take my covenant on your lips?
17 For you hate discipline,
        and you cast my words behind you.
18 If you see a thief, you are pleased with him,
        and you keep company with adulterers.

19 "You give your mouth free rein for evil,
        and your tongue frames deceit.
20 You sit and speak against your brother;
        you slander your own mother's son.

21   These things you have done, and I have been silent;
           you thought that I was one like yourself.
       But now I rebuke you and lay the charge before you.

22   "Mark this, then, you who forget God,
           lest I tear you apart, and there be none to deliver!
23   The one who offers thanksgiving as his sacrifice
           glorifies me;
       to one who orders his way rightly
       I will show the salvation of God!"

§

Deep within the human heart resides the desire to buy God off. We know we fall short. We know we do not measure up. We know, deep within, that God exists and that we have offended his holiness. And bubbling up from within, desperately hoping to make amends, are our unspoken hopes of leveling things out. Surely there is something we can do to make things right?

The entire sacrificial system of the Old Testament was God's way of driving home to his people the horror of sin and the need for it to be punished—if not by the guilty one, then by an animal bearing that guilt. Yet the story of the Old Testament is a story of Israel's misusing the sacrificial system, using it to attempt to buy God off in a coldly transactional way rather than allowing it to move them to deeper contrition and trust in him. This is a repeated theme, for example, in the book of Jeremiah.

The burden of this psalm is that the sacrifices that are misused to appease God are already God's. We can never benefit God—he can only benefit us. God does not want empty ritual—he wants our hearts. God does not ask us to give him gifts—he asks us to give him ourselves. God does not want the aroma of burning animals—he wants the aroma of heartfelt thanksgiving (vv. 14, 23).

Most of all, he wants us to honor him simply by crying out for help: "Call upon me in the day of trouble; I will deliver you, and you shall glorify me" (v. 15). We glorify God by being delivered by him—which reminds us of the deepest reason for the sacrificial system. All of the sacrifices were anticipating a final sacrifice that would truly take away sins (Heb. 10:1–7). Every priest was preparing for a final priest who would never die (Heb. 7:23–24). All of the offerings were fulfilled in a final offering put forth once and for all (Heb. 10:10). We dare not try to buy God off; God has taken care of everything himself, in his own Son.

PSALM 51

To the choirmaster. A Psalm of David, when Nathan the prophet went to him, after he had gone in to Bathsheba.

1   Have mercy on me, O God,
        according to your steadfast love;
    according to your abundant mercy
        blot out my transgressions.
2   Wash me thoroughly from my iniquity,
        and cleanse me from my sin!

3   For I know my transgressions,
        and my sin is ever before me.

4 Against you, you only, have I sinned
    and done what is evil in your sight,
  so that you may be justified in your words
    and blameless in your judgment.
5 Behold, I was brought forth in iniquity,
    and in sin did my mother conceive me.
6 Behold, you delight in truth in the inward being,
    and you teach me wisdom in the secret heart.

7 Purge me with hyssop, and I shall be clean;
    wash me, and I shall be whiter than snow.
8 Let me hear joy and gladness;
    let the bones that you have broken rejoice.
9 Hide your face from my sins,
    and blot out all my iniquities.
10 Create in me a clean heart, O God,
    and renew a right spirit within me.
11 Cast me not away from your presence,
    and take not your Holy Spirit from me.
12 Restore to me the joy of your salvation,
    and uphold me with a willing spirit.

13 Then I will teach transgressors your ways,
    and sinners will return to you.
14 Deliver me from bloodguiltiness, O God,
    O God of my salvation,
    and my tongue will sing aloud of your righteousness.
15 O Lord, open my lips,
    and my mouth will declare your praise.
16 For you will not delight in sacrifice, or I would give it;
    you will not be pleased with a burnt offering.

17   The sacrifices of God are a broken spirit;
            a broken and contrite heart, O God, you will not
                despise.

18   Do good to Zion in your good pleasure;
            build up the walls of Jerusalem;
19   then will you delight in right sacrifices,
            in burnt offerings and whole burnt offerings;
            then bulls will be offered on your altar.

∽

Who among us does not know the need to go to Psalm 51 and make it ours? David prayed this psalm after commit-ting adultery with Bathsheba, but his words and heart of repen-tance are universally relevant to all who feel the weight of their sin.

Note the pervasive metaphor used throughout the psalm: David feels *dirty*. He needs God to make him clean. "Wash me" (vv. 2, 7), he begs. "Cleanse me" (v. 3). "Purge me" (v. 7). "Blot out all my iniquities" (v. 9). But this is a dirtiness that cannot be washed off in a shower. It is inside us.

Do you feel dirty? The good news of the gospel is that you can be rinsed clean. David pleads for God to have mercy on him (v. 1). Is this an empty, hopeless plea? By no means. Look at the next words: "according to your steadfast love" (v. 1). David is asking for God to be who he is. He is asking God to act in a way that is consistent with himself. David knows he is a God of "abundant mercy" (v. 1), so he asks for mercy accordingly.

Is this who you know God to be? Is this who you know yourself to be? Do you know yourself to be dirty? A sinner? All that God asks of you is to bring the sacrifice of a "broken and contrite heart" (v. 17). He gave his own Son as the final sacrifice so that your brokenness could be the only prerequisite to receiving God's abundant mercy. Amid your dirtiness, you are free to breathe again. He is the God of abundant mercy. He proved it in Jesus. This is who he is. In Christ, you are rinsed clean—invincibly, permanently, irreversibly.

PSALM 52

To the choirmaster. A Maskil of David, when
Doeg, the Edomite, came and told Saul, "David
has come to the house of Ahimelech."

1 Why do you boast of evil, O mighty man?
     The steadfast love of God endures all the day.
2 Your tongue plots destruction,
     like a sharp razor, you worker of deceit.
3 You love evil more than good,
     and lying more than speaking what is right.   *Selah*
4 You love all words that devour,
     O deceitful tongue.

5 But God will break you down forever;
     he will snatch and tear you from your tent;
     he will uproot you from the land of the living. *Selah*
6 The righteous shall see and fear,
     and shall laugh at him, saying,
7 "See the man who would not make
     God his refuge,

but trusted in the abundance of his riches
and sought refuge in his own destruction!"

8   But I am like a green olive tree
in the house of God.
I trust in the steadfast love of God
forever and ever.
9   I will thank you forever,
because you have done it.
I will wait for your name, for it is good,
in the presence of the godly.

∽

David draws his imagery in this psalm from the realm of the botanical. He reflects on God's uprooting the evil from the land (v. 5) while comparing himself to a green, vibrant olive tree (v. 8; note also 1:3).

And why is David a "green olive tree"? Has he disciplined himself to just the right amount of exercise? Has he been careful about his diet? Has he received a windfall of money? Note what he says: "I am like a green olive tree in the house of God. I trust in the steadfast love of God forever and ever" (52:8). He goes on to explain further that he is waiting on God, hoping in him (v. 9). This is one of the great secrets at the heart of the life of a believer. The breakthrough to inner health and calm is fundamentally not activity on our part but, in a sense, passivity—looking to God, trusting him, leaning on him.

What does it really mean to trust God? To trust God means to live your life *as if God actually exists and is who he says he is*. It is to conduct your existence in such a way that what you say that you believe about God aligns with how you use words, money, your body, and other people. It is to leave your final welfare in God's hands rather than your own. To do otherwise is to welcome your own destruction (v. 7). We can trust in ourselves and perish eternally, or we can trust in the Lord, and—because of the redemptive work of Christ—live eternally.

PSALM 53

To the choirmaster: according to Mahalath. A Maskil of David.

1   The fool says in his heart, "There is no God."
        They are corrupt, doing abominable iniquity;
        there is none who does good.

2   God looks down from heaven
        on the children of man
    to see if there are any who understand,
        who seek after God.

3   They have all fallen away;
        together they have become corrupt;
    there is none who does good,
        not even one.

4   Have those who work evil no knowledge,
        who eat up my people as they eat bread,
        and do not call upon God?

5   There they are, in great terror,
          where there is no terror!
     For God scatters the bones of him who encamps against
               you;
          you put them to shame, for God has rejected them.

6   Oh, that salvation for Israel would come out of Zion!
          When God restores the fortunes of his people,
          let Jacob rejoice, let Israel be glad.

৸

Some people are given Nobel prizes. Others are jailed for life. If there is one thing that seems clear in society today, it is that there is a sharp divide between good people and bad people.

And at one level this is of course true. Some follow the law; others do not. Some respect civil authority; others flout it and are incarcerated accordingly.

But the Bible provides a deeper diagnosis of the human condition. Due to God's common grace, many people around the world live basically upright lives as far as civil laws are concerned, yet Scripture teaches that beneath external conformity to civil law lies a deep, dark sickness that has infected every human being. The Bible calls this sickness sin. And the Bible teaches that sin manifests itself in an almost infinite diversity of ways.

This psalm drives home this sobering diagnosis of universal human sinfulness: "There is none who does good, not even one" (v. 3). We cannot finally divide the world into "good" and "bad." As the Russian writer Aleksandr Solzhenitsyn put it, "The line dividing good and evil cuts through the heart of every human being."

Do you know this about yourself? Do you feel your deep wickedness, the way your heart naturally curves toward itself? Do you see *yourself* in Psalm 53, or only your neighbors, enemies, and others? If you feel yourself to be under the indictment of this psalm, this is all that is needed to receive the mercy of God in Jesus Christ. To the degree that you know your sin, to that degree you may enjoy amazing grace.

PSALM 54

To the choirmaster: with stringed instruments.
A Maskil of David, when the Ziphites went and
told Saul, "Is not David hiding among us?"

1   O God, save me by your name,
        and vindicate me by your might.
2   O God, hear my prayer;
        give ear to the words of my mouth.

3   For strangers have risen against me;
        ruthless men seek my life;
        they do not set God before themselves.   *Selah*

4   Behold, God is my helper;
        the Lord is the upholder of my life.
5   He will return the evil to my enemies;
        in your faithfulness put an end to them.

6   With a freewill offering I will sacrifice to you;
        I will give thanks to your name, O LORD, for it is
            good.
7   For he has delivered me from every trouble,
        and my eye has looked in triumph on my enemies.

∽

David has been hiding from Saul among the Ziphites. And the Ziphites, instead of protecting David, reveal his location to Saul. David wrote this psalm out of that experience.

It is one thing to be treated badly by those you know to be your enemies. It is another thing, a deeper pain, to be treated badly by those you thought to be your friends. Ponder your own life. Have you been betrayed? By friends? Perhaps by family? Maybe even by your own parents? This psalm is for you.

Consider where David's heart turns: "Behold, God is my helper; the Lord is the upholder of my life" (v. 4). Instead of looking around for some other person or group of people to protect him the way the Ziphites failed to, David looks to God. His eyes go up, not out.

Perhaps you think, "I can't possibly pray what David prays to end the psalm, announcing deliverance from all my troubles." But if you are in Christ, consider that amid all your present troubles, God has delivered you from the only enemy who could really harm you, the one enemy who could harm your soul, eternally, in hell. He has delivered you from Satan and the sting of death. You are free. You are promised that one day—if not today, then very soon—you will say, with David, "My eye has looked in triumph on my enemies" (v. 7).

PSALM 55

*To the choirmaster: with stringed
instruments. A Maskil of David.*

1   Give ear to my prayer, O God,
     and hide not yourself from my plea for mercy!
2   Attend to me, and answer me;
     I am restless in my complaint and I moan,
3   because of the noise of the enemy,
     because of the oppression of the wicked.
  For they drop trouble upon me,
     and in anger they bear a grudge against me.

4   My heart is in anguish within me;
     the terrors of death have fallen upon me.
5   Fear and trembling come upon me,
     and horror overwhelms me.
6   And I say, "Oh, that I had wings like a dove!
     I would fly away and be at rest;
7   yes, I would wander far away;
     I would lodge in the wilderness;   *Selah*
8   I would hurry to find a shelter
     from the raging wind and tempest."

9   Destroy, O Lord, divide their tongues;
     for I see violence and strife in the city.
10   Day and night they go around it
     on its walls,

and iniquity and trouble are within it;
11   ruin is in its midst;
oppression and fraud
    do not depart from its marketplace.

12 For it is not an enemy who taunts me—
    then I could bear it;
it is not an adversary who deals insolently with me—
    then I could hide from him.
13 But it is you, a man, my equal,
    my companion, my familiar friend.
14 We used to take sweet counsel together;
    within God's house we walked in the throng.
15 Let death steal over them;
    let them go down to Sheol alive;
    for evil is in their dwelling place and in their heart.

16 But I call to God,
    and the LORD will save me.
17 Evening and morning and at noon
    I utter my complaint and moan,
    and he hears my voice.
18 He redeems my soul in safety
    from the battle that I wage,
    for many are arrayed against me.
19 God will give ear and humble them,
    he who is enthroned from of old,   *Selah*
because they do not change
    and do not fear God.

20 My companion stretched out his hand against his friends;
    he violated his covenant.

21	His speech was smooth as butter,
	yet war was in his heart;
	his words were softer than oil,
	yet they were drawn swords.

21 His speech was smooth as butter,
   yet war was in his heart;
his words were softer than oil,
   yet they were drawn swords.

22 Cast your burden on the Lord,
   and he will sustain you;
he will never permit
   the righteous to be moved.

23 But you, O God, will cast them down
   into the pit of destruction;
men of blood and treachery
   shall not live out half their days.
But I will trust in you.

∽

David has been betrayed by the one person who ought never to have breached his trust—"you, a man, my equal, my companion, my familiar friend" (v. 13). This is not, as in the previous psalm, the Ziphites—a group of strangers. This is David's close ally, his dear friend.

The pain of betrayal! Many of us can attest firsthand to David's expression of pain: "My heart is in anguish within me" (v. 4). Why does close personal betrayal hurt so much? It is because we have disclosed our heart to this brother or sister. We have opened up. We have loved. We have unveiled who we are deep within. We have risked openness, honesty. Over time, a profound bond has formed. We have enjoyed the deep joy of human fellowship, as those made in God's image and created for communion with others. We have been *friends*.

Such betrayal happens every day on this earth, but there is one Friend who we know will never betray us: "Cast your burden on the LORD, and he will sustain you" (v. 22). Open up to him, fellowship with him, pour out your heart to him. He will not let you down. He proved it by sending his Son, the friend of sinners, who experienced betrayal but never did nor never will betray anyone who comes to him for help.

PSALM 56

To the choirmaster: according to The Dove on Far-off Terebinths. A Miktam of David, when the Philistines seized him in Gath.

1   Be gracious to me, O God, for man tramples on me;
         all day long an attacker oppresses me;
2   my enemies trample on me all day long,
         for many attack me proudly.
3   When I am afraid,
         I put my trust in you.
4   In God, whose word I praise,
         in God I trust; I shall not be afraid.
         What can flesh do to me?

5   All day long they injure my cause;
         all their thoughts are against me for evil.

6   They stir up strife, they lurk;
        they watch my steps,
        as they have waited for my life.
7   For their crime will they escape?
        In wrath cast down the peoples, O God!

8   You have kept count of my tossings;
        put my tears in your bottle.
        Are they not in your book?
9   Then my enemies will turn back
        in the day when I call.
        This I know, that God is for me.
10   In God, whose word I praise,
        in the LORD, whose word I praise,
11   in God I trust; I shall not be afraid.
        What can man do to me?

12   I must perform my vows to you, O God;
        I will render thank offerings to you.
13   For you have delivered my soul from death,
        yes, my feet from falling,
     that I may walk before God
        in the light of life.

∽

We are all, by nature, timid. There is no such thing as a naturally fearless and brave person—if there were, that person would not be brave. Bravery is the *overcoming* of fear, not the non-existence of fear. Notice the temptations to fear in this psalm. "When I am afraid ..." (v. 3); "I shall not be afraid" (vv. 4, 11). In light of these temptations, how does David respond?

This psalm lists different reasons not to be afraid. One striking remark from David addresses the *tender nearness* of God. Consider the beautiful imagery David uses: "You have kept count of my tossings; put my tears in your bottle" (v. 8). This word-picture arrests us. Consider every tear that has fallen from your face. Every single one. They have each been marked by heaven. God has noticed every one.

He is not aloof, distant, uncaring. We know this because a millennium after David wrote this psalm, God incarnate entered into our space and time. He himself wept (John 11:35). He himself endured anguish (Matt. 26:37–39). Jesus Christ is the living proof, in flesh and blood, that God cares deeply about our problems and pain and tears.

PSALM 57

To the choirmaster: according to Do Not Destroy. A Miktam of David, when he fled from Saul, in the cave.

1   Be merciful to me, O God, be merciful to me,
        for in you my soul takes refuge;
    in the shadow of your wings I will take refuge,
        till the storms of destruction pass by.
2   I cry out to God Most High,
        to God who fulfills his purpose for me.
3   He will send from heaven and save me;
        he will put to shame him who tramples on me. *Selah*
    God will send out his steadfast love and his faithfulness!

4   My soul is in the midst of lions;
         I lie down amid fiery beasts—
     the children of man, whose teeth are spears and arrows,
         whose tongues are sharp swords.

5   Be exalted, O God, above the heavens!
         Let your glory be over all the earth!

6   They set a net for my steps;
         my soul was bowed down.
     They dug a pit in my way,
         but they have fallen into it themselves.   *Selah*
7   My heart is steadfast, O God,
         my heart is steadfast!
     I will sing and make melody!
8   Awake, my glory!
     Awake, O harp and lyre!
         I will awake the dawn!
9   I will give thanks to you, O Lord, among the peoples;
         I will sing praises to you among the nations.
10   For your steadfast love is great to the heavens,
         your faithfulness to the clouds.

11   Be exalted, O God, above the heavens!
         Let your glory be over all the earth!

∽

David has been forced to flee from Saul and is hiding in a cave. Yet his prayer in this psalm testifies that *God* is his cave: "In you my soul takes refuge" (v. 1). David has taken refuge in a solitary cave, and yet there his mind is brought to rest on the deeper truth that God is his true refuge. In the darkness of that moment, his heart takes solace in God.

And how specifically is David comforting himself? In the glorification of God. He states twice, once in the middle and once at the end of the psalm, "Be exalted, O God, above the heavens! Let your glory be over all the earth!" (vv. 5, 11). The placement and repetition of these two statements make clear that this is the major thrust of this psalm. This is David's deepest desire in this dark moment: the exaltation of God.

In the midst of difficulty, the Holy Spirit delights to bring us into this settled place of contentment: as long as God is exalted, all is well. As long as he is known and lifted up and honored, my own welfare need not worry me too much.

Of course, the great consolation of the gospel and the message of the whole Bible is that God delights to glorify himself in the deliverance of his people. The two activities are one. This is why David begins this psalm by asking for personal mercy but ends it by asking for divine glory. In the cross of Christ we see this supremely, where Jesus is "lifted up" on the cross—physically lifted up, yes, but, more deeply, "lifted up" in the sense of being glorified and honored (John 3:14; 8:28; 12:32). And in that lifting up, gracious deliverance for sinners is achieved.

PSALM 58

*To the choirmaster: according to Do Not
Destroy. A Miktam of David.*

1 Do you indeed decree what is right, you gods?
    Do you judge the children of man uprightly?
2 No, in your hearts you devise wrongs;
    your hands deal out violence on earth.

3 The wicked are estranged from the womb;
    they go astray from birth, speaking lies.
4 They have venom like the venom of a serpent,
    like the deaf adder that stops its ear,
5 so that it does not hear the voice of charmers
    or of the cunning enchanter.

6 O God, break the teeth in their mouths;
    tear out the fangs of the young lions, O LORD!
7 Let them vanish like water that runs away;
    when he aims his arrows, let them be blunted.
8 Let them be like the snail that dissolves into slime,
    like the stillborn child who never sees the sun.
9 Sooner than your pots can feel the heat of thorns,
    whether green or ablaze, may he sweep them away!

10 The righteous will rejoice when he sees the vengeance;
    he will bathe his feet in the blood of the wicked.

11   Mankind will say, "Surely there is a reward for the
              righteous;
        surely there is a God who judges on earth."

℘

The graphic, almost savage imagery of this psalm catches us off guard. Surely the Bible is too holy a book for such violent retribution toward the wicked at the hands of the righteous!

Such a response is understandable. But we must take the Scripture whole, or else not at all. If we received only those parts of the Bible that we found palatable, we would be in fact not sitting under the Bible in submission but standing over it in authority, making ourselves the final arbiter of what God could say. We would become the teacher, God the pupil. Moreover, if God never wrote these kinds of things into the Bible, would it not be *harder* to receive it as a word to us in our real world? The glory of a psalm like this is its realism, its earthiness, its utter honesty about the horrors of life in this fallen world.

Above all we must recognize that the psalmist is calling for evil to be judged not simply out of mean vindictiveness but out of a cry for justice. Wrongs must be righted. This is only proper. David is being ill-treated. If God exists, this ill-treatment must be judged and dealt with. David is calling for the wicked to receive what they deserve, not worse than they deserve.

Have you been ill-treated? Are you in the midst of ill-treatment, even now? Pray, with David, "Surely there is a God who judges on earth" (v. 11). God will right all wrongs. The final judgment of God is a deeply liberating doctrine. All will be put to right. We can release the need to judge now. We can leave it in his wise hands.

PSALM 59

To the choirmaster: according to Do Not Destroy.
A Miktam of David, when Saul sent men to
watch his house in order to kill him.

1 Deliver me from my enemies, O my God;
    protect me from those who rise up against me;
2 deliver me from those who work evil,
    and save me from bloodthirsty men.

3 For behold, they lie in wait for my life;
    fierce men stir up strife against me.
For no transgression or sin of mine, O Lord,
4   for no fault of mine, they run and make ready.
Awake, come to meet me, and see!
5   You, Lord God of hosts, are God of Israel.
Rouse yourself to punish all the nations;
    spare none of those who treacherously plot evil. *Selah*

6 Each evening they come back,
    howling like dogs
    and prowling about the city.
7 There they are, bellowing with their mouths
    with swords in their lips—
    for "Who," they think, "will hear us?"

8 But you, O Lord, laugh at them;
    you hold all the nations in derision.

9   O my Strength, I will watch for you,
        for you, O God, are my fortress.
10 My God in his steadfast love will meet me;
        God will let me look in triumph on my enemies.

11 Kill them not, lest my people forget;
        make them totter by your power and bring them
            down,
        O Lord, our shield!
12 For the sin of their mouths, the words of their lips,
        let them be trapped in their pride.
    For the cursing and lies that they utter,
13   consume them in wrath;
        consume them till they are no more,
    that they may know that God rules over Jacob
        to the ends of the earth.   *Selah*

14 Each evening they come back,
        howling like dogs
        and prowling about the city.
15 They wander about for food
        and growl if they do not get their fill.

16 But I will sing of your strength;
        I will sing aloud of your steadfast love in the morning.
    For you have been to me a fortress
        and a refuge in the day of my distress.
17 O my Strength, I will sing praises to you,
        for you, O God, are my fortress,
        the God who shows me steadfast love.

S ometimes in the Psalms David acknowledges that his present affliction is the result of his own sin. Other times, such as here, his adversity, he testifies, is "for no fault of mine" (v. 4).

We find this to be true in our own lives as well. All of life is under the curse of the fall, and sometimes it is hard to draw a neat line between the two, but there are certainly pains we endure that come directly from our own folly, and other pains we walk through that are no fault of our own. When you reflect on the pain in your life that is caused by others, how do you handle it? If you, like David here, are being attacked verbally by others (v. 7), what do you do? How do you avoid sliding into the seductive emotional relief of bitterness?

The only final solution here is the gospel—the final endpoint of what David describes in this psalm as God's "steadfast love" (vv. 10, 17). This refers to God's covenant loyalty to those who trust in him. The only way to fight off resentment is to consider that we have deeply offended God, and *he* did not deserve it. We have done to God what verbal attackers do to us. If we have pains we do not deserve, how much more does the holy God not deserve the pains of our own failure to defend him and praise him and follow him wholeheartedly?

Bathe your heart in the gospel of undeserved grace. Watch how your resentment melts.

PSALM 60

To the choirmaster: according to Shushan Eduth. A Miktam
of David; for instruction; when he strove with Aram-naharaim
and with Aram-zobah, and when Joab on his return struck
down twelve thousand of Edom in the Valley of Salt.

1   O God, you have rejected us, broken our defenses;
        you have been angry; oh, restore us.
2   You have made the land to quake; you have torn it
            open;
        repair its breaches, for it totters.
3   You have made your people see hard things;
        you have given us wine to drink that made us
            stagger.

4   You have set up a banner for those who fear you,
        that they may flee to it from the bow.   *Selah*
5   That your beloved ones may be delivered,
        give salvation by your right hand and answer us!

6   God has spoken in his holiness:
        "With exultation I will divide up Shechem
        and portion out the Vale of Succoth.
7   Gilead is mine; Manasseh is mine;
        Ephraim is my helmet;
        Judah is my scepter.
8   Moab is my washbasin;
        upon Edom I cast my shoe;
        over Philistia I shout in triumph."

<table>
<tr><td>9</td><td>Who will bring me to the fortified city?
    Who will lead me to Edom?</td></tr>
<tr><td>10</td><td>Have you not rejected us, O God?
    You do not go forth, O God, with our armies.</td></tr>
<tr><td>11</td><td>Oh, grant us help against the foe,
    for vain is the salvation of man!</td></tr>
<tr><td>12</td><td>With God we shall do valiantly;
    it is he who will tread down our foes.</td></tr>
</table>

⌇

God placed Adam and Eve on a small portion of the earth, but their mandate was to spread out and subdue all of it (Gen. 1:26–28). They rebelled against God, who later called Abraham to go to the land he would show him (Gen. 12:1–3). Abraham's descendants, the Israelites, would wind up in captivity in Egypt, but God brought them back to the land through Moses. Even after settling the Promised Land, however, Israel continued to rebel against God and suffer invasions and war and eventually exile out of the land.

This psalm picks up this whole-Bible theme of the land. David is in the midst of fighting the Edomites, a southern neighbor of Israel. At stake is God's ancient promise to Abraham that God would give Abraham's people—over which David then ruled— the Promised Land.

Ultimately, through Jesus Christ, God fulfills his promises to Abraham, and the New Testament indicates that God's way of continuing to fulfill his land promises is through faithful Christian witness, extending not just to the Promised Land of Israel but to the end of the earth (Matt. 28:18–20; Acts 1:8). If you are in Christ, you will one day rule over the entire globe. The final fulfillment of the promise to Abraham, which you too inherit if you are in Christ, is the inheritance of the entire world (Matt. 5:5; Rom. 4:13). All things are yours (1 Cor. 3:21).

PSALM 61

To the choirmaster: with stringed instruments. Of David.

1   Hear my cry, O God,
    listen to my prayer;
2   from the end of the earth I call to you
    when my heart is faint.
    Lead me to the rock
      that is higher than I,
3   for you have been my refuge,
    a strong tower against the enemy.

4   Let me dwell in your tent forever!
    Let me take refuge under the shelter of your wings!
                               Selah
5   For you, O God, have heard my vows;
    you have given me the heritage of those who fear
      your name.

6   Prolong the life of the king;
    may his years endure to all generations!
7   May he be enthroned forever before God;
    appoint steadfast love and faithfulness to watch over
      him!

8   So will I ever sing praises to your name,
        as I perform my vows day after day.

♪

When we are in trouble, God often feels distant. Notice that David says he is crying out to God "from the end of the earth" (v. 2). He is wandering far from what is familiar, and God seems far off. But David remembers his past history with God: "You have been my refuge, a strong tower" (v. 3); "You, O God, have heard my vows" (v. 5). When in distress, David clings to what he knows has been true of God over the course of David's life.

Now, therefore, David does not curl up in feelings of futility or hopelessness. He goes to God, trusting that his voice will be heard: "Hear my cry, O God" (v. 1). He asks the Lord to deliver him: "Lead me to the rock that is higher than I" (v. 2). In other words, David is asking God to take him to a place of safety that he himself cannot attain on his own strength. Picture a rising flood. David needs God to guide him to a rock that gets him higher than he himself could reach, lest he drown.

How do you handle distress—emotional, psychological, physical, financial? What is your heart-impulse when you feel swamped by adversity? Cry out to the Lord. He will lead you to a place of safety. Perhaps it will not be the safety you expect; perhaps it will not be immediate deliverance from your present trials. But at bottom he will assure you of your final and ultimate safety—in the arms of Jesus Christ, the true rock that is higher than what you yourself could attain. This rock not only lifts you above the floodwaters of your earthly adversity; it lifts you all the way up into heaven, by grace instead of on the basis of your own resources.

PSALM 62

To the choirmaster: according to Jeduthun. A Psalm of David.

1   For God alone my soul waits in silence;
        from him comes my salvation.
2   He alone is my rock and my salvation,
        my fortress; I shall not be greatly shaken.

3   How long will all of you attack a man
        to batter him,
        like a leaning wall, a tottering fence?
4   They only plan to thrust him down from his high
            position.
        They take pleasure in falsehood.
    They bless with their mouths,
        but inwardly they curse.   *Selah*

5   For God alone, O my soul, wait in silence,
        for my hope is from him.
6   He only is my rock and my salvation,
        my fortress; I shall not be shaken.
7   On God rests my salvation and my glory;
        my mighty rock, my refuge is God.

8   Trust in him at all times, O people;
        pour out your heart before him;
        God is a refuge for us.   *Selah*

9   Those of low estate are but a breath;
        those of high estate are a delusion;
    in the balances they go up;
        they are together lighter than a breath.
10 Put no trust in extortion;
        set no vain hopes on robbery;
        if riches increase, set not your heart on them.

11 Once God has spoken;
        twice have I heard this:
    that power belongs to God,
12   and that to you, O Lord, belongs steadfast love.
    For you will render to a man
        according to his work.

§

The theme of this psalm is that God is not simply our only hope and safety when we die; he is our only hope and safety while we live as well. The conviction into which this psalm is settling us is that the Lord himself is our deepest, our truest, our only stable refuge. Into what are you funneling all of your heart's anxieties? What are you banking on? What do you spend extra money on? What do you daydream about? The answer to these questions reveals our real refuge.

Pain has a special way of exposing where our trust truly lies. But pain also brings us into our only secure trust: the Lord himself. Three hundred years ago, hymn-writer Anne Steele (1716–1778) endured a series of horrors throughout her life, especially early on. Her mother died when she was three; Anne was injured early in life and remained an invalid all her days; and her fiancé drowned in a river the day before their wedding, when Anne was twenty-one. How do you keep getting out of bed day after day amid such pain? The answer is Psalm 62: "On God rests my salvation and my glory; my mighty rock, my refuge is God" (v. 7). One of Anne Steele's hymns captures this beautifully:

Dear refuge of my weary soul,
On Thee, when sorrows rise,
On Thee, when waves of trouble roll,
My fainting hope relies.
To Thee I tell each rising grief,
For Thou alone canst heal;
Thy Word can bring a sweet relief
For every pain I feel.

Hast Thou not bid me seek Thy face,
And shall I seek in vain?
And can the ear of sovereign grace
Be deaf when I complain?
No, still the ear of sovereign grace
Attends the mourner's prayer;
O may I ever find access
To breathe my sorrows there.

PSALM 63

A Psalm of David, when he was in the wilderness of Judah.

1   O God, you are my God; earnestly I seek you;
      my soul thirsts for you;
    my flesh faints for you,
      as in a dry and weary land where there is no water.
2   So I have looked upon you in the sanctuary,
      beholding your power and glory.
3   Because your steadfast love is better than life,
      my lips will praise you.
4   So I will bless you as long as I live;
      in your name I will lift up my hands.

5   My soul will be satisfied as with fat and rich food,
      and my mouth will praise you with joyful lips,
6   when I remember you upon my bed,
      and meditate on you in the watches of the night;
7   for you have been my help,
      and in the shadow of your wings I will sing for joy.
8   My soul clings to you;
      your right hand upholds me.

9   But those who seek to destroy my life
      shall go down into the depths of the earth;
10 they shall be given over to the power of the sword;
      they shall be a portion for jackals.

11   But the king shall rejoice in God;
            all who swear by him shall exult,
            for the mouths of liars will be stopped.

∽

Y ou were made for God.
        The heart of Christianity is not a set of doctrines to
believe, even though sound doctrine is vital. Nor is the heart of
Christianity an activity to pursue, even though the Christian faith
is necessarily active. Nor is it essentially a set of disciplines, even
though without reading the Bible and praying we will not get far
in the Christian life. The heart of Christianity is—to use a phrase
from John Bunyan, the old Puritan preacher and writer—"to
live upon God." You were made for God. To know him. Enjoy
him. Revere him. Draw strength from him. Trust him. Love him.

    Consider the language of Psalm 63. David speaks of God as
the thirst-quenching water for his dry and barren soul (v. 1). He
speaks of God as the delicious meal for his hungry soul (v. 5).
He speaks of God as his shade and protection, like the wings of
a great bird (v. 7). David needs one thing in life. God. Not truths
about God, in the first place. Rather, God himself.

    And what specifically is it in knowing God that gives David
life and strength? "Because your steadfast love is better than life,
my lips will praise you" (v. 3). It is God's steadfast love that does
so. The Hebrew word is *hesed*: God's covenant loyalty, his refusal
to give up on those whom he has taken to himself. And how do
you know that God will never give up on you? Because he sent
his Son to prove it.

PSALM 64

To the choirmaster. A Psalm of David.

1   Hear my voice, O God, in my complaint;
           preserve my life from dread of the enemy.
2   Hide me from the secret plots of the wicked,
           from the throng of evildoers,
3   who whet their tongues like swords,
           who aim bitter words like arrows,
4   shooting from ambush at the blameless,
           shooting at him suddenly and without fear.
5   They hold fast to their evil purpose;
           they talk of laying snares secretly,
      thinking, "Who can see them?"
6   They search out injustice,
      saying, "We have accomplished a diligent search."
           For the inward mind and heart of a man are deep.

7   But God shoots his arrow at them;
           they are wounded suddenly.
8   They are brought to ruin, with their own tongues
                     turned against them;
           all who see them will wag their heads.
9   Then all mankind fears;
           they tell what God has brought about
           and ponder what he has done.

10   Let the righteous one rejoice in the Lord
        and take refuge in him!
    Let all the upright in heart exult!

§

There are few places in Scripture where the destructive power of the tongue is more vividly described than here. Accusations are being conjured up in a sinister plot to ruin a righteous man's reputation. But note the rhythm of this psalm: the first half speaks of the words of evil people as arrows (vv. 3–4), while the last half speaks of the words of God as arrows (v. 7). The overall point is that we dare not seek to respond with verbal arrows of our own. Justice is God's to give. We can either seek justice now, and be further hardened, or let God exact justice in his good time, and be softened now in our own hearts.

Consider our use of words. How do we respond when others speak ill of us? What do we do when we learn someone is quietly plotting against us? When gossip gets back to us, and we learn someone we thought was a trusted friend actually is not?

Our words reveal what is truly happening in our hearts, far better than any X-ray. When our immediate verbal response is to respond to evil with evil, we demonstrate that we are not in tune with the gospel. For the gospel is a word of grace to us, and enjoying such grace is the only way to respond with words of grace to others. God will bring all cruel words to justice. For now our job is to "rejoice in the Lord and take refuge in him" (v. 10).

PSALM 65

To the choirmaster. A Psalm of David. A Song.

1   Praise is due to you, O God, in Zion,
     and to you shall vows be performed.
2   O you who hear prayer,
     to you shall all flesh come.
3   When iniquities prevail against me,
     you atone for our transgressions.
4   Blessed is the one you choose and bring near,
     to dwell in your courts!
    We shall be satisfied with the goodness of your house,
     the holiness of your temple!

5   By awesome deeds you answer us with righteousness,
     O God of our salvation,
    the hope of all the ends of the earth
     and of the farthest seas;
6   the one who by his strength established the mountains,
     being girded with might;
7   who stills the roaring of the seas,
     the roaring of their waves,
     the tumult of the peoples,
8   so that those who dwell at the ends of the earth are
        in awe at your signs.
    You make the going out of the morning and the
        evening to shout for joy.

9   You visit the earth and water it;
         you greatly enrich it;
      the river of God is full of water;
         you provide their grain,
         for so you have prepared it.
10   You water its furrows abundantly,
         settling its ridges,
      softening it with showers,
         and blessing its growth.
11   You crown the year with your bounty;
         your wagon tracks overflow with abundance.
12   The pastures of the wilderness overflow,
         the hills gird themselves with joy,
13   the meadows clothe themselves with flocks,
         the valleys deck themselves with grain,
         they shout and sing together for joy.

∽

This psalm shouts of satisfaction in the immense productivity of the land. Canaan is performing like it was supposed to perform, like it was promised to perform—like a land flowing with milk and honey. David must have been overjoyed to see his domain overflowing with abundant life.

Yet how rarely is life like that today? Our jobs get boring. Toys break. Bodies ache. Clearly, if we look for full satisfaction in this world, we will be frustrated. Instead, we must look for the new earth, when we will feast with the Lord Jesus in his presence and truly "dwell in your courts" and "be satisfied with the goodness of your house" (v. 4). After all, because of his death and resurrection, Christ is making all things new and will usher into a land overflowing with abundant life, which the Bible describes as a great feast (Rev. 19:6–9).

In short, God cares for you. He does not care about our souls alone, although that is the most important thing about us. He cares also about our physical nourishment. Yet why did he give us food, ultimately? Not only for our enjoyment but more deeply to tell us who he is—our true sustenance, our deepest nourishment. Jesus said, "I am the bread of life; whoever comes to me shall not hunger, and whoever believes in me shall never thirst" (John 6:35). This psalm whets our appetite for the feasting on Christ yet to come.

PSALM 66

To the choirmaster. A Song. A Psalm.

1   Shout for joy to God, all the earth;
2   sing the glory of his name;
       give to him glorious praise!
3   Say to God, "How awesome are your deeds!
      So great is your power that your enemies come
         cringing to you.
4   All the earth worships you
      and sings praises to you;
       they sing praises to your name."   *Selah*

5   Come and see what God has done:
        he is awesome in his deeds toward the children
            of man.
6   He turned the sea into dry land;
        they passed through the river on foot.
    There did we rejoice in him,
7   who rules by his might forever,
    whose eyes keep watch on the nations—
        let not the rebellious exalt themselves.   *Selah*

8   Bless our God, O peoples;
        let the sound of his praise be heard,
9   who has kept our soul among the living
        and has not let our feet slip.
10 For you, O God, have tested us;
        you have tried us as silver is tried.
11 You brought us into the net;
        you laid a crushing burden on our backs;
12 you let men ride over our heads;
        we went through fire and through water;
    yet you have brought us out to a place of abundance.

13 I will come into your house with burnt offerings;
        I will perform my vows to you,
14 that which my lips uttered
        and my mouth promised when I was in trouble.
15 I will offer to you burnt offerings of fattened animals,
        with the smoke of the sacrifice of rams;
    I will make an offering of bulls and goats.   *Selah*

16 Come and hear, all you who fear God,
        and I will tell what he has done for my soul.

17   I cried to him with my mouth,
          and high praise was on my tongue.
18   If I had cherished iniquity in my heart,
          the Lord would not have listened.
19   But truly God has listened;
          he has attended to the voice of my prayer.

20   Blessed be God,
          because he has not rejected my prayer
          or removed his steadfast love from me!

~

This song is a hymn to the God of Israel, praising his gracious deliverance in times past. The psalmist recalls the exodus, for example, where God "turned the sea into dry land" (v. 6). The psalm also acknowledges the harrowing experiences in Israel's history—"we went through fire and through water" (v. 12)—but in it all it recognizes that God has "brought us out to a place of abundance" (v. 12).

How true this is to the life of the faithful. God brings us into meaningful depth with him not through ease but through difficulty. It is tears, not smiles, that form the anvil on which solid joy in God is forged. We thank God for the mountaintop experiences with him. But it is in the valley where we find him nearest and dearest to us.

Are you in a valley now? Do you feel now that you are fighting your way "through fire and through water"—emotionally, relationally, parentally, maritally, financially, physically? There is no easy, pat answer to this. No quick formula. But take comfort in Psalm 66. Through tears he brings us "to a place of abundance." This was, after all, the very pattern of Christ's own life—through the sufferings and tears of Gethsemane into the place of abundance and of reigning resurrection life. If our Savior walked this path, let us not be averse to following him.

PSALM 67

To the choirmaster: with stringed
instruments. A Psalm. A Song.

1   May God be gracious to us and bless us
        and make his face to shine upon us,   *Selah*
2   that your way may be known on earth,
        your saving power among all nations.
3   Let the peoples praise you, O God;
        let all the peoples praise you!

4   Let the nations be glad and sing for joy,
        for you judge the peoples with equity
        and guide the nations upon earth.   *Selah*
5   Let the peoples praise you, O God;
        let all the peoples praise you!

6   The earth has yielded its increase;
        God, our God, shall bless us.
7   God shall bless us;
        let all the ends of the earth fear him!

~s~

Why has God's grace come to you? For the same reason that it came to the Israelites of old: so that this same grace can stream out to the nations. Consider your neighbors. Unless they are Jews, these people all around you are "the nations." Maybe they even come from vastly different ethnicities despite living in close proximity. This is a beautiful picture of those God has graced with this psalm.

The psalm starts in verse 1 with an echo of the old Aaronic blessing from Numbers 6:24–26:

> The LORD bless you and keep you;
>> the LORD makes his face to shine upon you and
>>> be gracious to you;
>> the LORD lift up his countenance upon you and
>>> give you peace.

Yet the psalm then immediately goes on to draw the nations of the earth into this ancient blessing. This is who God is. He is not a parochial, narrow-minded God. His welcome to sinners is wide. He asks only for our penitent faith, our trusting contrition—all he asks is that we humble ourselves enough to know of our need for his saving mercy. The psalmist prays that "God's saving power" would be known throughout all the earth (v. 2).

For us today, this saving power has been climactically displayed in the Lord Jesus Christ. In Jesus and his work on our behalf, we see the length to which God would go to draw men and women everywhere into the blessing of enjoying the radiant face of God shining down on them.

PSALM 68

To the choirmaster. A Psalm of David. A Song.

1   God shall arise, his enemies shall be scattered;
      and those who hate him shall flee before him!

2   As smoke is driven away, so you shall drive them away;
      as wax melts before fire,
      so the wicked shall perish before God!

3   But the righteous shall be glad;
      they shall exult before God;
      they shall be jubilant with joy!

4   Sing to God, sing praises to his name;
      lift up a song to him who rides through the deserts;
    his name is the LORD;
      exult before him!

5   Father of the fatherless and protector of widows
      is God in his holy habitation.

6   God settles the solitary in a home;
      he leads out the prisoners to prosperity,
      but the rebellious dwell in a parched land.

7   O God, when you went out before your people,
      when you marched through the wilderness,   *Selah*

8   the earth quaked, the heavens poured down rain,
      before God, the One of Sinai,
      before God, the God of Israel.

9   Rain in abundance, O God, you shed abroad;
      you restored your inheritance as it languished;

10 your flock found a dwelling in it;
   in your goodness, O God, you provided for the needy.

11 The Lord gives the word;
   the women who announce the news are a great host:
12   "The kings of the armies—they flee, they flee!"
 The women at home divide the spoil—
13   though you men lie among the sheepfolds—
 the wings of a dove covered with silver,
   its pinions with shimmering gold.
14 When the Almighty scatters kings there,
   let snow fall on Zalmon.

15 O mountain of God, mountain of Bashan;
   O many-peaked mountain, mountain of Bashan!
16 Why do you look with hatred, O many-peaked
     mountain,
   at the mount that God desired for his abode,
   yes, where the LORD will dwell forever?
17 The chariots of God are twice ten thousand,
   thousands upon thousands;
   the Lord is among them; Sinai is now in the sanctuary.
18 You ascended on high,
   leading a host of captives in your train
   and receiving gifts among men,
 even among the rebellious, that the LORD God may
     dwell there.

19 Blessed be the Lord,
   who daily bears us up;
   God is our salvation.   *Selah*

20 Our God is a God of salvation,
   and to GOD, the Lord, belong deliverances from death.
21 But God will strike the heads of his enemies,
   the hairy crown of him who walks in his guilty ways.
22 The Lord said,
   "I will bring them back from Bashan,
   I will bring them back from the depths of the sea,
23 that you may strike your feet in their blood,
   that the tongues of your dogs may have their portion
   from the foe."

24 Your procession is seen, O God,
   the procession of my God, my King, into the
   sanctuary—
25 the singers in front, the musicians last,
   between them virgins playing tambourines:
26 "Bless God in the great congregation,
   the LORD, O you who are of Israel's fountain!"
27 There is Benjamin, the least of them, in the lead,
   the princes of Judah in their throng,
   the princes of Zebulun, the princes of Naphtali.

28 Summon your power, O God,
   the power, O God, by which you have worked for us.
29 Because of your temple at Jerusalem
   kings shall bear gifts to you.
30 Rebuke the beasts that dwell among the reeds,
   the herd of bulls with the calves of the peoples.
   Trample underfoot those who lust after tribute;
   scatter the peoples who delight in war.
31 Nobles shall come from Egypt;
   Cush shall hasten to stretch out her hands to God.

32   O kingdoms of the earth, sing to God;
          sing praises to the Lord,   *Selah*
33   to him who rides in the heavens, the ancient heavens;
          behold, he sends out his voice, his mighty voice.
34   Ascribe power to God,
          whose majesty is over Israel,
          and whose power is in the skies.
35   Awesome is God from his sanctuary;
          the God of Israel—he is the one who gives power
              and strength to his people.
      Blessed be God!

∽

God defies our neat categories. Consider this psalm: in it the Lord is spoken of as both terrifically mighty and gently saving. He is both ferocious and meek.

He is mighty: "God shall arise, his enemies shall be scattered" (v. 1); "When you marched through the wilderness, the earth quaked" (vv. 7–8); "The kings of the armies—they flee" (v. 12); "The chariots of God are twice ten thousand" (v. 17); "Trample underfoot those who lust after tribute" (v. 30). This is a God before whom the universe trembles.

But he is also gentle: "Father of the fatherless and protector of widows is God" (v. 5); "God settles the solitary in a home; he leads out the prisoners to prosperity" (v. 6); "Blessed be the Lord, who daily bears us up" (v. 19); "He is the one who gives power and strength to his people" (v. 35). This is a God who delights to draw near in comfort to the weak.

How are we to think about these two realities? What difference does it make that God is both mighty and merciful, both powerful and gentle? All the difference in the world. It means he is *able* to deliver us from all our difficulties and sins, and it means he *enjoys* delivering us. If he were mighty but not merciful, he could save us but would not. If he were merciful but not mighty, he would like to save us but could not.

And in Jesus, we see these two realities of who God is merge beautifully. Jesus is both lion and lamb, both omnipotent and gracious. He can be trusted. We can bank everything on him. He *can* rescue you, and he *wants* to.

PSALM 69

To the choirmaster: according to Lilies. Of David.

1   Save me, O God!
        For the waters have come up to my neck.
2   I sink in deep mire,
        where there is no foothold;
    I have come into deep waters,
        and the flood sweeps over me.
3   I am weary with my crying out;
        my throat is parched.
    My eyes grow dim
        with waiting for my God.

4   More in number than the hairs of my head
        are those who hate me without cause;
    mighty are those who would destroy me,
        those who attack me with lies.

What I did not steal
    must I now restore?
5 O God, you know my folly;
    the wrongs I have done are not hidden from you.

6 Let not those who hope in you be put to shame
        through me,
    O Lord GOD of hosts;
  let not those who seek you be brought to dishonor
        through me,
    O God of Israel.
7 For it is for your sake that I have borne reproach,
    that dishonor has covered my face.
8 I have become a stranger to my brothers,
    an alien to my mother's sons.

9 For zeal for your house has consumed me,
      and the reproaches of those who reproach you have
        fallen on me.
10 When I wept and humbled my soul with fasting,
    it became my reproach.
11 When I made sackcloth my clothing,
    I became a byword to them.
12 I am the talk of those who sit in the gate,
    and the drunkards make songs about me.

13 But as for me, my prayer is to you, O LORD.
    At an acceptable time, O God,
      in the abundance of your steadfast love answer me
        in your saving faithfulness.
14 Deliver me
    from sinking in the mire;

let me be delivered from my enemies
and from the deep waters.

15   Let not the flood sweep over me,
or the deep swallow me up,
or the pit close its mouth over me.

16   Answer me, O LORD, for your steadfast love is good;
according to your abundant mercy, turn to me.
17   Hide not your face from your servant,
for I am in distress; make haste to answer me.
18   Draw near to my soul, redeem me;
ransom me because of my enemies!

19   You know my reproach,
and my shame and my dishonor;
my foes are all known to you.
20   Reproaches have broken my heart,
so that I am in despair.
I looked for pity, but there was none,
and for comforters, but I found none.
21   They gave me poison for food,
and for my thirst they gave me sour wine to drink.

22   Let their own table before them become a snare;
and when they are at peace, let it become a trap.
23   Let their eyes be darkened, so that they cannot see,
and make their loins tremble continually.
24   Pour out your indignation upon them,
and let your burning anger overtake them.
25   May their camp be a desolation;
let no one dwell in their tents.

26 For they persecute him whom you have struck down,
and they recount the pain of those you have
wounded.
27 Add to them punishment upon punishment;
may they have no acquittal from you.
28 Let them be blotted out of the book of the living;
let them not be enrolled among the righteous.

29 But I am afflicted and in pain;
let your salvation, O God, set me on high!

30 I will praise the name of God with a song;
I will magnify him with thanksgiving.
31 This will please the LORD more than an ox
or a bull with horns and hoofs.
32 When the humble see it they will be glad;
you who seek God, let your hearts revive.
33 For the LORD hears the needy
and does not despise his own people who are
prisoners.

34 Let heaven and earth praise him,
the seas and everything that moves in them.
35 For God will save Zion
and build up the cities of Judah,
and people shall dwell there and possess it;
36 the offspring of his servants shall inherit it,
and those who love his name shall dwell in it.

The entire Bible is fulfilled in our loving Savior, Jesus Christ, the friend of sinners. He himself said that all the psalms were about him (Luke 24:44). How does Psalm 69 fit into that?

Consider David's plea. He is in deep distress. He is crying out to God for deliverance. He feels hated, ridiculed. Do you see that Jesus is the final answer to David's prayer? Do you see that as you pray Psalm 69, Jesus Christ is the concrete answer David hoped in but could see only vaguely?

No one was ever hated without cause more than Jesus was (v. 4). No one ever bore more reproach for the sake of God than Jesus did (v. 7). He became a stranger to his own family, just as David felt here, and perhaps as you feel now (v. 8; Matt. 12:49). He was ridiculed (Ps. 69:12; Matt. 27:29). David prays not to be overwhelmed (Ps. 69:14–15) and that God would not hide his face from him (v. 17). Jesus prayed that too (Matt. 26:39). Yet note the great difference between what David prayed and what Jesus prayed. Although Jesus endured all of David's hardships and more, Jesus' prayer for deliverance was not answered as he might have liked.

Why does this matter for you? Consider this: in your time of distress, you can pray Psalm 69 and know with confidence that God will somehow answer and deliver you, because Jesus prayed for deliverance but faced the cross nevertheless. Jesus endured separation from God on our behalf so that we never need to. David prays to be ransomed (v. 18); you and I truly were, through the finished work of Christ on the cross. You may open your heart to him without any fear of rejection or silence.

PSALM 70

To the choirmaster. Of David, for the memorial offering.

1   Make haste, O God, to deliver me!
        O LORD, make haste to help me!
2   Let them be put to shame and confusion
        who seek my life!
    Let them be turned back and brought to dishonor
        who delight in my hurt!
3   Let them turn back because of their shame
        who say, "Aha, Aha!"

4   May all who seek you
        rejoice and be glad in you!
    May those who love your salvation
        say evermore, "God is great!"
5   But I am poor and needy;
        hasten to me, O God!
    You are my help and my deliverer;
        O LORD, do not delay!

§

There are two, and only two, basic approaches to life. We can attempt to handle life's adversities either through self-resourced deliverance or through looking outside ourselves for deliverance. We can look in or we can look out.

Psalms, especially psalms of lament such as this one, train us to look outside ourselves to God. The ringing note on which the psalm begins and ends points to deliverance beyond what David himself can muster. "Make haste, O God, to deliver me!" (v. 1); "You are my help and my deliverer; O LORD, do not delay!" (v. 5).

Consider your own life. On what do you rely, moment by moment? True communion with God is the lifelong process of growing more and more deeply in dependence upon God: leaning on him, trusting in him, counting on him. But to get there, you must see yourself the way David sees himself: "I am poor and needy" (v. 5). To the degree that you feel yourself sufficient and competent, to that degree you will not cry out to God. To the degree that you feel yourself weak and inadequate, to that degree you will call out for his help and deliverance—a prayer his heart delights to answer.

PSALM 71

1   In you, O LORD, do I take refuge;
        let me never be put to shame!
2   In your righteousness deliver me and rescue me;
        incline your ear to me, and save me!
3   Be to me a rock of refuge,
        to which I may continually come;
    you have given the command to save me,
        for you are my rock and my fortress.

4   Rescue me, O my God, from the hand of the wicked,
        from the grasp of the unjust and cruel man.

5   For you, O Lord, are my hope,
        my trust, O LORD, from my youth.
6   Upon you I have leaned from before my birth;
        you are he who took me from my mother's womb.
    My praise is continually of you.

7   I have been as a portent to many,
        but you are my strong refuge.
8   My mouth is filled with your praise,
        and with your glory all the day.
9   Do not cast me off in the time of old age;
        forsake me not when my strength is spent.
10 For my enemies speak concerning me;
        those who watch for my life consult together
11 and say, "God has forsaken him;
        pursue and seize him,
        for there is none to deliver him."

12 O God, be not far from me;
        O my God, make haste to help me!
13 May my accusers be put to shame and consumed;
        with scorn and disgrace may they be covered
        who seek my hurt.
14 But I will hope continually
        and will praise you yet more and more.
15 My mouth will tell of your righteous acts,
        of your deeds of salvation all the day,
        for their number is past my knowledge.
16 With the mighty deeds of the Lord GOD I will come;
        I will remind them of your righteousness, yours
            alone.

17   O God, from my youth you have taught me,
        and I still proclaim your wondrous deeds.
18   So even to old age and gray hairs,
        O God, do not forsake me,
   until I proclaim your might to another generation,
        your power to all those to come.
19   Your righteousness, O God,
        reaches the high heavens.
   You who have done great things,
        O God, who is like you?
20   You who have made me see many troubles and calamities
        will revive me again;
   from the depths of the earth
        you will bring me up again.
21   You will increase my greatness
        and comfort me again.

22   I will also praise you with the harp
        for your faithfulness, O my God;
   I will sing praises to you with the lyre,
        O Holy One of Israel.
23   My lips will shout for joy,
        when I sing praises to you;
        my soul also, which you have redeemed.
24   And my tongue will talk of your righteous help all
        the day long,
   for they have been put to shame and disappointed
        who sought to do me hurt.

This is the prayer of a saint in winter, who in his old age realizes that life is mostly over for him: "Do not cast me off in the time of old age" (v. 9), he prays. "So even to old age and gray hairs, O God, do not forsake me" (v. 18). As we continue to age, this psalm instructs us in how to walk with God.

We are reminded that our time on earth is filled with strife; God has brought into the psalmist's life "many troubles and calamities" (v. 20). The psalmists are realists. They do not skate over hardships, smiling all the way. They know what it feels like to spend time in "the depths of the earth" (v. 20).

Yet through all of the pains, the psalmist has not grown cynical. Cynicism is a great temptation as we walk through life and move toward death. As difficulties pile up, as relationships sour, as hopes and goals fail to materialize, it is easy to throw in the towel emotionally and settle into cold-hearted cynicism. The psalmist, however, teaches us that pain is not meant to numb us and cause our hearts to withdraw; pain is meant to draw our hearts up to God: "From the depths of the earth *you will bring me up again*" (v. 20).

Adversity is not intended to diminish our hope in God. Adversity is intended to heighten our hope in him. We are brought to remember that God is all we have, and that he is enough.

PSALM 72

Of Solomon.

1   Give the king your justice, O God,
        and your righteousness to the royal son!
2   May he judge your people with righteousness,
        and your poor with justice!
3   Let the mountains bear prosperity for the people,
        and the hills, in righteousness!
4   May he defend the cause of the poor of the people,
        give deliverance to the children of the needy,
        and crush the oppressor!

5   May they fear you while the sun endures,
        and as long as the moon, throughout all generations!
6   May he be like rain that falls on the mown grass,
        like showers that water the earth!
7   In his days may the righteous flourish,
        and peace abound, till the moon be no more!

8   May he have dominion from sea to sea,
        and from the River to the ends of the earth!
9   May desert tribes bow down before him,
        and his enemies lick the dust!
10   May the kings of Tarshish and of the coastlands
        render him tribute;
    may the kings of Sheba and Seba
        bring gifts!

11 May all kings fall down before him,
    all nations serve him!

12 For he delivers the needy when he calls,
    the poor and him who has no helper.
13 He has pity on the weak and the needy,
    and saves the lives of the needy.
14 From oppression and violence he redeems their life,
    and precious is their blood in his sight.

15 Long may he live;
    may gold of Sheba be given to him!
May prayer be made for him continually,
    and blessings invoked for him all the day!
16 May there be abundance of grain in the land;
    on the tops of the mountains may it wave;
    may its fruit be like Lebanon;
and may people blossom in the cities
    like the grass of the field!
17 May his name endure forever,
    his fame continue as long as the sun!
May people be blessed in him,
    all nations call him blessed!

18 Blessed be the LORD, the God of Israel,
    who alone does wondrous things.
19 Blessed be his glorious name forever;
    may the whole earth be filled with his glory!
        Amen and Amen!

20 The prayers of David, the son of Jesse, are ended.

S olomon wrote this psalm. David wrote most of the psalms, but this one was written by his son. What does Solomon say? He asks for divine blessing to carry forward the promises made to David—God's covenant promises to be with him always, to give him a never-ending kingdom, to give him heaven's blessing, to establish his rule over the nations.

Solomon would have been keenly aware of the blessings to David, and he doubtless would have felt some measure of inadequacy in filling his father's shoes. Indeed, the story of 1 Kings tells us of Solomon's great wisdom and strong start but also recounts the ways in which Solomon's reign did not end well. He fell into idolatry toward the end of his life, and with his sons the kingdom began to crack in two due to civil war.

As we read this psalm today, however, we can lift our eyes from Solomon's reign to that of the Davidic heir—someone "greater than Solomon" (Luke 11:31) who would come a thousand years later. Solomon prayed in Psalm 72 that he would reign in righteousness (vv. 1–2), defend the cause of the needy (v. 4), enjoy dominion "from sea to sea" (v. 8), see the nations bowing down to him (vv. 9–11), and have a name that would last forever (v. 17).

Only one king ever lived up to this lofty prayer. In the Lord Jesus, we see the supreme promises of God come to climactic realization.

BOOK THREE

PSALM 73

A Psalm of Asaph.

1   Truly God is good to Israel,
        to those who are pure in heart.
2   But as for me, my feet had almost stumbled,
        my steps had nearly slipped.
3   For I was envious of the arrogant
        when I saw the prosperity of the wicked.

4   For they have no pangs until death;
        their bodies are fat and sleek.
5   They are not in trouble as others are;
        they are not stricken like the rest of mankind.
6   Therefore pride is their necklace;
        violence covers them as a garment.
7   Their eyes swell out through fatness;
        their hearts overflow with follies.
8   They scoff and speak with malice;
        loftily they threaten oppression.
9   They set their mouths against the heavens,
        and their tongue struts through the earth.
10   Therefore his people turn back to them,
        and find no fault in them.
11   And they say, "How can God know?
        Is there knowledge in the Most High?"
12   Behold, these are the wicked;
        always at ease, they increase in riches.

13   All in vain have I kept my heart clean
       and washed my hands in innocence.

14   For all the day long I have been stricken
       and rebuked every morning.

15   If I had said, "I will speak thus,"
       I would have betrayed the generation of your
          children.

16   But when I thought how to understand this,
       it seemed to me a wearisome task,

17   until I went into the sanctuary of God;
       then I discerned their end.

18   Truly you set them in slippery places;
       you make them fall to ruin.

19   How they are destroyed in a moment,
       swept away utterly by terrors!

20   Like a dream when one awakes,
       O Lord, when you rouse yourself, you despise them
          as phantoms.

21   When my soul was embittered,
       when I was pricked in heart,

22   I was brutish and ignorant;
       I was like a beast toward you.

23   Nevertheless, I am continually with you;
       you hold my right hand.

24   You guide me with your counsel,
       and afterward you will receive me to glory.

25   Whom have I in heaven but you?
       And there is nothing on earth that I desire besides
          you.

26   My flesh and my heart may fail,
        but God is the strength of my heart and my portion
           forever.

27   For behold, those who are far from you shall perish;
        you put an end to everyone who is unfaithful to you.
28   But for me it is good to be near God;
        I have made the Lord GOD my refuge,
        that I may tell of all your works.

∽

This psalm, written by Asaph, expresses dismay at the prospering of the wicked. How can those who pursue such cruelty and shameless evil enjoy such richness of life? It is only when Asaph lifts his eyes to God that he sees the total picture (v. 17). When the final destruction of the wicked is considered, their present prosperity takes on new proportions—it is seen to be brief, fleeting. The evil are prospering today, then snuffed out after a few seconds of this short life's existence.

Yet we are still stuck in the present, watching day after day as the wicked flourish. How do we survive emotionally? This psalm gives us the beautiful solution: "Whom have I in heaven but you? And there is nothing on earth I desire besides you. My flesh and my heart may fail, but God is the strength of my heart and my portion forever" (vv. 25–26).

How would you put this in your own words? Consider what Asaph is saying: with God, you are invincible. Nothing can touch you. Your greatest enjoyment—God—can never be taken away from you. In heaven, God is all you want and need. On earth, God is all you want and need. In death or in life, in sickness or in health, even as your body wastes away toward the grave, God is all you want and need.

Be at peace. Your true happiness is beyond the reach of any evil this life can bring.

PSALM 74

A Maskil of Asaph.

1   O God, why do you cast us off forever?
      Why does your anger smoke against the sheep
            of your pasture?
2   Remember your congregation, which you have
            purchased of old,
         which you have redeemed to be the tribe of
            your heritage!
      Remember Mount Zion, where you have dwelt.
3   Direct your steps to the perpetual ruins;
      the enemy has destroyed everything in the sanctuary!

4   Your foes have roared in the midst of your meeting
            place;
      they set up their own signs for signs.
5   They were like those who swing axes
      in a forest of trees.
6   And all its carved wood
      they broke down with hatchets and hammers.

7   They set your sanctuary on fire;
        they profaned the dwelling place of your name,
        bringing it down to the ground.
8   They said to themselves, "We will utterly subdue
            them";
        they burned all the meeting places of God in the
            land.

9   We do not see our signs;
        there is no longer any prophet,
        and there is none among us who knows how long.
10 How long, O God, is the foe to scoff?
        Is the enemy to revile your name forever?
11 Why do you hold back your hand, your right hand?
        Take it from the fold of your garment and destroy
            them!

12 Yet God my King is from of old,
        working salvation in the midst of the earth.
13 You divided the sea by your might;
        you broke the heads of the sea monsters on the
            waters.
14 You crushed the heads of Leviathan;
        you gave him as food for the creatures of the
            wilderness.
15 You split open springs and brooks;
        you dried up ever-flowing streams.
16 Yours is the day, yours also the night;
        you have established the heavenly lights and the sun.
17 You have fixed all the boundaries of the earth;
        you have made summer and winter.

18 Remember this, O Lord, how the enemy scoffs,
        and a foolish people reviles your name.
19 Do not deliver the soul of your dove to the wild beasts;
        do not forget the life of your poor forever.

20 Have regard for the covenant,
        for the dark places of the land are full of the
            habitations of violence.
21 Let not the downtrodden turn back in shame;
        let the poor and needy praise your name.

22 Arise, O God, defend your cause;
        remember how the foolish scoff at you all the day!
23 Do not forget the clamor of your foes,
        the uproar of those who rise against you, which goes
            up continually!

႙

This psalm is a community lament. Have you ever suffered with others through something terrible? An unexpected death in the family? A betrayal by church leadership? A natural disaster? God's people at the time of this psalm had just endured the destruction of the very heart and center of their life together—the temple. "They set your sanctuary on fire; they profaned the dwelling place of your name" (v. 7).

The psalmist cries out for God's deliverance throughout this psalm (vv. 1–3, 18, 22), remembering God's covenant promises and deliverance in the past (vv. 12–15). You and I read this psalm today with deeper insight into the ways of God than was possible for God's people at the time of Asaph. For we see that the greatest destruction directed toward God's people came not upon the people as a whole but upon a representative Israelite. In the fullness of time, the temple was again destroyed—not the temple made by human hands but the true and final temple, the temple of the body of Jesus Christ, in which God's presence was most clearly displayed (John 2:19–22).

And why? Was this final temple destroyed at the whim of an invading army? No, it was the pre-ordained plan of God, set in motion from time immemorial, so that the hosts of heaven and hell would stand and wonder at the glory of the love of God. In the destruction of Jesus, your own destruction is assured to be behind you instead of in front of you. When you look at the cross, you see your punishment being carried out, so that before you is only peace with God and an eternity with him.

PSALM 75

*To the choirmaster: according to Do Not
Destroy. A Psalm of Asaph. A Song.*

1   We give thanks to you, O God;
      we give thanks, for your name is near.
   We recount your wondrous deeds.

2   "At the set time that I appoint
      I will judge with equity.
3   When the earth totters, and all its inhabitants,
      it is I who keep steady its pillars.   *Selah*
4   I say to the boastful, 'Do not boast,'
      and to the wicked, 'Do not lift up your horn;
5   do not lift up your horn on high,
      or speak with haughty neck.'"

6   For not from the east or from the west
      and not from the wilderness comes lifting up,
7   but it is God who executes judgment,
      putting down one and lifting up another.
8   For in the hand of the Lord there is a cup
      with foaming wine, well mixed,
   and he pours out from it,
      and all the wicked of the earth
      shall drain it down to the dregs.

9   But I will declare it forever;
      I will sing praises to the God of Jacob.

10   All the horns of the wicked I will cut off,
                but the horns of the righteous shall be lifted up.

∽

God is the ultimate judge. No one else is. Only God. That is the message of this psalm. Where does this truth land on your own life today?

Perhaps you find yourself haunted by a past in which you were a victim of some form of abuse. God will judge. Maybe your life today is plagued by animosity from family members toward you. God will judge. Perhaps you feel discouraged when you read or listen to the news and hear the media, and those whom they interview, twisting the truth. God will judge. All will be put right.

Or maybe you find yourself tormented by a conscience that knows you yourself to be the perpetrator of evil—of selfishness, of mean words, or relational withdrawal, of deceit. If so, repent and seek restitution with those whom you have wronged. But beneath it all, take heart in the greatest truth of God's judgment: God judged his own righteous Son in place of us unrighteous rebels, so that any who turns to take refuge in him gets the future that Jesus deserves. This, above all else, is reason to give thanks to God for his wondrous deeds (v. 1).

PSALM 76

To the choirmaster: with stringed instruments.
A Psalm of Asaph. A Song.

1   In Judah God is known;
      his name is great in Israel.

2   His abode has been established in Salem,
      his dwelling place in Zion.

3   There he broke the flashing arrows,
      the shield, the sword, and the weapons of war.   *Selah*

4   Glorious are you, more majestic
      than the mountains full of prey.

5   The stouthearted were stripped of their spoil;
      they sank into sleep;
   all the men of war
      were unable to use their hands.

6   At your rebuke, O God of Jacob,
      both rider and horse lay stunned.

7   But you, you are to be feared!
      Who can stand before you
      when once your anger is roused?

8   From the heavens you uttered judgment;
      the earth feared and was still,

9   when God arose to establish judgment,
      to save all the humble of the earth.   *Selah*

10   Surely the wrath of man shall praise you;
           the remnant of wrath you will put on like a belt.
11   Make your vows to the LORD your God and perform
               them;
           let all around him bring gifts
           to him who is to be feared,
12   who cuts off the spirit of princes,
           who is to be feared by the kings of the earth.

∽

This psalm begins by recounting the dwelling place of God (vv. 1–3). God dwelt in "Salem" (an old name for Jerusalem) and thus in the temple that was on "Zion" (the mountain on which Jerusalem stood) (v. 2). It is in Israel and Judah that "God [was] known" (v. 1).

Is that how God is known today? Through his presence in a certain city in the Middle East, in a temple, on a certain mountain? No. For at just the right time, God came in the person of Jesus Christ, the final temple. As a result, the New Testament teaches that God now lives not in a temple on a mountain on the other side of the globe but in *you and me, who are united to Christ*. We are the temple in which God dwells, of which Jesus is the chief cornerstone, the key foundation (Eph. 2:19–22).

Consider this in light of the rest of this psalm, which goes on to recount the fearsome majesty of God (Ps. 76:4–9). It is *this* God who has taken up residence inside of you. How can this be? It is because the ferocious wrath of God landed on Christ, not us. As a result, God can take up residence within us without threatening his holiness or justice. And, one day, this wrath will pour out on everyone who does not bow the knee to Christ as king and deliverer (vv. 10–12).

PSALM 77

To the choirmaster: according to Jeduthun. A Psalm of Asaph.

1 I cry aloud to God,
   aloud to God, and he will hear me.
2 In the day of my trouble I seek the Lord;
   in the night my hand is stretched out without
     wearying;
   my soul refuses to be comforted.
3 When I remember God, I moan;
   when I meditate, my spirit faints.   *Selah*

4 You hold my eyelids open;
   I am so troubled that I cannot speak.
5 I consider the days of old,
   the years long ago.
6 I said, "Let me remember my song in the night;
   let me meditate in my heart."
   Then my spirit made a diligent search:
7 "Will the Lord spurn forever,
   and never again be favorable?
8 Has his steadfast love forever ceased?
   Are his promises at an end for all time?
9 Has God forgotten to be gracious?
   Has he in anger shut up his compassion?" *Selah*

10 Then I said, "I will appeal to this,
   to the years of the right hand of the Most High."

11 I will remember the deeds of the LORD;
　　yes, I will remember your wonders of old.
12 I will ponder all your work,
　　and meditate on your mighty deeds.
13 Your way, O God, is holy.
　　What god is great like our God?
14 You are the God who works wonders;
　　you have made known your might among the
　　　　peoples.
15 You with your arm redeemed your people,
　　the children of Jacob and Joseph. *Selah*

16 When the waters saw you, O God,
　　when the waters saw you, they were afraid;
　　indeed, the deep trembled.
17 The clouds poured out water;
　　the skies gave forth thunder;
　　your arrows flashed on every side.
18 The crash of your thunder was in the whirlwind;
　　your lightnings lighted up the world;
　　the earth trembled and shook.
19 Your way was through the sea,
　　your path through the great waters;
　　yet your footprints were unseen.
20 You led your people like a flock
　　by the hand of Moses and Aaron.

The rhythm of this psalm is the troubles of the present considered in light of the deliverances of the past. The first half of the psalm expresses Asaph's troubles (vv. 1–9); the second half remembers God's past salvations (vv. 10–20).

This is one vital strategy when you find yourself immersed in difficulty. An estranged relationship. A habitual sin. A public embarrassment. Sustained depression. A physical malady. A tormented conscience. When these are present realities, consider your past. Have you not seen God help you? Have you not felt his comforting and strengthening presence through the Holy Spirit? Have you not experienced times of sweetness in Scripture?

And above all, have you not seen his supreme deliverance of you through the gospel of Jesus Christ, in which God sent his Son to suffer and die in your place? Note what Asaph writes toward the end of this psalm: "Your way was through the sea" (v. 19). How implausible that would have seemed to Israel as they stood with their backs to the sea and the Egyptians pursuing them. Yet God's ways run counter to our intuitions. He works in defiance of what our puny minds can predict. The cross is the supreme instance of this. In the Old Testament, his way was through the sea. In the New Testament, his way is through the cross. The gracious provision of God confounds us even as it delivers us.

PSALM 78

A Maskil of Asaph.

1 Give ear, O my people, to my teaching;
  incline your ears to the words of my mouth!
2 I will open my mouth in a parable;
  I will utter dark sayings from of old,
3 things that we have heard and known,
  that our fathers have told us.
4 We will not hide them from their children,
  but tell to the coming generation
the glorious deeds of the LORD, and his might,
  and the wonders that he has done.

5 He established a testimony in Jacob
  and appointed a law in Israel,
which he commanded our fathers
  to teach to their children,
6 that the next generation might know them,
  the children yet unborn,
and arise and tell them to their children,
7   so that they should set their hope in God
and not forget the works of God,
  but keep his commandments;
8 and that they should not be like their fathers,
  a stubborn and rebellious generation,
a generation whose heart was not steadfast,
  whose spirit was not faithful to God.

9   The Ephraimites, armed with the bow,
        turned back on the day of battle.
10 They did not keep God's covenant,
        but refused to walk according to his law.
11 They forgot his works
        and the wonders that he had shown them.
12 In the sight of their fathers he performed wonders
        in the land of Egypt, in the fields of Zoan.
13 He divided the sea and let them pass through it,
        and made the waters stand like a heap.
14 In the daytime he led them with a cloud,
        and all the night with a fiery light.
15 He split rocks in the wilderness
        and gave them drink abundantly as from the deep.
16 He made streams come out of the rock
        and caused waters to flow down like rivers.

17 Yet they sinned still more against him,
        rebelling against the Most High in the desert.
18 They tested God in their heart
        by demanding the food they craved.
19 They spoke against God, saying,
        "Can God spread a table in the wilderness?
20 He struck the rock so that water gushed out
        and streams overflowed.
    Can he also give bread
        or provide meat for his people?"

21 Therefore, when the LORD heard, he was full of wrath;
        a fire was kindled against Jacob;
        his anger rose against Israel,

22 because they did not believe in God
        and did not trust his saving power.
23 Yet he commanded the skies above
        and opened the doors of heaven,
24 and he rained down on them manna to eat
        and gave them the grain of heaven.
25 Man ate of the bread of the angels;
        he sent them food in abundance.
26 He caused the east wind to blow in the heavens,
        and by his power he led out the south wind;
27 he rained meat on them like dust,
        winged birds like the sand of the seas;
28 he let them fall in the midst of their camp,
        all around their dwellings.
29 And they ate and were well filled,
        for he gave them what they craved.
30 But before they had satisfied their craving,
        while the food was still in their mouths,
31 the anger of God rose against them,
        and he killed the strongest of them
        and laid low the young men of Israel.

32 In spite of all this, they still sinned;
        despite his wonders, they did not believe.
33 So he made their days vanish like a breath,
        and their years in terror.
34 When he killed them, they sought him;
        they repented and sought God earnestly.
35 They remembered that God was their rock,
        the Most High God their redeemer.
36 But they flattered him with their mouths;
        they lied to him with their tongues.

37 Their heart was not steadfast toward him;
   they were not faithful to his covenant.
38 Yet he, being compassionate,
   atoned for their iniquity
   and did not destroy them;
   he restrained his anger often
   and did not stir up all his wrath.
39 He remembered that they were but flesh,
   a wind that passes and comes not again.
40 How often they rebelled against him in the wilderness
   and grieved him in the desert!
41 They tested God again and again
   and provoked the Holy One of Israel.
42 They did not remember his power
   or the day when he redeemed them from the foe,
43 when he performed his signs in Egypt
   and his marvels in the fields of Zoan.
44 He turned their rivers to blood,
   so that they could not drink of their streams.
45 He sent among them swarms of flies, which devoured
      them,
   and frogs, which destroyed them.
46 He gave their crops to the destroying locust
   and the fruit of their labor to the locust.
47 He destroyed their vines with hail
   and their sycamores with frost.
48 He gave over their cattle to the hail
   and their flocks to thunderbolts.
49 He let loose on them his burning anger,
   wrath, indignation, and distress,
   a company of destroying angels.

50 He made a path for his anger;
he did not spare them from death,
but gave their lives over to the plague.
51 He struck down every firstborn in Egypt,
the firstfruits of their strength in the tents of Ham.
52 Then he led out his people like sheep
and guided them in the wilderness like a flock.
53 He led them in safety, so that they were not afraid,
but the sea overwhelmed their enemies.
54 And he brought them to his holy land,
to the mountain which his right hand had won.
55 He drove out nations before them;
he apportioned them for a possession
and settled the tribes of Israel in their tents.

56 Yet they tested and rebelled against the Most High God
and did not keep his testimonies,
57 but turned away and acted treacherously like their fathers;
they twisted like a deceitful bow.
58 For they provoked him to anger with their high places;
they moved him to jealousy with their idols.
59 When God heard, he was full of wrath,
and he utterly rejected Israel.
60 He forsook his dwelling at Shiloh,
the tent where he dwelt among mankind,
61 and delivered his power to captivity,
his glory to the hand of the foe.
62 He gave his people over to the sword
and vented his wrath on his heritage.
63 Fire devoured their young men,
and their young women had no marriage song.

64 Their priests fell by the sword,
     and their widows made no lamentation.
65 Then the Lord awoke as from sleep,
     like a strong man shouting because of wine.
66 And he put his adversaries to rout;
     he put them to everlasting shame.

67 He rejected the tent of Joseph;
     he did not choose the tribe of Ephraim,
68 but he chose the tribe of Judah,
     Mount Zion, which he loves.
69 He built his sanctuary like the high heavens,
     like the earth, which he has founded forever.
70 He chose David his servant
     and took him from the sheepfolds;
71 from following the nursing ewes he brought him
     to shepherd Jacob his people,
     Israel his inheritance.
72 With upright heart he shepherded them
     and guided them with his skillful hand.

᧥

This is a "historical psalm," recounting God's faithfulness to his people over many generations and events. Asaph recounts the giving of the law, Israel's wandering in the wilderness, water from the rock, manna from heaven, the miracles in Egypt, and other events. In all this Asaph is concerned to highlight the grace of God despite the ongoing rebellion of God's people: "In spite of all this, they still sinned; despite his wonders, they did not believe" (v. 32).

Consider your own life. What events from your own life are evidence of God's abundant grace, in spite of your own sinfulness? What mentors has he provided for you? What church home? What family? What books? What sermons? Above all, consider your own conversion and new birth, the great event in which you became God's child.

Consider the past two thousand years. Ponder the great events of history and how time and again God delivered his people. Think of the pastors, the theologians, the missionaries, and the thousands of unknown faithful Christians whom God has used to extend the gospel throughout the world and, in your own time, to you.

Finally, consider the events of this psalm. Think of the events of the Old Testament. But above all think of the great Event to which the whole Old Testament, including all that is recounted in this psalm, points: the coming of Jesus Christ. He is the rock that, when broken, gushes forth water (1 Cor. 10:4). He is the manna from heaven that provides true nourishment (John 6:49–51). He is the one in whom the entire Old Testament law is fulfilled (Matt. 5:17). In him you are restored to your true self. Your sins are forgiven. You are promised an eternity in the new earth. Read this psalm and praise God for his goodness to Israel—and to you.

PSALM 79

A Psalm of Asaph.

1   O God, the nations have come into your inheritance;
        they have defiled your holy temple;
        they have laid Jerusalem in ruins.
2   They have given the bodies of your servants
        to the birds of the heavens for food,
        the flesh of your faithful to the beasts of the earth.
3   They have poured out their blood like water
        all around Jerusalem,
        and there was no one to bury them.
4   We have become a taunt to our neighbors,
        mocked and derided by those around us.

5   How long, O Lord? Will you be angry forever?
        Will your jealousy burn like fire?
6   Pour out your anger on the nations
        that do not know you,
    and on the kingdoms
        that do not call upon your name!
7   For they have devoured Jacob
        and laid waste his habitation.

8   Do not remember against us our former iniquities;
        let your compassion come speedily to meet us,
        for we are brought very low.
9   Help us, O God of our salvation,
        for the glory of your name;

deliver us, and atone for our sins,
>   for your name's sake!
10 Why should the nations say,
>   "Where is their God?"
>   Let the avenging of the outpoured blood of your servants
>   be known among the nations before our eyes!

11 Let the groans of the prisoners come before you;
>   according to your great power, preserve those
>   doomed to die!
12 Return sevenfold into the lap of our neighbors
>   the taunts with which they have taunted you, O Lord!
13 But we your people, the sheep of your pasture,
>   will give thanks to you forever;
>   from generation to generation we will recount your
>   praise.

ᔓ

The community cries out for relief in this moving lament. "How long, O Lord? Will you be angry forever?" (v. 5). The people of God have been torn to bits, and Jerusalem has been destroyed. But this is not a matter of mere victimhood. Asaph understands, on behalf of the people, that Israel herself is culpable. He asks God not to remember their sins (v. 8) but to atone for their sinful deeds (v. 9).

Such is life in this perplexing fallen world. Disaster strikes. Pain suddenly swallows us up. Yet we are not mere victims. We are acutely aware of much of our own sinfulness and failure. We do not feel free to ask God for relief from the pain overwhelming us; after all, we are so error-laden ourselves. Surely we deserve this pain? Perhaps somehow this is God's paying us back? Maybe we have brought divine anger down on us in this catastrophe?

As we pray this psalm today, we have a unique advantage over God's people in Asaph's time. For we see that if we are united to Christ by faith, then no disaster that ever washes into our lives is because of God's frustrated anger. All of that was poured out on Christ at the cross. God may be disciplining us; he may be chastening us; he may be testing us. But it is all out of love. Jesus has washed away any reason for God to be angry with us in a punishing kind of way.

Everything in your life, good and pain, comfortable and painful, is from the hand of a loving Father.

PSALM 80

To the choirmaster: according to Lilies.
A Testimony. Of Asaph, a Psalm.

1   Give ear, O Shepherd of Israel,
        you who lead Joseph like a flock.
    You who are enthroned upon the cherubim, shine forth.
2   Before Ephraim and Benjamin and Manasseh,
    stir up your might
        and come to save us!

3   Restore us, O God;
        let your face shine, that we may be saved!

4   O LORD God of hosts,
        how long will you be angry with your people's
            prayers?
5   You have fed them with the bread of tears
        and given them tears to drink in full measure.
6   You make us an object of contention for our neighbors,
        and our enemies laugh among themselves.

7   Restore us, O God of hosts;
        let your face shine, that we may be saved!

8   You brought a vine out of Egypt;
        you drove out the nations and planted it.
9   You cleared the ground for it;
        it took deep root and filled the land.
10 The mountains were covered with its shade,
        the mighty cedars with its branches.
11 It sent out its branches to the sea
        and its shoots to the River.
12 Why then have you broken down its walls,
        so that all who pass along the way pluck its fruit?
13 The boar from the forest ravages it,
        and all that move in the field feed on it.

14 Turn again, O God of hosts!
        Look down from heaven, and see;
    have regard for this vine,
15   the stock that your right hand planted,
        and for the son whom you made strong for yourself.
16 They have burned it with fire; they have cut it down;
        may they perish at the rebuke of your face!

17   But let your hand be on the man of your right hand,
          the son of man whom you have made strong for
          yourself!
18   Then we shall not turn back from you;
          give us life, and we will call upon your name!

19   Restore us, O LORD God of hosts!
          Let your face shine, that we may be saved!

§

The people of God feel forsaken. Their eyes are dry from weeping (vv. 4–5). They are taunted by other nations (v. 6). They feel as if God is deeply disappointed with them (v. 4).

The psalmist peers through that present adversity to reflect on what God did in delivering the people from Egypt. The metaphor carried through the second half of the psalm is that of a vine. Israel is described as a vine that God took and planted in the promised land to spread out and bless the surrounding regions with its shade; however, the vine was torn down, and others plucked its fruit. The psalmist asks God to look again upon this vine, Israel, and cause it to flourish.

God did so. But not in the way that any human could have ever dreamed up. God was insistent that his people flourish, but they could never have done so if left to their own resources. They needed deep deliverance, not just from Egyptian captivity but from sin's captivity. When Jesus Christ came to earth, he called *himself* the vine (John 15:1). In other words, he came to do what Israel failed to do. He came to spread the shade of his blessing far and wide. United to him by faith, we too become part of that life-giving vine and we bear fruit (John 15:4–5).

Do you feel forsaken, as if you keep disappointing God? Consider what God has done for you if you are in Christ. You are vitally connected to the life of heaven. Trust him. Enjoy him. Bear fruit. It is who you now are.

PSALM 81

To the choirmaster: according to The Gittith. Of Asaph.

1 Sing aloud to God our strength;
    shout for joy to the God of Jacob!
2 Raise a song; sound the tambourine,
    the sweet lyre with the harp.
3 Blow the trumpet at the new moon,
    at the full moon, on our feast day.

4 For it is a statute for Israel,
    a rule of the God of Jacob.
5 He made it a decree in Joseph
    when he went out over the land of Egypt.
  I hear a language I had not known:
6 "I relieved your shoulder of the burden;
    your hands were freed from the basket.
7 In distress you called, and I delivered you;
    I answered you in the secret place of thunder;
    I tested you at the waters of Meribah.   *Selah*
8 Hear, O my people, while I admonish you!
    O Israel, if you would but listen to me!

9   There shall be no strange god among you;
         you shall not bow down to a foreign god.
10   I am the LORD your God,
         who brought you up out of the land of Egypt.
         Open your mouth wide, and I will fill it.

11   "But my people did not listen to my voice;
         Israel would not submit to me.
12   So I gave them over to their stubborn hearts,
         to follow their own counsels.
13   Oh, that my people would listen to me,
         that Israel would walk in my ways!
14   I would soon subdue their enemies
         and turn my hand against their foes.
15   Those who hate the LORD would cringe toward him,
         and their fate would last forever.
16   But he would feed you with the finest of the wheat,
         and with honey from the rock I would satisfy you."

∽

The long, sad story of human history is of man's endless quest to find something other than God to satisfy his deepest soul-longings. Conquest, power, material possessions, sexual freedom, even religion—we will latch onto anything that leaves us feeling like we are in control and that allows us to avoid being confronted by the One who made us.

But it is only by losing ourselves in God that we will find our true selves. He alone satisfies. Look at how the psalmist puts it: "Open your mouth wide, and [God] will fill it" (v. 10); "He would feed you with the finest of the wheat, and with honey from the rock [God] would satisfy you" (v. 16). Is this your view of God?

When Christ came, he said he came to give life (John 10:10); he said he was the fountain of living water (John 4:14), the bread from heaven (John 6:38). *You were made for him.*

The fifth-century theologian Augustine put it this way:

> So what should we do in sharing the love of God, whose full enjoyment constitutes the happy life? It is God from whom all those who love him derive both their existence and their love; it is God who frees us from any fear that he can fail to satisfy anyone to whom he becomes known; it is God who wants himself to be loved, not in order to gain any reward for himself but to give to those who love him an eternal reward— namely himself.

Walk with God. Enjoy him. Ponder his love. This is your fullest humanity.

PSALM 82

A Psalm of Asaph.

1   God has taken his place in the divine council;
         in the midst of the gods he holds judgment:
2   "How long will you judge unjustly
         and show partiality to the wicked?   *Selah*
3   Give justice to the weak and the fatherless;
         maintain the right of the afflicted and the destitute.

4   Rescue the weak and the needy;
        deliver them from the hand of the wicked."

5   They have neither knowledge nor understanding,
        they walk about in darkness;
        all the foundations of the earth are shaken.

6   I said, "You are gods,
        sons of the Most High, all of you;
7   nevertheless, like men you shall die,
        and fall like any prince."

8   Arise, O God, judge the earth;
        for you shall inherit all the nations!

৽

In the midst of a lofty vision of God's authority and divine right to rule and judge, this psalm considers the weakest and neediest in the community. The psalm goes way up high and then comes way down low.

How does your life match up with the call of verses 3 and 4? "Give justice to the weak and the fatherless. . . . Rescue the weak and the needy." Some might ascribe such activity to "mercy ministry," and so it is—but such mercy ministry should not be left as an optional element of the Christian life. Why? Because in aiding the weakest in our communities we are acting out in a small way what God has done for us in Christ. *We* are weak—spiritually. We have tasted what it is to be poor and destitute and needy. We were in sin's chains. But God sent his Son to break those chains.

Having been delivered from the greatest bondage—spiritual bondage—we become delighted and privileged to care for those in a lesser but real bondage—physical and material bondage.

PSALM 83

A Song. A Psalm of Asaph.

1   O God, do not keep silence;
       do not hold your peace or be still, O God!
2   For behold, your enemies make an uproar;
       those who hate you have raised their heads.
3   They lay crafty plans against your people;
       they consult together against your treasured ones.
4   They say, "Come, let us wipe them out as a nation;
       let the name of Israel be remembered no more!"
5   For they conspire with one accord;
       against you they make a covenant—
6   the tents of Edom and the Ishmaelites,
       Moab and the Hagrites,
7   Gebal and Ammon and Amalek,
       Philistia with the inhabitants of Tyre;
8   Asshur also has joined them;
       they are the strong arm of the children of Lot.   *Selah*

9   Do to them as you did to Midian,
       as to Sisera and Jabin at the river Kishon,

10   who were destroyed at En-dor,
            who became dung for the ground.
11   Make their nobles like Oreb and Zeeb,
            all their princes like Zebah and Zalmunna,
12   who said, "Let us take possession for ourselves
            of the pastures of God."

13   O my God, make them like whirling dust,
            like chaff before the wind.
14   As fire consumes the forest,
            as the flame sets the mountains ablaze,
15   so may you pursue them with your tempest
            and terrify them with your hurricane!
16   Fill their faces with shame,
            that they may seek your name, O LORD.
17   Let them be put to shame and dismayed forever;
            let them perish in disgrace,
18   that they may know that you alone,
            whose name is the LORD,
            are the Most High over all the earth.

᾽

God sometimes hides his face from the world, but his hidden-
ness does not mean he is absent. In this psalm, God's silence
lures in ten nations, symbolizing all of the opponents of God's
people, so that he might destroy those nations with one blow
(Ps. 83:3–8; cf. 2 Chron. 20:13–23). At the same time, despite all
of the efforts of the world to wipe out his people, God has always
preserved his chosen ones (Ps. 83:4–5; Rom. 11:1–6). And, being
grafted into their olive tree, Gentiles are now heirs to the same

promises of protection (Rom. 11:24). They are his "treasured" property (Ps. 83:3, 12; Rom. 9:23).

Not only does God promise to preserve his disadvantaged people, he also delights in prevailing over their opponents for the sake of his people's deliverance. Asaph's first example of an unlikely victory is Midian's defeat by Gideon, the youngest leader of the weakest tribe of Israel (Judg. 6:1–40). Second is the defeat of Sisera, in which the mighty commander under Jabin, who had tormented Israel for twenty years, was destroyed by a homemaker (Judg. 4:17–22).

The ultimate reason to live confidently in a hostile world is that Jesus Christ has prevailed over our greatest enemies: sin, guilt, Satan, and death. In Christ we are invincible, for Jesus was raised bodily, and we are now united to him by faith. Our future could not be brighter, whatever adversity washes over us in this fallen world.

PSALM 84

To the choirmaster: according to The Gittith.
A Psalm of the Sons of Korah.

1   How lovely is your dwelling place,
         O LORD of hosts!
2   My soul longs, yes, faints
         for the courts of the LORD;
     my heart and flesh sing for joy
         to the living God.

3   Even the sparrow finds a home,
           and the swallow a nest for herself,
           where she may lay her young,
     at your altars, O Lord of hosts,
           my King and my God.
4   Blessed are those who dwell in your house,
           ever singing your praise!   *Selah*

5   Blessed are those whose strength is in you,
           in whose heart are the highways to Zion.
6   As they go through the Valley of Baca
           they make it a place of springs;
           the early rain also covers it with pools.
7   They go from strength to strength;
           each one appears before God in Zion.

8   O Lord God of hosts, hear my prayer;
           give ear, O God of Jacob!   *Selah*
9   Behold our shield, O God;
           look on the face of your anointed!

10   For a day in your courts is better
           than a thousand elsewhere.
     I would rather be a doorkeeper in the house of my God
           than dwell in the tents of wickedness.
11   For the Lord God is a sun and shield;
           the Lord bestows favor and honor.
     No good thing does he withhold
           from those who walk uprightly.
12   O Lord of hosts,
           blessed is the one who trusts in you!

$\backsim$

I n his book *The Saints' Knowledge of Christ's Love*, the Puritan preacher John Bunyan writes, "I have often seen, that the afflicted are always the best sort of Christians." He goes on to explain that what we see as good providences (health, success, ease) frequently have minimal spiritual value, while what we see as bad providences (pain, trial, darkness) are often our deepest sources of spiritual nourishment and growth.

Seasoned Christians know this to be true. We see it here in Psalm 84: the psalmist cries out, seeking to dwell with God (vv. 1–4), for the presence of God is our true strength (v. 5). Then note what the psalmist says: "As they go through the Valley of Baca they make it a place of springs....They go from strength to strength" (vv. 6–7). We do not know exactly where the Valley of Baca was—but we know it was a valley! Valleys in the Bible often symbolize lowness, darkness, and adversity (remember 23:4). Yet those whose strength is in God "make it a place of springs" (84:6). When God is your supreme value, your ultimate good—when you would rather have a lowly place *with* God than a comfortable place *without* him (v. 10)—then no matter what pain washes into your life, your deepest joy cannot be threatened. You are safe. Nothing can touch you. Even the valleys of life become places of fruitfulness.

But what if you do not sense God to be your greatest treasure? We all go through times like these. And that is why texts such as verse 11 are in the Bible—to recalibrate our hearts: "The LORD God is a sun and a shield; the LORD bestows favor and honor. No good thing does he withhold from those who walk uprightly." God is above you, illumining—"a sun." God is before you, protecting—"a shield." God is for you, dignifying—he "bestows favor and honor." God is with you, lavishing—"no good thing does he withhold."

235

PSALM 85

To the choirmaster. A Psalm of the Sons of Korah.

1   Lord, you were favorable to your land;
        you restored the fortunes of Jacob.

2   You forgave the iniquity of your people;
        you covered all their sin.   *Selah*

3   You withdrew all your wrath;
        you turned from your hot anger.

4   Restore us again, O God of our salvation,
        and put away your indignation toward us!

5   Will you be angry with us forever?
        Will you prolong your anger to all generations?

6   Will you not revive us again,
        that your people may rejoice in you?

7   Show us your steadfast love, O Lord,
        and grant us your salvation.

8   Let me hear what God the Lord will speak,
        for he will speak peace to his people, to his saints;
        but let them not turn back to folly.

9   Surely his salvation is near to those who fear him,
        that glory may dwell in our land.

10   Steadfast love and faithfulness meet;
        righteousness and peace kiss each other.

11   Faithfulness springs up from the ground,
        and righteousness looks down from the sky.

12   Yes, the LORD will give what is good,
         and our land will yield its increase.
13   Righteousness will go before him
         and make his footsteps a way.

∽

The Christian life is not static, like a spiritual plateau. Instead, it is up and down. One season we find ourselves trusting heartily in God, worshiping him, enjoying him. The next season, sometimes for no apparent reason, our heart feels cold and stiff. We know the right things to say, we continue to go through the motions, but it feels dead and dry.

Psalm 85 is in the Bible for you to pray in such seasons of emptiness. The psalmist reflects on God's past goodness (vv. 1–3) and then asks for a divine work of renewal (vv. 4–9). He knows what it is to love God in a richly heartfelt way, but something has dried up within him, and he longs for it to return. In praying for this renewal, the psalmist leads us in acknowledging that we cannot manufacture inner renewal on our own. We need God to intervene. We need him to work.

Are you feeling dead and dry? Pray Psalm 85. Meditate on it in the morning and in the evening. After all, God has proven that he will not let such a prayer go unanswered. How did he prove it? By showing, in the fullness of time, exactly how "righteousness and peace" would "kiss each other" (v. 10). He sent Jesus Christ, his only Son, to satisfy the righteous requirements of the law and, in so doing, provide true and lasting peace for any who humbles himself enough to receive it. Jesus has wiped away any reason for God to withhold his renewing grace from you.

PSALM 86

A Prayer of David.

1   Incline your ear, O LORD, and answer me,
       for I am poor and needy.
2   Preserve my life, for I am godly;
       save your servant, who trusts in you—you are my God.
3   Be gracious to me, O Lord,
       for to you do I cry all the day.
4   Gladden the soul of your servant,
       for to you, O Lord, do I lift up my soul.
5   For you, O Lord, are good and forgiving,
       abounding in steadfast love to all who call upon you.
6   Give ear, O LORD, to my prayer;
       listen to my plea for grace.
7   In the day of my trouble I call upon you,
       for you answer me.

8   There is none like you among the gods, O Lord,
       nor are there any works like yours.
9   All the nations you have made shall come
       and worship before you, O Lord,
       and shall glorify your name.
10   For you are great and do wondrous things;
       you alone are God.
11   Teach me your way, O LORD,
       that I may walk in your truth;
       unite my heart to fear your name.

12   I give thanks to you, O Lord my God, with my whole
                 heart,
         and I will glorify your name forever.
13   For great is your steadfast love toward me;
         you have delivered my soul from the depths of Sheol.

14   O God, insolent men have risen up against me;
         a band of ruthless men seeks my life,
         and they do not set you before them.
15   But you, O Lord, are a God merciful and gracious,
         slow to anger and abounding in steadfast love and
                 faithfulness.
16   Turn to me and be gracious to me;
         give your strength to your servant,
         and save the son of your maidservant.
17   Show me a sign of your favor,
         that those who hate me may see and be put to shame
         because you, LORD, have helped me and comforted me.

℘

This psalm is a sustained plea for God's grace and mercy to
wash over the psalmist. And notice the nature of the appeal:
the psalmist appeals not to his own goodness as that which will
trigger God's grace, but to God's goodness. "For you, O Lord, are
good and forgiving" (v. 5). "But you, O Lord, are a God merciful
and gracious, slow to anger and abounding in steadfast love and
faithfulness" (v. 15).

How do you think about your own life? Ponder your weaknesses, your failures, your fickleness, your mistakes—your sins. Our
lives are haunted through and through by a profound brokenness,
a far-reaching sickness that curves us in on ourselves and darkens

our thoughts toward God and others. Do you feel your sinfulness? How strange, then, that we often subtly seek to influence God's view of us with our own obedience or morality.

The message of the Bible is that God saves sinners. God does the saving. And he saves only those who know themselves to be sinners. When Jesus Christ was born, human history began to see in concrete form what was only shadowy in Psalm 86. For Jesus was God's grace and mercy *as a human*. In Jesus God's goodness could be touched, seen, hugged. And he went to a cross and perished in order to win over for every penitent sinner the full and free love of God, in endless supply amid all of our weakness.

As you ponder your sinfulness, ponder his graciousness—a grace that ever outstrips even your sin.

PSALM 87

A Psalm of the Sons of Korah. A Song.

1   On the holy mount stands the city he founded;
2   the LORD loves the gates of Zion
        more than all the dwelling places of Jacob.
3   Glorious things of you are spoken,
        O city of God.   *Selah*

4   Among those who know me I mention Rahab and
        Babylon;
        behold, Philistia and Tyre, with Cush—
      "This one was born there," they say.
5   And of Zion it shall be said,
      "This one and that one were born in her";
      for the Most High himself will establish her.
6   The LORD records as he registers the peoples,
      "This one was born there."   *Selah*

7   Singers and dancers alike say,
      "All my springs are in you."

∽

In 1779 the English pastor John Newton wrote a hymn based on this psalm. The first stanza goes like this:

    Glorious things of thee are spoken,
    Zion, city of our God;

He, whose Word cannot be broken,
Formed thee for His own abode:
On the Rock of Ages founded,
What can shake thy sure repose?
With salvation's walls surrounded,
Thou may'st smile at all thy foes.

Newton captures exactly what this psalm is celebrating. Throughout the Bible, God's city represents a place of safety and refuge. Indeed, the city of God becomes one of the chief metaphors for salvation itself. "Glorious things" are not spoken of Zion simply because of architectural beauty or geographical location. Zion represents God himself, in all his mercy, offered to sinners. In him we take refuge. Newton ends his hymn on just this note:

Blest inhabitants of Zion,
Washed in the Redeemer's blood!
Jesus, whom their souls rely on,
Makes them kings and priests to God;
'Tis His love His people raises
Over self to reign as kings,
And as priests, His solemn praises
Each for a thank off'ring brings.

PSALM 88

A Song. A Psalm of the Sons of Korah. To the
choirmaster: according to Mahalath Leannoth.
A Maskil of Heman the Ezrahite.

1   O LORD, God of my salvation,
      I cry out day and night before you.
2   Let my prayer come before you;
      incline your ear to my cry!

3   For my soul is full of troubles,
      and my life draws near to Sheol.
4   I am counted among those who go down to the pit;
      I am a man who has no strength,
5   like one set loose among the dead,
      like the slain that lie in the grave,
   like those whom you remember no more,
      for they are cut off from your hand.
6   You have put me in the depths of the pit,
      in the regions dark and deep.
7   Your wrath lies heavy upon me,
      and you overwhelm me with all your waves.   *Selah*

8   You have caused my companions to shun me;
      you have made me a horror to them.
   I am shut in so that I cannot escape;
9   my eye grows dim through sorrow.
   Every day I call upon you, O LORD;
      I spread out my hands to you.

10   Do you work wonders for the dead?
          Do the departed rise up to praise you?   *Selah*
11   Is your steadfast love declared in the grave,
          or your faithfulness in Abaddon?
12   Are your wonders known in the darkness,
          or your righteousness in the land of forgetfulness?

13   But I, O LORD, cry to you;
          in the morning my prayer comes before you.
14   O LORD, why do you cast my soul away?
          Why do you hide your face from me?
15   Afflicted and close to death from my youth up,
          I suffer your terrors; I am helpless.
16   Your wrath has swept over me;
          your dreadful assaults destroy me.
17   They surround me like a flood all day long;
          they close in on me together.
18   You have caused my beloved and my friend to shun me;
          my companions have become darkness.

ᔤ

One of the great wonders of the Bible is that it accommodates the darkest experiences any of us could walk through. We will never experience a difficulty that goes deeper than what the Bible addresses. Every pain is accounted for, acknowledged, in Scripture. We are even, as here in this psalm, given words to pray in such emotionally debilitating times.

In Psalm 88 we see the depths of anguish of a heart tormented by feelings of the wrath and anger of God. Divine wrath feels like a flood in which the psalmist is submerged (vv. 16–17). So profound is his disillusionment that even his dearest friends have forsaken him (v. 18). He feels as if God has utterly turned away (v. 14). He is alone. He feels as though he might as well be dead (vv. 3–5). And indeed, this is the only psalm that ends on a note of darkness instead of on a note of praise or hope.

What are we to make of this? Did the psalmist lose all faith in God? We can remember that he addresses God as the "God of my salvation" and uses the covenant name Yahweh ("the LORD") in addressing him (vv. 1, 13). Indeed, the very fact that the psalmist sat down and wrote out this prayer to God signifies a fundamental trust in the Lord and in his goodness.

For us today, we see with the full light of day the length to which God was willing to go to ensure that we would never be truly alone, no matter our folly, no matter our stupidity. For Jesus endured Psalm 88. He *really* endured it. On our behalf. He was shunned by his companions, the disciples. He not only was like one *among* the dead; he *was* dead. But he burst through the other side, into the dawn of resurrection life. United to him by faith, we too join him in resurrection life now (Eph. 2:6) and in the promised hope of final physical resurrection when he comes again (1 Cor. 15:53).

PSALM 89

A Maskil of Ethan the Ezrahite.

1   I will sing of the steadfast love of the LORD, forever;
     with my mouth I will make known your faithfulness
       to all generations.

2   For I said, "Steadfast love will be built up forever;
     in the heavens you will establish your faithfulness."

3   You have said, "I have made a covenant with my chosen
       one;
     I have sworn to David my servant:

4   'I will establish your offspring forever,
     and build your throne for all generations.'"   *Selah*

5   Let the heavens praise your wonders, O LORD,
     your faithfulness in the assembly of the holy ones!

6   For who in the skies can be compared to the LORD?
     Who among the heavenly beings is like the LORD,

7   a God greatly to be feared in the council of the holy
       ones,
     and awesome above all who are around him?

8   O LORD God of hosts,
     who is mighty as you are, O LORD,
     with your faithfulness all around you?

9   You rule the raging of the sea;
     when its waves rise, you still them.

10 You crushed Rahab like a carcass;
     you scattered your enemies with your mighty arm.

11 The heavens are yours; the earth also is yours;
   the world and all that is in it, you have founded them.
12 The north and the south, you have created them;
   Tabor and Hermon joyously praise your name.
13 You have a mighty arm;
   strong is your hand, high your right hand.
14 Righteousness and justice are the foundation of your
        throne;
   steadfast love and faithfulness go before you.
15 Blessed are the people who know the festal shout,
   who walk, O LORD, in the light of your face,
16 who exult in your name all the day
   and in your righteousness are exalted.
17 For you are the glory of their strength;
   by your favor our horn is exalted.
18 For our shield belongs to the LORD,
   our king to the Holy One of Israel.

19 Of old you spoke in a vision to your godly one, and said:
   "I have granted help to one who is mighty;
   I have exalted one chosen from the people.
20 I have found David, my servant;
   with my holy oil I have anointed him,
21 so that my hand shall be established with him;
   my arm also shall strengthen him.
22 The enemy shall not outwit him;
   the wicked shall not humble him.
23 I will crush his foes before him
   and strike down those who hate him.
24 My faithfulness and my steadfast love shall be with him,
   and in my name shall his horn be exalted.

25	I will set his hand on the sea
	and his right hand on the rivers.
26	He shall cry to me, 'You are my Father,
	my God, and the Rock of my salvation.'
27	And I will make him the firstborn,
	the highest of the kings of the earth.
28	My steadfast love I will keep for him forever,
	and my covenant will stand firm for him.
29	I will establish his offspring forever
	and his throne as the days of the heavens.
30	If his children forsake my law
	and do not walk according to my rules,
31	if they violate my statutes
	and do not keep my commandments,
32	then I will punish their transgression with the rod
	and their iniquity with stripes,
33	but I will not remove from him my steadfast love
	or be false to my faithfulness.
34	I will not violate my covenant
	or alter the word that went forth from my lips.
35	Once for all I have sworn by my holiness;
	I will not lie to David.
36	His offspring shall endure forever,
	his throne as long as the sun before me.
37	Like the moon it shall be established forever,
	a faithful witness in the skies." *Selah*

38	But now you have cast off and rejected;
	you are full of wrath against your anointed.
39	You have renounced the covenant with your servant;
	you have defiled his crown in the dust.

40 You have breached all his walls;
        you have laid his strongholds in ruins.
41 All who pass by plunder him;
        he has become the scorn of his neighbors.
42 You have exalted the right hand of his foes;
        you have made all his enemies rejoice.
43 You have also turned back the edge of his sword,
        and you have not made him stand in battle.
44 You have made his splendor to cease
        and cast his throne to the ground.
45 You have cut short the days of his youth;
        you have covered him with shame.   *Selah*

46 How long, O LORD? Will you hide yourself forever?
        How long will your wrath burn like fire?
47 Remember how short my time is!
        For what vanity you have created all the children of
            man!
48 What man can live and never see death?
        Who can deliver his soul from the power of Sheol?
                                                   Selah

49 Lord, where is your steadfast love of old,
        which by your faithfulness you swore to David?
50 Remember, O Lord, how your servants are mocked,
        and how I bear in my heart the insults of all the
            many nations,
51 with which your enemies mock, O LORD,
        with which they mock the footsteps of your anointed.

52 Blessed be the LORD forever!
                    Amen and Amen.

$\backsim$

Perhaps when you read the psalms that recount God's promises to David you feel a bit removed from it all. How do God's actions toward a single king centuries ago speak to me? "Perhaps I see who God is and how he acts and am encouraged by that. But I don't myself enjoy the promises and blessings of David," you might think.

One key to understanding the Old Testament, however, is the principle of corporate solidarity. Simply put, in the biblical worldview, the one stands for the many and the many are represented by the one. The king of Israel, in other words, represented the people; as went the king, so went the people. The whole nation of Israel had a vested interest, therefore, in the flourishing of their king.

And this principle of corporate solidarity stretches past the time of ancient Israel into all of human history. Everyone is born in Adam. At conversion, our fundamental identity is transferred over to Christ. And as goes Christ, so go we! Consider, therefore, the significance of Psalm 89 and the way it cries out for the Davidic kingship to be blessed (vv. 1–37) amid great national distress (vv. 38–52). Do you begin to see how deeply relevant the Davidic throne is to your own life? Jesus was the final Davidic heir (Matt. 1:1; 2 Tim. 2:8); he was the one in whom all the Davidic promises came to decisive fulfillment. He is *the* king, the leader of God's people whose throne truly will never come to an end. And if you trust in Christ, his fate belongs also to you. You will share in his resurrection, his glory, his rule.

BOOK FOUR

PSALM 90

A Prayer of Moses, the man of God.

1   Lord, you have been our dwelling place
        in all generations.
2   Before the mountains were brought forth,
        or ever you had formed the earth and the world,
        from everlasting to everlasting you are God.

3   You return man to dust
        and say, "Return, O children of man!"
4   For a thousand years in your sight
        are but as yesterday when it is past,
        or as a watch in the night.

5   You sweep them away as with a flood; they are like
            a dream,
        like grass that is renewed in the morning:
6   in the morning it flourishes and is renewed;
        in the evening it fades and withers.

7   For we are brought to an end by your anger;
        by your wrath we are dismayed.
8   You have set our iniquities before you,
        our secret sins in the light of your presence.

9   For all our days pass away under your wrath;
        we bring our years to an end like a sigh.

10   The years of our life are seventy,
         or even by reason of strength eighty;
      yet their span is but toil and trouble;
         they are soon gone, and we fly away.
11   Who considers the power of your anger,
         and your wrath according to the fear of you?

12   So teach us to number our days
         that we may get a heart of wisdom.
13   Return, O LORD! How long?
         Have pity on your servants!
14   Satisfy us in the morning with your steadfast love,
         that we may rejoice and be glad all our days.
15   Make us glad for as many days as you have afflicted us,
         and for as many years as we have seen evil.
16   Let your work be shown to your servants,
         and your glorious power to their children.
17   Let the favor of the Lord our God be upon us,
         and establish the work of our hands upon us;
         yes, establish the work of our hands!

∽

The transience of human life is the theme of this psalm, set against the eternal existence of God. We might live seventy or eighty years (v. 10) as our life comes and then slips away with frightful speed. For God, however, who existed before the first mountain was formed (v. 2), a thousand years are like a single day (v. 4).

This psalm is a sober reminder of the folly of planting all of our hopes in this passing world. To the young, life on this earth seems as if it will stretch on forever. The middle-aged find their own mortality suddenly staring them in the face as it sinks in that they are now more than halfway through their time on this earth. The elderly ponder, and frequently comment on, the perplexing speed with which their lives have come and gone. God, on the other hand, is self-existent and endlessly alive and active. He had no beginning and will have no end. His eternality defies time itself.

How, though, does this help us? First, it settles us into the prayer that we would use well the little time we have: "Teach us to number our days" (v. 12). Time is a precious commodity, not to be squandered. Second, more deeply, this psalm instructs us to ask the Lord to grant us by his grace a significance that transcends and outstrips our brief lives. This is the note on which the psalm ends: "Let the favor of the Lord our God be upon us, and establish the work of our hands upon us; yes, establish the work of our hands!" (v. 17). For those who trust in God, he delights to dignify our brief lives with everlasting impact.

Love those whom you see today. Dignify them. Rejoice in them. You are planting seeds that will grow and blossom into eternity.

PSALM 91

1   He who dwells in the shelter of the Most High
        will abide in the shadow of the Almighty.
2   I will say to the LORD, "My refuge and my fortress,
        my God, in whom I trust."

3   For he will deliver you from the snare of the fowler
        and from the deadly pestilence.
4   He will cover you with his pinions,
        and under his wings you will find refuge;
        his faithfulness is a shield and buckler.
5   You will not fear the terror of the night,
        nor the arrow that flies by day,
6   nor the pestilence that stalks in darkness,
        nor the destruction that wastes at noonday.

7   A thousand may fall at your side,
        ten thousand at your right hand,
        but it will not come near you.
8   You will only look with your eyes
        and see the recompense of the wicked.

9   Because you have made the LORD your dwelling place—
        the Most High, who is my refuge—
10   no evil shall be allowed to befall you,
        no plague come near your tent.

11   For he will command his angels concerning you
         to guard you in all your ways.
12   On their hands they will bear you up,
         lest you strike your foot against a stone.
13   You will tread on the lion and the adder;
         the young lion and the serpent you will trample
            underfoot.

14   "Because he holds fast to me in love, I will deliver him;
         I will protect him, because he knows my name.
15   When he calls to me, I will answer him;
         I will be with him in trouble;
         I will rescue him and honor him.
16   With long life I will satisfy him
         and show him my salvation."

∽

This psalm is a song of deep consolation to the one looking to God for rest amid the adversities of life. Its consistent theme is the rest and peace God gives. Amid the storms of life, God is a safe and serene harbor. Have you experienced this? Or are you internally frenetic? Do you see the Lord himself, your Heavenly Father, ruling over all that washes into your life, hard and easy, good and bad? Do you see him nurturing you along in life, loving you, protecting you, working all for good? Rest in him again today.

After all, the Lord Jesus proved that this is who God is. Jesus said, "Come to me, all who labor and are heavy laden, and I will give you rest" (Matt. 11:28). Dwelling in the shelter of the Most High slows down the frantic spinning of our hearts. Life with God blankets our fast-paced lives with inner shalom. He is the God of peace (Rom. 15:33; 16:20; 1 Cor. 14:33). This is the whole reason Jesus came, as announced by the angels at his birth (Luke 2:14).

The eighteenth-century hymn writer Charles Wesley captured it well in his hymn "Thou Hidden Source of Calm Repose":

> Jesus, my all in all thou art;
> My rest in toil, my ease in pain,
> The healing of my broken heart.
> In war my peace, in loss my gain;
> My smile beneath the tyrant's frown,
> In shame my glory, and my crown.
>
> In want my plentiful supply;
> In weakness my almighty power,
> In bonds my perfect liberty.
> My light in Satan's darkest hour;
> In grief my joy unspeakable,
> My life in death, my heaven in hell.

PSALM 92

A Psalm. A Song for the Sabbath.

1   It is good to give thanks to the Lord,
      to sing praises to your name, O Most High;
2   to declare your steadfast love in the morning,
      and your faithfulness by night,
3   to the music of the lute and the harp,
      to the melody of the lyre.
4   For you, O Lord, have made me glad by your work;
      at the works of your hands I sing for joy.

5   How great are your works, O Lord!
      Your thoughts are very deep!
6   The stupid man cannot know;
      the fool cannot understand this:
7   that though the wicked sprout like grass
      and all evildoers flourish,
    they are doomed to destruction forever;
8   but you, O Lord, are on high forever.
9   For behold, your enemies, O Lord,
      for behold, your enemies shall perish;
      all evildoers shall be scattered.

10   But you have exalted my horn like that of the wild ox;
      you have poured over me fresh oil.
11   My eyes have seen the downfall of my enemies;
      my ears have heard the doom of my evil assailants.

12   The righteous flourish like the palm tree
         and grow like a cedar in Lebanon.
13   They are planted in the house of the Lord;
         they flourish in the courts of our God.
14   They still bear fruit in old age;
         they are ever full of sap and green,
15   to declare that the Lord is upright;
         he is my rock, and there is no unrighteousness in him.

∾

The prescript for this psalm tells us it is meant for the Sabbath. What comes into your mind when you hear the word "Sabbath"? Perhaps you think simply of Sunday, or of church. Perhaps you think of Christians who treat the Sabbath in a very conscientious way and are careful to do no work. Maybe not much at all comes into your mind; you know it is associated with ancient Judaism, but not much else.

The Sabbath is something built into the very creation of the world; we see the first Sabbath in the opening two chapters of the Bible, as God himself rests on the seventh day. The Sabbath has been put in place for God's people to show us that he is a God of rest and that in trusting him we ourselves find our true rest. The Sabbath was not instituted merely to be another rule for God's people to keep (Mark 2:27). It is a gracious gift in order for God's people to gain a foretaste of the final rest in the new heavens and new earth we will one day enjoy. That is when we will experience the concluding description of this psalm: "The righteous flourish like the palm tree. . . . They are planted in the house of the Lord; they flourish in the courts of our God. They still bear fruit in old age; they are ever full of sap and green" (vv. 12–14).

Are you in haste? Are you frantic on the inside? Do you paint smiles over internal distress? That is not what Christ came to offer. Instead he came to offer eternal rest (Heb. 4:9), which we anticipate each and every Lord's Day as we rest from our worldly labors. Bring to Jesus your worries, your cares. Unload your burdens on him. Above all, give him your sins. He died and rose again to give us rest for our souls now and, one day, rest for both soul and body, perfectly, forever, unendingly.

PSALM 93

1   The LORD reigns; he is robed in majesty;
        the LORD is robed; he has put on strength as his belt.
    Yes, the world is established; it shall never be moved.
2   Your throne is established from of old;
        you are from everlasting.

3   The floods have lifted up, O LORD,
        the floods have lifted up their voice;
        the floods lift up their roaring.
4   Mightier than the thunders of many waters,
        mightier than the waves of the sea,
        the LORD on high is mighty!

5   Your decrees are very trustworthy;
        holiness befits your house,
        O LORD, forevermore.

⟨flourish⟩

Any of us could easily sit down and begin to list out on a piece of paper various disasters that might overwhelm us: earthquake, flood, fire, heat, cold, disease, accident, lightning strike. The purpose of this short psalm is to remind us that whatever the scariest catastrophe we can imagine, God is greater. "The floods lift up their roaring" (v. 3), but God himself is the creator of water. "The waves of the sea" are intimidating (v. 4), but God made the oceans.

This psalm even speaks of the earth as God's throne. On it he sits, ruling, comfortable, issuing commands and decrees. He orders the world; the world does not order him. As those who belong to him, we take courage today in his fatherly oversight of our lives, for his "decrees are very trustworthy" (v. 5). He does not do things flippantly or out of impulse. Indeed, the supreme expression of just how trustworthy he is can be seen in his sending of his own Son for his people, to redeem them and to love life back into them.

PSALM 94

1   O LORD, God of vengeance,
        O God of vengeance, shine forth!
2   Rise up, O judge of the earth;
        repay to the proud what they deserve!
3   O LORD, how long shall the wicked,
        how long shall the wicked exult?
4   They pour out their arrogant words;
        all the evildoers boast.
5   They crush your people, O LORD,
        and afflict your heritage.
6   They kill the widow and the sojourner,
        and murder the fatherless;
7   and they say, "The LORD does not see;
        the God of Jacob does not perceive."

8   Understand, O dullest of the people!
        Fools, when will you be wise?
9   He who planted the ear, does he not hear?
        He who formed the eye, does he not see?
10   He who disciplines the nations, does he not rebuke?
        He who teaches man knowledge—
11   the LORD—knows the thoughts of man,
        that they are but a breath.

12   Blessed is the man whom you discipline, O LORD,
        and whom you teach out of your law,

13   to give him rest from days of trouble,
        until a pit is dug for the wicked.

14   For the LORD will not forsake his people;
        he will not abandon his heritage;

15   for justice will return to the righteous,
        and all the upright in heart will follow it.

16   Who rises up for me against the wicked?
        Who stands up for me against evildoers?

17   If the LORD had not been my help,
        my soul would soon have lived in the land of silence.

18   When I thought, "My foot slips,"
        your steadfast love, O LORD, held me up.

19   When the cares of my heart are many,
        your consolations cheer my soul.

20   Can wicked rulers be allied with you,
        those who frame injustice by statute?

21   They band together against the life of the righteous
        and condemn the innocent to death.

22   But the LORD has become my stronghold,
        and my God the rock of my refuge.

23   He will bring back on them their iniquity
        and wipe them out for their wickedness;
        the LORD our God will wipe them out.

U ntil believers arrive in the new heavens and the new earth, we will be on the receiving end of ostracism, ridicule, rejection, and even physical violence. It is our privilege to follow the Lord Jesus in this way, as he himself promised (John 15:18–25). But this has always been true of God's people, going all the way back to faithful Abel's being persecuted by faithless Cain (Genesis 4).

Here in Psalm 94 we see the psalmist grieving over the violence and injustice directed at the faithful. He cries out to God for justice. In doing so he gives believers words to speak to God today when in similar angst.

The bottom-line promise to which the psalmist clings is that "The LORD will not forsake his people" (v. 14). Even the psalmist's use of the covenant name "LORD" ("Yahweh"), speaks to the covenant loyalty and commitment by which God has bound himself to his people. It is these covenant promises in which the psalmist finds relief: "When the cares of my heart are many, your consolations cheer my soul" (v. 19).

Do you have heart-cares today? Does it feel like your foot is slipping (v. 18)—like the very earth beneath you is becoming unstable and slippery in light of the many worries and anxieties pressing down upon you? Let the psalmist lead you in considering God's consolations. For, if you are in Christ, you have in full sight the supreme consolation of God—the coming of Jesus Christ to love and deliver you from all your sins, and his indwelling Spirit to comfort and direct you all your days.

PSALM 95

1   Oh come, let us sing to the LORD;
      let us make a joyful noise to the rock of our salvation!

2   Let us come into his presence with thanksgiving;
      let us make a joyful noise to him with songs of praise!

3   For the LORD is a great God,
      and a great King above all gods.

4   In his hand are the depths of the earth;
      the heights of the mountains are his also.

5   The sea is his, for he made it,
      and his hands formed the dry land.

6   Oh come, let us worship and bow down;
      let us kneel before the LORD, our Maker!

7   For he is our God,
      and we are the people of his pasture,
      and the sheep of his hand.
    Today, if you hear his voice,

8   do not harden your hearts, as at Meribah,
      as on the day at Massah in the wilderness,

9   when your fathers put me to the test
      and put me to the proof, though they had seen my
        work.

10   For forty years I loathed that generation
      and said, "They are a people who go astray in their
        heart,
      and they have not known my ways."

11 Therefore I swore in my wrath,
    "They shall not enter my rest."

∽

Do you learn from the mistakes of those who have gone before you?

That is the call of Psalm 95. The psalmist reminds God's people of "Meribah" and "Massah" (v. 8), where the Israelites grumbled against Moses (and ultimately against God) for a lack of water (Ex. 17:1–7). The psalmist encourages God's people to come to God in contrition and worship instead, recognizing him as their Maker and Deliverer—after all, "they had seen my work" (Ps. 95:9).

Are you grumbling today? Murmuring? Do you find yourself nursing wounds, wondering why God has made your life so hard? Repent. Consider that God is the one who formed the earth and made you. Above all, consider the divine "work" that you have experienced: the gracious giving of his own Son to suffer for your sins and restore you to himself. As the writer of Hebrews encourages, let Psalm 95 calm your grumbling and settle you into the glad joy of knowing both the rest that comes from the gospel now and the final rest that will come one day soon in the new earth (Heb. 3:7–11).

PSALM 96

¹ Oh sing to the LORD a new song;
  sing to the LORD, all the earth!
² Sing to the LORD, bless his name;
  tell of his salvation from day to day.
³ Declare his glory among the nations,
  his marvelous works among all the peoples!
⁴ For great is the LORD, and greatly to be praised;
  he is to be feared above all gods.
⁵ For all the gods of the peoples are worthless idols,
  but the LORD made the heavens.
⁶ Splendor and majesty are before him;
  strength and beauty are in his sanctuary.

⁷ Ascribe to the LORD, O families of the peoples,
  ascribe to the LORD glory and strength!
⁸ Ascribe to the LORD the glory due his name;
  bring an offering, and come into his courts!
⁹ Worship the LORD in the splendor of holiness;
  tremble before him, all the earth!

¹⁰ Say among the nations, "The LORD reigns!
  Yes, the world is established; it shall never be moved;
  he will judge the peoples with equity."

¹¹ Let the heavens be glad, and let the earth rejoice;
  let the sea roar, and all that fills it;
¹²   let the field exult, and everything in it!

Then shall all the trees of the forest sing for joy
13   before the Lord, for he comes,
        for he comes to judge the earth.
    He will judge the world in righteousness,
        and the peoples in his faithfulness.

∽

"Splendor and majesty are before him; strength and beauty are in his sanctuary" (v. 6). This psalm exults in God's supreme rule over all the earth, inviting the Gentiles ("the nations," "the peoples," v. 3) to join his people in celebrating his might and reign. As we read and pray this psalm, we too are led in worship. Our hearts are calmed and lifted up. We remember who God is.

And we remember the point on which the psalm concludes—God's mighty rule will one day come to final fruition by establishing forever what is right. All wrongs will be addressed. All debts will be paid. "He will judge the world in righteousness" (v. 13). Every stabbing memory, every grievous wound, will be restored. The very trees will rejoice on that day (v. 12).

This final, cleansing judgment can be a hopeful reality for you instead of a threatening one because, at the cross of Jesus Christ, God has already taken care of your own sins and need for judgment. Final judgment is now to be anticipated with eagerness, not feared with trepidation.

PSALM 97

1   The LORD reigns, let the earth rejoice;
    let the many coastlands be glad!
2   Clouds and thick darkness are all around him;
    righteousness and justice are the foundation of his
        throne.
3   Fire goes before him
    and burns up his adversaries all around.
4   His lightnings light up the world;
    the earth sees and trembles.
5   The mountains melt like wax before the LORD,
    before the Lord of all the earth.

6   The heavens proclaim his righteousness,
    and all the peoples see his glory.
7   All worshipers of images are put to shame,
    who make their boast in worthless idols;
    worship him, all you gods!

8   Zion hears and is glad,
    and the daughters of Judah rejoice,
    because of your judgments, O LORD.
9   For you, O LORD, are most high over all the earth;
    you are exalted far above all gods.

10   O you who love the LORD, hate evil!
    He preserves the lives of his saints;
    he delivers them from the hand of the wicked.

11 Light is sown for the righteous,
        and joy for the upright in heart.
12 Rejoice in the LORD, O you righteous,
        and give thanks to his holy name!

∽

How small God can seem! How big evil can appear! In this fallen world it is often difficult to believe that God is as great as we believe him to be. Psalms such as this one reorient our hearts as we are brought back to a big vision of God: "You, O LORD, are most high over all the earth" (v. 9). This is a God who consumes his enemies like fire (v. 3) and before whom the mountains are like melting wax candles (v. 5).

Is your vision of God diminishing? Do you find the ceiling of your view of his glory lowering? Confess your small-mindedness to God and perhaps also to a trusted Christian friend. Consider who he is. Glory in him again. Ponder him in the mornings. As you do so, do you realize what is happening? Not only is he preserving your life as each day goes by (v. 10); light is being "sown" for you (v. 11). In other words, your final radiance and glory is taking root as you seek God each day. And one day your resplendence will dazzle the angels. In his essay "The Weight of Glory," C. S. Lewis put it this way: "The dullest and most uninteresting person you can talk to may one day be a creature which, if you saw it now, you would be strongly tempted to worship." Lewis goes on to say: "There are no ordinary people. You have never talked to a mere mortal."

PSALM 98

A Psalm.

1   Oh sing to the LORD a new song,
         for he has done marvelous things!
     His right hand and his holy arm
         have worked salvation for him.
2   The LORD has made known his salvation;
         he has revealed his righteousness in the sight of the
             nations.
3   He has remembered his steadfast love and faithfulness
         to the house of Israel.
     All the ends of the earth have seen
         the salvation of our God.

4   Make a joyful noise to the LORD, all the earth;
         break forth into joyous song and sing praises!
5   Sing praises to the LORD with the lyre,
         with the lyre and the sound of melody!
6   With trumpets and the sound of the horn
         make a joyful noise before the King, the LORD!

7   Let the sea roar, and all that fills it;
         the world and those who dwell in it!
8   Let the rivers clap their hands;
         let the hills sing for joy together
9   before the LORD, for he comes
         to judge the earth.

He will judge the world with righteousness,
and the peoples with equity.

∽

Amid the many deities and pagan religions of Old Testament times, the God of the Jews stands out, for at least two reasons.

First, he is not a parochial, regional God. He is not one God among many. He is Lord of all the earth: "Make a joyful noise to the LORD, all the earth" (v. 4); "All the ends of the earth have seen the salvation of our God" (v. 3); "He will judge the world with righteousness, and the peoples with equity" (v. 9).

Second, he defies all other religions by accomplishing his people's safety unilaterally; that is, his power achieves it, not that of his followers. Every other religion is transactional: the follower acts a certain way out of loyalty to the god, and then the god responds with favor. Trace every religion down to the root, and this is what you find. When we come to the God of the Bible, however, "His right hand and his holy arm have worked salvation for him. The LORD has made known his salvation" (vv. 1–2). Believers in this God cannot manipulate him. We only receive.

Do you know this and feel this to be true of your own life in Christ? If you are not ethnically Jewish, then you are living evidence that God is the God of all the earth and of all peoples. You have been welcomed in. And do you know and feel that he and he alone has accomplished your gracious rescue? As the old hymn puts it, "Nothing in my hand I bring; simply to thy cross I cling." God's global grace is reason for deep encouragement. Anyone can get in on this—as long as he does not try to barter with God but rather humbles himself enough to simply receive his love freely.

PSALM 99

1   The LORD reigns; let the peoples tremble!
    He sits enthroned upon the cherubim; let the earth
        quake!
2   The LORD is great in Zion;
    he is exalted over all the peoples.
3   Let them praise your great and awesome name!
    Holy is he!
4   The King in his might loves justice.
    You have established equity;
you have executed justice
    and righteousness in Jacob.
5   Exalt the LORD our God;
    worship at his footstool!
    Holy is he!

6   Moses and Aaron were among his priests,
    Samuel also was among those who called upon his
        name.
    They called to the LORD, and he answered them.
7   In the pillar of the cloud he spoke to them;
    they kept his testimonies
    and the statute that he gave them.

8   O LORD our God, you answered them;
    you were a forgiving God to them,
    but an avenger of their wrongdoings.

9 Exalt the L<small>ORD</small> our God,
   and worship at his holy mountain;
   for the L<small>ORD</small> our God is holy!

∽

This psalm exalts the Lord in his glory and splendor, reflecting on his living presence in the temple, where "he sits enthroned upon the cherubim" (that is, in the ark, which sat in the temple, v. 1). The psalmist remembers Moses and Aaron, who "were among his priests" (v. 6). Samuel, too, acted in a priestly function as he mediated God's word and presence to the people in his time (v. 6).

This can all seem quite foreign and ancient to us, but consider what is true of us today if we are in Christ. The New Testament says that we are priests. That is, we all, each one of us, hold that lofty office of mediating God's Word and presence to the world around us. The priests in the Old Testament were a portion of the people, mediating God to the rest of the people, but all within Israel. Christians today are a portion of the world's people, mediating God to the rest of the people. The Old Testament gives us these categories and helps us to see who we truly are.

We today are led by the psalmist to "exalt the L<small>ORD</small> our God" (v. 9), but we do it with the greater knowledge that we are priests to the world—and this is true only because God sent his own Son to become the true and final great high priest, the priest who offered the ultimate sacrifice of his own life (Heb. 7:27). As a result, we delight to tell the world of God's great love.

PSALM 100

A Psalm for giving thanks.

1   Make a joyful noise to the LORD, all the earth!
2   Serve the LORD with gladness!
         Come into his presence with singing!

3   Know that the LORD, he is God!
         It is he who made us, and we are his;
         we are his people, and the sheep of his pasture.

4   Enter his gates with thanksgiving,
         and his courts with praise!
         Give thanks to him; bless his name!

5   For the LORD is good;
         his steadfast love endures forever,
         and his faithfulness to all generations.

§

A miserable Christian is a contradiction in terms. To be sure, life is hard. The pain that accumulates throughout one's journey in this world is a strong temptation to cynicism. The Christian life is not one of painted-on smiles, pretending that all is right in the world when in truth there are horrors all around. Sometimes the pain in life is so great that the thought of rejoicing seems not only distant but a mockery to our true emotional state.

Yet we must receive what the Bible says in passages such as Psalm 100 because the Bible itself acknowledges the deep pain of life, not only in other books (such as Ecclesiastes) but even in the Psalms. And even more deeply, the Bible gives us resources for wading through the pain of life with a joy and calm that transcends the darkness. As this psalm concludes, "The LORD is good; his steadfast love endures forever, and his faithfulness to all generations" (v. 5). Your pain never outpaces his love. Your difficulty is surrounded by the deeper reality of his goodness. He proved it by sending his own Son for you. Even in the pain of life, we lift our hearts and our voices to the Lord.

PSALM 101

A Psalm of David.

1   I will sing of steadfast love and justice;
         to you, O LORD, I will make music.
2   I will ponder the way that is blameless.
         Oh when will you come to me?
      I will walk with integrity of heart
         within my house;
3   I will not set before my eyes
         anything that is worthless.
      I hate the work of those who fall away;
         it shall not cling to me.
4   A perverse heart shall be far from me;
         I will know nothing of evil.

5 Whoever slanders his neighbor secretly
       I will destroy.
   Whoever has a haughty look and an arrogant heart
       I will not endure.

6 I will look with favor on the faithful in the land,
       that they may dwell with me;
   he who walks in the way that is blameless
       shall minister to me.

7 No one who practices deceit
       shall dwell in my house;
   no one who utters lies
       shall continue before my eyes.

8 Morning by morning I will destroy
       all the wicked in the land,
   cutting off all the evildoers
       from the city of the LORD.

&

To walk with God is to grow in personal integrity. More than this, it is to *love* integrity. The more one grows in Christ and journeys through this world in communion with him, the deeper one's desire to be an integrated human being will be—to bring into alignment our passions, words, thoughts, finances, and so on.

And what is the root of the psalmist's desire? A longing for God: "Oh when will you come to me?" (v. 2). It is impossible to move through life with a primary focus on the things of this world yet still grow in integrity. But when one keeps one's eyes focused on God—his character, his promises, his mighty rule, his heart of grace for sinners—all of life comes into accord. Things fall into place. The disordered loves of our naturally idolatrous hearts become ordered. And now, united to Christ and indwelt by the Spirit, we grow to love the noble life of truth, honor, justice, and virtue.

PSALM 102

A Prayer of one afflicted, when he is faint and
pours out his complaint before the LORD.

1   Hear my prayer, O LORD;
    let my cry come to you!
2   Do not hide your face from me
      in the day of my distress!
    Incline your ear to me;
      answer me speedily in the day when I call!

3   For my days pass away like smoke,
      and my bones burn like a furnace.
4   My heart is struck down like grass and has withered;
      I forget to eat my bread.
5   Because of my loud groaning
      my bones cling to my flesh.
6   I am like a desert owl of the wilderness,
      like an owl of the waste places;
7   I lie awake;
      I am like a lonely sparrow on the housetop.

8   All the day my enemies taunt me;
       those who deride me use my name for a curse.
9   For I eat ashes like bread
       and mingle tears with my drink,
10   because of your indignation and anger;
       for you have taken me up and thrown me down.
11   My days are like an evening shadow;
       I wither away like grass.

12   But you, O Lord, are enthroned forever;
       you are remembered throughout all generations.
13   You will arise and have pity on Zion;
       it is the time to favor her;
       the appointed time has come.
14   For your servants hold her stones dear
       and have pity on her dust.
15   Nations will fear the name of the Lord,
       and all the kings of the earth will fear your glory.
16   For the Lord builds up Zion;
       he appears in his glory;
17   he regards the prayer of the destitute
       and does not despise their prayer.

18   Let this be recorded for a generation to come,
       so that a people yet to be created may praise the
         Lord:
19   that he looked down from his holy height;
       from heaven the Lord looked at the earth,
20   to hear the groans of the prisoners,
       to set free those who were doomed to die,
21   that they may declare in Zion the name of the Lord,
       and in Jerusalem his praise,

22   when peoples gather together,
          and kingdoms, to worship the LORD.

23   He has broken my strength in midcourse;
          he has shortened my days.
24   "O my God," I say, "take me not away
          in the midst of my days—
      you whose years endure
          throughout all generations!"

25   Of old you laid the foundation of the earth,
          and the heavens are the work of your hands.
26   They will perish, but you will remain;
          they will all wear out like a garment.
      You will change them like a robe, and they will pass away,
27   but you are the same, and your years have no end.
28   The children of your servants shall dwell secure;
          their offspring shall be established before you.

∽

This psalm, as the title says, is a "prayer of one afflicted, when he is faint and pours out his complaint before the LORD." Is this your present condition? Perhaps we could even put it this way—is this ever *not* your condition? Certainly, times of heightened adversity come. In this psalm, some tragedy has befallen the psalmist in the prime of his life (vv. 23–24). Yet pain is not something we experience *some* of the time. Pain is something we experience in some part of life *all* of the time.

The consolation toward which this psalm beckons us is the permanence and stability of God himself. Throughout the psalm we read of the transience of humanity over against the established and enduring reality of God: "They will perish, but you will remain" (v. 26).

Yet it is not the bare permanence of God that is the comfort in this psalm. It is the permanence of God as funneled into the future of his people, a future that cannot be threatened by our mortality or hindered by what may befall us. As the psalm ends: "The children of your servants shall dwell secure; their offspring shall be established before you" (v. 28). The grace of God grants a significance that transcends our brief little lives. For we have been united to Christ. His future now determines our future.

PSALM 103

Of David.

1   Bless the LORD, O my soul,
        and all that is within me,
        bless his holy name!
2   Bless the LORD, O my soul,
        and forget not all his benefits,
3   who forgives all your iniquity,
        who heals all your diseases,
4   who redeems your life from the pit,
        who crowns you with steadfast love and mercy,
5   who satisfies you with good
        so that your youth is renewed like the eagle's.

6   The LORD works righteousness
        and justice for all who are oppressed.
7   He made known his ways to Moses,
        his acts to the people of Israel.
8   The LORD is merciful and gracious,
        slow to anger and abounding in steadfast love.
9   He will not always chide,
        nor will he keep his anger forever.
10 He does not deal with us according to our sins,
        nor repay us according to our iniquities.
11 For as high as the heavens are above the earth,
        so great is his steadfast love toward those who fear
            him;
12 as far as the east is from the west,
        so far does he remove our transgressions from us.
13 As a father shows compassion to his children,
        so the LORD shows compassion to those who fear
            him.
14 For he knows our frame;
        he remembers that we are dust.

15 As for man, his days are like grass;
        he flourishes like a flower of the field;
16 for the wind passes over it, and it is gone,
        and its place knows it no more.
17 But the steadfast love of the LORD is from everlasting
            to everlasting on those who fear him,
        and his righteousness to children's children,
18 to those who keep his covenant
        and remember to do his commandments.
19 The LORD has established his throne in the heavens,
        and his kingdom rules over all.

20   Bless the LORD, O you his angels,
           you mighty ones who do his word,
           obeying the voice of his word!
21   Bless the LORD, all his hosts,
           his ministers, who do his will!
22   Bless the LORD, all his works,
           in all places of his dominion.
     Bless the LORD, O my soul!

∽

Who is God? Who is he, really? What is at the center of his heart? This psalm, as much as any place in the Bible, opens up to us who he most deeply is.

What is it, above all else, that weary sinners most need to know? What is oxygen to us in our distressed, pain-riddled lives? The radiant sun of divine favor, shining down on God's children. While the clouds of sin and failure may darken our feelings of that favor, it cannot be lessened any more than a tiny, wispy cloud can threaten the existence of the sun. The sun is shining. It cannot stop. Be at peace.

The Lord looks on his children with utterly unflappable affection (v. 13). Consider the affection of the fatherly heart of God. Let this psalm wash over you. Growth in the Christian life is the process of bringing your sense of self, your swirling internal world of fretful panic arising out of gospel deficit, into alignment with the more fundamental truth that "The LORD is merciful and gracious, slow to anger and abounding in steadfast love" (v. 8). In Christ, God proved it.

We are sinners. We sin. But in Christ our basic identity is not sinner but cleansed, whole. And as we step out into a new day in soul-calm because of that free gift of cleansing, we find that strangely, startlingly, we begin to "do his commandments" (v. 18).

PSALM 104

1 Bless the LORD, O my soul!
    O LORD my God, you are very great!
You are clothed with splendor and majesty,
2   covering yourself with light as with a garment,
    stretching out the heavens like a tent.
3 He lays the beams of his chambers on the waters;
he makes the clouds his chariot;
    he rides on the wings of the wind;
4 he makes his messengers winds,
    his ministers a flaming fire.

5 He set the earth on its foundations,
    so that it should never be moved.
6 You covered it with the deep as with a garment;
    the waters stood above the mountains.
7 At your rebuke they fled;
    at the sound of your thunder they took to flight.
8 The mountains rose, the valleys sank down
    to the place that you appointed for them.
9 You set a boundary that they may not pass,
    so that they might not again cover the earth.

10   You make springs gush forth in the valleys;
         they flow between the hills;
11   they give drink to every beast of the field;
         the wild donkeys quench their thirst.
12   Beside them the birds of the heavens dwell;
         they sing among the branches.
13   From your lofty abode you water the mountains;
         the earth is satisfied with the fruit of your work.

14   You cause the grass to grow for the livestock
         and plants for man to cultivate,
     that he may bring forth food from the earth
15   and wine to gladden the heart of man,
     oil to make his face shine
         and bread to strengthen man's heart.

16   The trees of the LORD are watered abundantly,
         the cedars of Lebanon that he planted.
17   In them the birds build their nests;
         the stork has her home in the fir trees.
18   The high mountains are for the wild goats;
         the rocks are a refuge for the rock badgers.

19   He made the moon to mark the seasons;
         the sun knows its time for setting.
20   You make darkness, and it is night,
         when all the beasts of the forest creep about.
21   The young lions roar for their prey,
         seeking their food from God.
22   When the sun rises, they steal away
         and lie down in their dens.

23 Man goes out to his work
  and to his labor until the evening.

24 O LORD, how manifold are your works!
  In wisdom have you made them all;
  the earth is full of your creatures.
25 Here is the sea, great and wide,
  which teems with creatures innumerable,
  living things both small and great.
26 There go the ships,
  and Leviathan, which you formed to play in it.

27 These all look to you,
  to give them their food in due season.
28 When you give it to them, they gather it up;
  when you open your hand, they are filled with good
    things.
29 When you hide your face, they are dismayed;
  when you take away their breath, they die
  and return to their dust.
30 When you send forth your Spirit, they are created,
  and you renew the face of the ground.

31 May the glory of the LORD endure forever;
  may the LORD rejoice in his works,
32 who looks on the earth and it trembles,
  who touches the mountains and they smoke!
33 I will sing to the LORD as long as I live;
  I will sing praise to my God while I have being.
34 May my meditation be pleasing to him,
  for I rejoice in the LORD.

35   Let sinners be consumed from the earth,
           and let the wicked be no more!
    Bless the Lord, O my soul!
    Praise the Lord!

The world in which we live is a God-belittling world. Everywhere we look we see ads, billboards, marketing, political speeches, financial advice, films, and many other elements of everyday life drawing our minds down from heaven to earth, down from God to ourselves, down from true joy to trite emotionalism.

This psalm trains us to do the opposite. Our minds are drawn from earth to heaven, from the worldly to the divine. We see God and are captivated by his power. Specifically, this psalm celebrates his work in the natural world. Consider what is mentioned as being under God's rule—water, clouds, wind, fire, mountains, thunder, valleys, springs, hills, beasts, birds, branches, fruit, livestock, food, wine, oil, bread, trees, wild goats, rock badgers, the sun, lions . . . nothing under the sun is outside of God's oversight!

Consider your life. Have you compartmentalized the Lord of heaven? Have you set him off as one part of your life, as you have your finances, work, entertainment, and so on? Return to what you know to be true. Rejoice, with the psalmist, in God's splendor and rule over every corner of our lives, all for our good and glory. "Praise the Lord!" (v. 35).

PSALM 105

1   Oh give thanks to the Lord; call upon his name;
     make known his deeds among the peoples!
2   Sing to him, sing praises to him;
     tell of all his wondrous works!
3   Glory in his holy name;
     let the hearts of those who seek the Lord rejoice!
4   Seek the Lord and his strength;
     seek his presence continually!
5   Remember the wondrous works that he has done,
     his miracles, and the judgments he uttered,
6   O offspring of Abraham, his servant,
     children of Jacob, his chosen ones!

7   He is the Lord our God;
     his judgments are in all the earth.
8   He remembers his covenant forever,
     the word that he commanded, for a thousand
       generations,
9   the covenant that he made with Abraham,
     his sworn promise to Isaac,
10   which he confirmed to Jacob as a statute,
     to Israel as an everlasting covenant,
11   saying, "To you I will give the land of Canaan
     as your portion for an inheritance."

12   When they were few in number,
     of little account, and sojourners in it,

13   wandering from nation to nation,
         from one kingdom to another people,
14   he allowed no one to oppress them;
         he rebuked kings on their account,
15   saying, "Touch not my anointed ones,
         do my prophets no harm!"

16   When he summoned a famine on the land
         and broke all supply of bread,
17   he had sent a man ahead of them,
         Joseph, who was sold as a slave.
18   His feet were hurt with fetters;
         his neck was put in a collar of iron;
19   until what he had said came to pass,
         the word of the LORD tested him.
20   The king sent and released him;
         the ruler of the peoples set him free;
21   he made him lord of his house
         and ruler of all his possessions,
22   to bind his princes at his pleasure
         and to teach his elders wisdom.

23   Then Israel came to Egypt;
         Jacob sojourned in the land of Ham.
24   And the LORD made his people very fruitful
         and made them stronger than their foes.
25   He turned their hearts to hate his people,
         to deal craftily with his servants.

26   He sent Moses, his servant,
         and Aaron, whom he had chosen.

27 They performed his signs among them
and miracles in the land of Ham.
28 He sent darkness, and made the land dark;
they did not rebel against his words.
29 He turned their waters into blood
and caused their fish to die.
30 Their land swarmed with frogs,
even in the chambers of their kings.
31 He spoke, and there came swarms of flies,
and gnats throughout their country.
32 He gave them hail for rain,
and fiery lightning bolts through their land.
33 He struck down their vines and fig trees,
and shattered the trees of their country.
34 He spoke, and the locusts came,
young locusts without number,
35 which devoured all the vegetation in their land
and ate up the fruit of their ground.
36 He struck down all the firstborn in their land,
the firstfruits of all their strength.

37 Then he brought out Israel with silver and gold,
and there was none among his tribes who stumbled.
38 Egypt was glad when they departed,
for dread of them had fallen upon it.

39 He spread a cloud for a covering,
and fire to give light by night.
40 They asked, and he brought quail,
and gave them bread from heaven in abundance.
41 He opened the rock, and water gushed out;
it flowed through the desert like a river.

42   For he remembered his holy promise,
          and Abraham, his servant.

43   So he brought his people out with joy,
          his chosen ones with singing.
44   And he gave them the lands of the nations,
          and they took possession of the fruit of the peoples'
              toil,
45   that they might keep his statutes
          and observe his laws.
      Praise the LORD!

ᔑ

The Bible is filled with both "indicatives and "imperatives."
Indicatives are statements of what God has done graciously to
deliver us. Imperatives are exhortations of how we should live as a
result. Indicatives are what God does; imperatives are what we do.
In many of Paul's letters, for example, Paul begins by recounting
indicatives (e.g., Ephesians 1–3) and then goes on to rehearse
imperatives (e.g., Ephesians 4–6). The Ten Commandments are
another example: because God has delivered the people from
Egypt (indicative: Ex. 20:1–2), the people should live in the following way (imperative: Ex. 20:3–17).

But it is never a "trade-off"—as if God has scratched my back
and so I scratch his. We do not pay God back. The very meaning
of grace is that we cannot pay it back. Consider Psalm 105. This
psalm is a long one, 45 verses long. And it is 44 verses of indicative
and one verse of imperative. For 44 verses the psalmist recounts
God's saving deliverances down through Israel's history. Time after
time God mercifully met them in their need, even though they
were "of little account" (v. 12). Only at the very end of the psalm

does the psalmist remind the people of their grateful response: "that they might keep his statutes and observe his laws" (v. 45).

This is the biblical rhythm. God's grace and our obedience are not equal balances on a scale. God's grace is inexhaustible, endless. God's grace always outpaces any grateful response on our part. It is precisely for this reason that we delight to live in holiness and reverence. He has been so good to us—supremely in Christ and the gospel, the greatest indicative of all.

PSALM 106

1   Praise the Lord!
     Oh give thanks to the Lord, for he is good,
       for his steadfast love endures forever!
2   Who can utter the mighty deeds of the Lord,
       or declare all his praise?
3   Blessed are they who observe justice,
       who do righteousness at all times!

4   Remember me, O Lord, when you show favor to your
         people;
     help me when you save them,
5   that I may look upon the prosperity of your chosen ones,
       that I may rejoice in the gladness of your nation,
       that I may glory with your inheritance.

6   Both we and our fathers have sinned;
       we have committed iniquity; we have done
          wickedness.
7   Our fathers, when they were in Egypt,
       did not consider your wondrous works;
      they did not remember the abundance of your steadfast
          love,
       but rebelled by the sea, at the Red Sea.
8   Yet he saved them for his name's sake,
       that he might make known his mighty power.
9   He rebuked the Red Sea, and it became dry,
       and he led them through the deep as through a desert.
10   So he saved them from the hand of the foe
       and redeemed them from the power of the enemy.
11   And the waters covered their adversaries;
       not one of them was left.
12   Then they believed his words;
       they sang his praise.

13   But they soon forgot his works;
       they did not wait for his counsel.
14   But they had a wanton craving in the wilderness,
       and put God to the test in the desert;
15   he gave them what they asked,
       but sent a wasting disease among them.

16   When men in the camp were jealous of Moses
       and Aaron, the holy one of the LORD,
17   the earth opened and swallowed up Dathan,
       and covered the company of Abiram.
18   Fire also broke out in their company;
       the flame burned up the wicked.

19	They made a calf in Horeb
	and worshiped a metal image.
20	They exchanged the glory of God
	for the image of an ox that eats grass.
21	They forgot God, their Savior,
	who had done great things in Egypt,
22	wondrous works in the land of Ham,
	and awesome deeds by the Red Sea.
23	Therefore he said he would destroy them—
	had not Moses, his chosen one,
	stood in the breach before him,
	to turn away his wrath from destroying them.

24	Then they despised the pleasant land,
	having no faith in his promise.
25	They murmured in their tents,
	and did not obey the voice of the Lord.
26	Therefore he raised his hand and swore to them
	that he would make them fall in the wilderness,
27	and would make their offspring fall among the nations,
	scattering them among the lands.

28	Then they yoked themselves to the Baal of Peor,
	and ate sacrifices offered to the dead;
29	they provoked the Lord to anger with their deeds,
	and a plague broke out among them.
30	Then Phinehas stood up and intervened,
	and the plague was stayed.
31	And that was counted to him as righteousness
	from generation to generation forever.

32 They angered him at the waters of Meribah,
  and it went ill with Moses on their account,
33 for they made his spirit bitter,
  and he spoke rashly with his lips.

34 They did not destroy the peoples,
  as the LORD commanded them,
35 but they mixed with the nations
  and learned to do as they did.
36 They served their idols,
  which became a snare to them.
37 They sacrificed their sons
  and their daughters to the demons;
38 they poured out innocent blood,
  the blood of their sons and daughters,
  whom they sacrificed to the idols of Canaan,
  and the land was polluted with blood.
39 Thus they became unclean by their acts,
  and played the whore in their deeds.

40 Then the anger of the LORD was kindled against his
      people,
  and he abhorred his heritage;
41 he gave them into the hand of the nations,
  so that those who hated them ruled over them.
42 Their enemies oppressed them,
  and they were brought into subjection under their
      power.
43 Many times he delivered them,
  but they were rebellious in their purposes
  and were brought low through their iniquity.

44 Nevertheless, he looked upon their distress,
        when he heard their cry.
45 For their sake he remembered his covenant,
        and relented according to the abundance of his
            steadfast love.
46 He caused them to be pitied
        by all those who held them captive.

47 Save us, O LORD our God,
        and gather us from among the nations,
    that we may give thanks to your holy name
        and glory in your praise.

48 Blessed be the LORD, the God of Israel,
        from everlasting to everlasting!
    And let all the people say, "Amen!"
        Praise the LORD!

∽

This psalm, like the previous one, is a lengthy recounting of Israel's past and of God's goodness. What is different about this psalm, though, is that it is filled with reminders of Israel's fickleness and failure. Throughout, sins are acknowledged (v. 6)—rebellion (v. 7), forgetfulness (v. 13), uncleanness (v. 15), jealousy (v. 16), judgment (v. 17), idolatry (v. 19), faithlessness (v. 24), murmuring (v. 25), angering God (v. 32), child sacrifice (v. 37). This is a wayward people. This is a sordid history.

The question therefore confronts us: How did God respond? Who is God toward wayward people?

"Nevertheless, he looked upon their distress, when he heard their cry. . . . [He] relented according to the abundance of his steadfast love" (vv. 44–45).

In short, *God is the one who defies our expectations.* He is the one for whom love and compassion pour out of his very heart. He does not harbor grudges. He enjoys washing sinners in a flood of love and mercy. This is who he is. In Jesus, he showed us that this is who he is. For Jesus came to you and me—to fickle, faltering, sinful you and me—and defied our expectations. He went through with it. He went to the cross. He endured the agony of separation from the Father so that you and I can stand under the fountain of a loving God. All it takes is asking for it. Opening yourself up to it. *This is who he is.*

"Praise the LORD!" (v. 48).

BOOK FIVE

PSALM 107

1 Oh give thanks to the LORD, for he is good,
    for his steadfast love endures forever!
2 Let the redeemed of the LORD say so,
    whom he has redeemed from trouble
3 and gathered in from the lands,
    from the east and from the west,
    from the north and from the south.

4 Some wandered in desert wastes,
    finding no way to a city to dwell in;
5 hungry and thirsty,
    their soul fainted within them.
6 Then they cried to the LORD in their trouble,
    and he delivered them from their distress.
7 He led them by a straight way
    till they reached a city to dwell in.
8 Let them thank the LORD for his steadfast love,
    for his wondrous works to the children of man!
9 For he satisfies the longing soul,
    and the hungry soul he fills with good things.

10 Some sat in darkness and in the shadow of death,
    prisoners in affliction and in irons,
11 for they had rebelled against the words of God,
    and spurned the counsel of the Most High.
12 So he bowed their hearts down with hard labor;
    they fell down, with none to help.

13 Then they cried to the LORD in their trouble,
    and he delivered them from their distress.
14 He brought them out of darkness and the shadow of
        death,
    and burst their bonds apart.
15 Let them thank the LORD for his steadfast love,
    for his wondrous works to the children of man!
16 For he shatters the doors of bronze
    and cuts in two the bars of iron.

17 Some were fools through their sinful ways,
    and because of their iniquities suffered affliction;
18 they loathed any kind of food,
    and they drew near to the gates of death.
19 Then they cried to the LORD in their trouble,
    and he delivered them from their distress.
20 He sent out his word and healed them,
    and delivered them from their destruction.
21 Let them thank the LORD for his steadfast love,
    for his wondrous works to the children of man!
22 And let them offer sacrifices of thanksgiving,
    and tell of his deeds in songs of joy!

23 Some went down to the sea in ships,
    doing business on the great waters;
24 they saw the deeds of the LORD,
    his wondrous works in the deep.
25 For he commanded and raised the stormy wind,
    which lifted up the waves of the sea.
26 They mounted up to heaven; they went down to the
        depths;
    their courage melted away in their evil plight;

27 they reeled and staggered like drunken men
  and were at their wits' end.
28 Then they cried to the LORD in their trouble,
  and he delivered them from their distress.
29 He made the storm be still,
  and the waves of the sea were hushed.
30 Then they were glad that the waters were quiet,
  and he brought them to their desired haven.
31 Let them thank the LORD for his steadfast love,
  for his wondrous works to the children of man!
32 Let them extol him in the congregation of the people,
  and praise him in the assembly of the elders.

33 He turns rivers into a desert,
  springs of water into thirsty ground,
34 a fruitful land into a salty waste,
  because of the evil of its inhabitants.
35 He turns a desert into pools of water,
  a parched land into springs of water.
36 And there he lets the hungry dwell,
  and they establish a city to live in;
37 they sow fields and plant vineyards
  and get a fruitful yield.
38 By his blessing they multiply greatly,
  and he does not let their livestock diminish.

39 When they are diminished and brought low
  through oppression, evil, and sorrow,
40 he pours contempt on princes
  and makes them wander in trackless wastes;
41 but he raises up the needy out of affliction
  and makes their families like flocks.

42   The upright see it and are glad,
           and all wickedness shuts its mouth.

43   Whoever is wise, let him attend to these things;
           let them consider the steadfast love of the LORD.

§

The point of Psalm 107 is captured in its final verse: "Whoever
is wise, let him attend to these things; let them consider
the steadfast love of the LORD" (v. 43). The entire psalm leads to
this conclusion, for the entire psalm is a recitation of concrete
examples of the steadfast love of the Lord—to those wandering
in barren places (vv. 4–9), to those sitting in darkness (vv. 10–16),
to those suffering for their own sinful folly (vv. 17–22), and to
those caught in a storm (vv. 23–32). We are to "consider the
steadfast love of the LORD." The Hebrew verb "consider" here
means to understand, to discern, to perceive. The point is that in
considering God's history of delivering his people, we are to see
in those rescues the steadfast love, the certain mercy, of the Lord.

The psalmist himself in verses 33–42 helps us to understand
how the steadfast love of the Lord operates. Ponder what is being
said: the psalmist is saying that the Lord saves his people through
reversals. It is the parched land that becomes a spring of water. It is
the hungry who establish a city. It is the needy who are raised up.

This vindication through reversal is not an anomaly of this
psalm. It is how God delights to work. He takes the high and
makes them low; he takes the low and makes them high. He
manifests his strength through weakness. Supremely, he manifests
his saving glory through a cursed cross. The gospel is the final
great reversal: the sinless one suffered condemnation so that the
sinful ones might not. Anyone who by God's grace can humble

himself to receive Christ's work as a free gift will be forgiven and glorified and will enjoy the new heavens and the new earth. But the only way in is to get low. The proud—those who believe they deserve heaven—are the very ones who do not.

PSALM 108

A Song. A Psalm of David.

1 My heart is steadfast, O God!
    I will sing and make melody with all my being!
2 Awake, O harp and lyre!
    I will awake the dawn!
3 I will give thanks to you, O LORD, among the peoples;
    I will sing praises to you among the nations.
4 For your steadfast love is great above the heavens;
    your faithfulness reaches to the clouds.

5 Be exalted, O God, above the heavens!
    Let your glory be over all the earth!
6 That your beloved ones may be delivered,
    give salvation by your right hand and answer me!

7 God has promised in his holiness:
    "With exultation I will divide up Shechem
    and portion out the Valley of Succoth.

8 Gilead is mine; Manasseh is mine;
       Ephraim is my helmet,
       Judah my scepter.
9 Moab is my washbasin;
       upon Edom I cast my shoe;
       over Philistia I shout in triumph."

10 Who will bring me to the fortified city?
        Who will lead me to Edom?
11 Have you not rejected us, O God?
        You do not go out, O God, with our armies.
12 Oh grant us help against the foe,
        for vain is the salvation of man!
13 With God we shall do valiantly;
        it is he who will tread down our foes.

‹›

"Vain is the salvation of man!" (v. 12). The Hebrew word translated "vain" means "empty" or "worthless." The deliverance that man can provide has zero weightiness behind it. It is of no accord. When life falls apart—when our sins overwhelm us, when darkness presses in and does not lift—what will our pathetically limited human resources provide? And most supremely, when we come to stand before God, the Holy One, what human cleverness or obedience or accomplishments will we dare parade before him? Vain is the salvation of man. Left to our own resources, we can only feel as David did: "Have you not rejected us, O God?" (v. 11). On the other hand, "With God we shall do valiantly" (v. 13).

Few have felt the impotence of humanly contrived methods of salvation more so than Martin Luther, the German reformer of the sixteenth century. In his book *The Bondage of the Will* he wrote:

> God has assuredly promised his grace to the humble, that is, to those who lament and despair of themselves. But no man can be thoroughly humbled until he knows that his salvation is utterly beyond his own powers, devices, endeavors, will, and works, and depends entirely on the choice, will, and work of another, namely, of God alone.
>
> For as long as he is persuaded that he himself can do even the least thing toward his salvation, he retains some self-confidence and does not altogether despair of himself, and therefore he is not humbled before God, but presumes that there is—or at least hopes or desires that there may be—some place, time, and work for him, by which he may at length attain to salvation. But when a man has no doubt that everything depends on the will of God, then he completely despairs of himself and chooses nothing for himself, but waits for God to work.

Vain is the salvation of man. But with God on our side, we shall triumph.

PSALM 109

To the choirmaster. A Psalm of David.

1   Be not silent, O God of my praise!
2   For wicked and deceitful mouths are opened against me,
         speaking against me with lying tongues.
3   They encircle me with words of hate,
         and attack me without cause.
4   In return for my love they accuse me,
         but I give myself to prayer.
5   So they reward me evil for good,
         and hatred for my love.

6   Appoint a wicked man against him;
         let an accuser stand at his right hand.
7   When he is tried, let him come forth guilty;
         let his prayer be counted as sin!
8   May his days be few;
         may another take his office!
9   May his children be fatherless
         and his wife a widow!
10   May his children wander about and beg,
         seeking food far from the ruins they inhabit!
11   May the creditor seize all that he has;
         may strangers plunder the fruits of his toil!
12   Let there be none to extend kindness to him,
         nor any to pity his fatherless children!

13 May his posterity be cut off;
              may his name be blotted out in the second
                      generation!
14 May the iniquity of his fathers be remembered before
              the LORD,
              and let not the sin of his mother be blotted out!
15 Let them be before the LORD continually,
              that he may cut off the memory of them from the
                      earth!

16 For he did not remember to show kindness,
              but pursued the poor and needy
              and the brokenhearted, to put them to death.
17 He loved to curse; let curses come upon him!
              He did not delight in blessing; may it be far from him!
18 He clothed himself with cursing as his coat;
              may it soak into his body like water,
              like oil into his bones!
19 May it be like a garment that he wraps around him,
              like a belt that he puts on every day!
20 May this be the reward of my accusers from the LORD,
              of those who speak evil against my life!

21 But you, O GOD my Lord,
              deal on my behalf for your name's sake;
              because your steadfast love is good, deliver me!
22 For I am poor and needy,
              and my heart is stricken within me.
23 I am gone like a shadow at evening;
              I am shaken off like a locust.
24 My knees are weak through fasting;
              my body has become gaunt, with no fat.

25   I am an object of scorn to my accusers;
            when they see me, they wag their heads.

26   Help me, O LORD my God!
            Save me according to your steadfast love!
27   Let them know that this is your hand;
            you, O LORD, have done it!
28   Let them curse, but you will bless!
            They arise and are put to shame, but your servant
               will be glad!
29   May my accusers be clothed with dishonor;
            may they be wrapped in their own shame as in a
               cloak!

30   With my mouth I will give great thanks to the LORD;
            I will praise him in the midst of the throng.
31   For he stands at the right hand of the needy one,
            to save him from those who condemn his soul to
               death.

§

We live in a world of accusation. Sometimes our accusers
are actual people, as is the case for David as he writes this
psalm: "Wicked and deceitful mouths are opened against me"
(v. 2). When he attempts to forgive and show his accusers love
(v. 4), they respond in intensified hatred, slander, and attacks. They
will not allow him a moment of peace. David's cry to God in
this psalm is clear: "End it! Cut them off! Shut them up!" To our
ears this sounds too harsh, selfish, impatient, unloving. How can
David ask that "his days be few" (v. 8) or for God to "cut off the
memory of them from the earth" (v. 15)? Is this even a Christian

310

prayer? We want to plead with David to show a bit more grace, perhaps pointing him to Jesus' words in Matthew 5 about loving our enemies and turning the other cheek. However, before we do, let us consider one more thing.

David is the king, anointed by God to rule over Israel. His accusers are, in reality, accusing the One who appointed him king. If God allowed the accusers to continue, peace would not come to God's king or his people. They must be stopped.

David's enemies are not the only accusers. We, too, live in a world of accusation. We find ourselves accused by others (Matt. 5:11–12), by ourselves (Rom. 7:21–24), and by Satan himself (Rev. 12:7–10). We are attacked on all fronts. Our accusers cry out that we are not pure, not worthy, not right, not enough. And perhaps we are not pure or worthy. But as with David, it is not our worthiness that matters. "God made [us] alive together with [Christ], having forgiven us all our trespasses, by canceling the record of debt that stood against us with its legal demands. This he set aside, nailing it to the cross. He disarmed the rulers and authorities and put them to open shame, by triumphing over them in him" (Col. 2:13–15).

The way God answered David's prayer is Jesus. In Jesus, the strength of our accusers is cut off. "Who shall bring any charge against God's elect? It is God who justifies. Who is to condemn? Christ Jesus is the one who died—more than that, who was raised—who is at the right hand of God, who indeed is interceding for us" (Rom. 8:33–34). When our crucified and risen king comes again, our accusers will be silenced once and for all. We will have peace.

PSALM 110

A Psalm of David.

1   The LORD says to my Lord:
     "Sit at my right hand,
  until I make your enemies your footstool."

2   The LORD sends forth from Zion
     your mighty scepter.
     Rule in the midst of your enemies!
3   Your people will offer themselves freely
     on the day of your power,
      in holy garments;
  from the womb of the morning,
     the dew of your youth will be yours.
4   The LORD has sworn
     and will not change his mind,
  "You are a priest forever
     after the order of Melchizedek."

5   The Lord is at your right hand;
     he will shatter kings on the day of his wrath.
6   He will execute judgment among the nations,
     filling them with corpses;
  he will shatter chiefs
     over the wide earth.
7   He will drink from the brook by the way;
     therefore he will lift up his head.

This psalm triumphantly looks to the future, to the Son of David who towers over David himself as God's ultimate solution to a world hostile toward its Creator. The first verse of this psalm is cited all throughout the New Testament, and especially throughout Hebrews, as ancient testimony fulfilled in Christ of God's promise of a coming Messiah who would establish justice over God's enemies once and for all.

How does this text integrate into your own life? Christ's enemies are your enemies, as you are his disciple aligned with him. Your greatest battle has been won. But what is this greatest battle? Your deepest struggle is against sin and death and condemnation. This transcends all other struggles. This is your real danger: separation from the Father because of your own rebellion. Conquest by Satan and the forces of hell, accusing you of your actual sinfulness.

And how is this battle won? By the fulfillment of verse 4: God has sent a priest who, unlike every other priest, will never die and will never have to offer a sacrifice for his own sin (Heb. 7:1–25). Instead, this priest has himself been the sacrifice for your sins.

Christ is your king, representing God to you, but he is also your priest, representing you to God. He is worthy of all our trust.

PSALM 111

1   Praise the LORD!
    I will give thanks to the LORD with my whole heart,
       in the company of the upright, in the congregation.

2   Great are the works of the LORD,
       studied by all who delight in them.

3   Full of splendor and majesty is his work,
       and his righteousness endures forever.

4   He has caused his wondrous works to be remembered;
       the LORD is gracious and merciful.

5   He provides food for those who fear him;
       he remembers his covenant forever.

6   He has shown his people the power of his works,
       in giving them the inheritance of the nations.

7   The works of his hands are faithful and just;
       all his precepts are trustworthy;

8   they are established forever and ever,
       to be performed with faithfulness and uprightness.

9   He sent redemption to his people;
       he has commanded his covenant forever.
       Holy and awesome is his name!

10 The fear of the LORD is the beginning of wisdom;
       all those who practice it have a good understanding.
       His praise endures forever!

The Bible is not mainly a book of advice, telling us what to do. It is mainly a book of redemption, telling us what God has done. The Bible is not commands with stories sprinkled in; it is a Story with commands sprinkled in. To be sure, we are called to the high summons of holiness and obedience, but even this is a grateful response from the heart to what God has done for us in his great grace.

Consider this psalm. Pause and notice its subject: God and his actions. "Great are the works of the LORD" (v. 2). And these works are "studied by all who delight in them"—we study what God himself has done. The next several verses begin with "He . . ." God does not passively wait in heaven for us to get his attention enough for him to act. He cannot be bribed. He is not distant, aloof. He is on the move, acting in "gracious and merciful" ways toward his people (v. 4).

The Bible is a message of gracious redemption from start to finish. Scripture is not an advice column at the back of the newspaper; it is the front page, declaring news of what God has done. "He sent redemption to his people" (v. 9). Yes he did—far more than the writer of Psalm 111 knew. The good news of the gospel is that God sent redemption in the tangible form of his own Son as a fully human person to launch the renewal and consummation of all things through his life, death, and resurrection.

PSALM 112

1   Praise the LORD!
Blessed is the man who fears the LORD,
     who greatly delights in his commandments!
2   His offspring will be mighty in the land;
     the generation of the upright will be blessed.
3   Wealth and riches are in his house,
     and his righteousness endures forever.
4   Light dawns in the darkness for the upright;
     he is gracious, merciful, and righteous.
5   It is well with the man who deals generously and lends;
     who conducts his affairs with justice.
6   For the righteous will never be moved;
     he will be remembered forever.
7   He is not afraid of bad news;
     his heart is firm, trusting in the LORD.
8   His heart is steady; he will not be afraid,
     until he looks in triumph on his adversaries.
9   He has distributed freely; he has given to the poor;
     his righteousness endures forever;
     his horn is exalted in honor.
10   The wicked man sees it and is angry;
     he gnashes his teeth and melts away;
     the desire of the wicked will perish!

This psalm walks us into steadiness of trust in the Lord. Most of us tend to trust in other things at a heart-level—bank accounts, reputation, family, intellectual ability, physical strength, or maybe even hopes for something in the future. We draw strength from these good earthly gifts in a way that is unhealthy because it relies on something that could be taken away at any moment.

Those who walk with God, on the other hand, are funneling their deepest hopes squarely onto God himself: "His heart is firm, trusting in the LORD" (v. 7). This is why "he is not afraid of bad news" (v. 7). Why? Because even the worst news can only threaten his earthly cares; nothing can take away God himself.

Ultimately, therefore, this life for him is but the breaking of the dawn: "Light dawns in the darkness for the upright" (v. 4). What does this mean? For those who trust in the Lord—those who take all of their cowering anxieties and cast them upon God—this life is like the first rays of sunshine coming over the horizon at five o'clock in the morning on a warm summer day. As Proverbs puts it, "The path of the righteous is like the light of dawn, which shines brighter and brighter until full day" (Prov. 4:18). Your radiant glory is just beginning. United to Christ and indwelt by the Spirit, this final radiance is graciously assured.

PSALM 113

1   Praise the LORD!
     Praise, O servants of the LORD,
       praise the name of the LORD!

2   Blessed be the name of the LORD
       from this time forth and forevermore!
3   From the rising of the sun to its setting,
       the name of the LORD is to be praised!

4   The LORD is high above all nations,
       and his glory above the heavens!
5   Who is like the LORD our God,
       who is seated on high,
6   who looks far down
       on the heavens and the earth?
7   He raises the poor from the dust
       and lifts the needy from the ash heap,
8   to make them sit with princes,
       with the princes of his people.
9   He gives the barren woman a home,
       making her the joyous mother of children.
     Praise the LORD!

We find ourselves praising all day long. Praise tumbles out of our mouths without our even knowing it. We praise musical ability, athletic prowess, a beautiful snowfall, a child's ability to take its first steps, a well-written book, a delicious dish. This psalm calls us to praise God. Why? Because the majestic God who rules over all (vv. 4–6) delights to take notice of the distraught and the needy (vv. 7–9). Who could have ever imagined that this is what the Creator is like? Who would have ever presumed him to be inclined in this way?

How about you? Have you seen his heart? Or do you view him as stoically distant and removed? Are you distraught? Are you perplexed by life? The Lord of heaven is drawn like a magnet to your distress. Open up to him. Welcome him into your need. "He raises the poor from the dust and lifts the needy from the ash heap" (v. 7).

Above all, remember that the great and high God proved once and for all that he loves to come down to meet distraught sinners in their need by coming in the person of the Son and becoming one who was himself low and distraught. He came for us. He came for *you*. He joined you in your lowly condition. Embrace him.

PSALM 114

1   When Israel went out from Egypt,
         the house of Jacob from a people of strange language,

2   Judah became his sanctuary,
         Israel his dominion.

3   The sea looked and fled;
         Jordan turned back.

4   The mountains skipped like rams,
         the hills like lambs.

5   What ails you, O sea, that you flee?
         O Jordan, that you turn back?

6   O mountains, that you skip like rams?
         O hills, like lambs?

7   Tremble, O earth, at the presence of the Lord,
         at the presence of the God of Jacob,

8   who turns the rock into a pool of water,
         the flint into a spring of water.

§

The natural elements can intimidate even mature adults. Many of us have driven through intense downpours of rain or been woken up to a peal of thunder right overhead. This psalm insists, however, that the Lord uses the natural elements to care for us, to serve us.

The supreme example of this, mentioned in the opening of the psalm, is the peeling back of the Red Sea for the people of Israel to pass through on dry land. But notice how the psalmist speaks: God did not just part the sea—"The sea looked and fled" (v. 3). God was in solidarity with his people against creation. He *scared* the sea away.

How can this solidarity be ours? How can we be assured of these truths as we walk through life, through whatever tempests assault us in our relationships, our finances, our work, our children? Especially when we are sinners who deserve to be overwhelmed by the storms of life? Only in the knowledge of the gospel—that Jesus Christ went through the ultimate storm on our behalf. When he was on the cross, the world went dark (Mark 15:33). Why? As a sign of God's judgment coming upon him. As a marker indicating that what was happening physically to the world was happening cosmically to the Son. He was being judged, in our place.

PSALM 115

1 Not to us, O LORD, not to us, but to your name give
        glory,
    for the sake of your steadfast love and your faithfulness!

2 Why should the nations say,
  "Where is their God?"
3 Our God is in the heavens;
    he does all that he pleases.

4 Their idols are silver and gold,
    the work of human hands.
5 They have mouths, but do not speak;
    eyes, but do not see.
6 They have ears, but do not hear;
    noses, but do not smell.
7 They have hands, but do not feel;
    feet, but do not walk;
    and they do not make a sound in their throat.
8 Those who make them become like them;
    so do all who trust in them.

9 O Israel, trust in the LORD!
    He is their help and their shield.
10 O house of Aaron, trust in the LORD!
    He is their help and their shield.
11 You who fear the LORD, trust in the LORD!
    He is their help and their shield.

12   The LORD has remembered us; he will bless us;
          he will bless the house of Israel;
          he will bless the house of Aaron;
13   he will bless those who fear the LORD,
          both the small and the great.

14   May the LORD give you increase,
          you and your children!
15   May you be blessed by the LORD,
          who made heaven and earth!

16   The heavens are the LORD's heavens,
          but the earth he has given to the children of man.
17   The dead do not praise the LORD,
          nor do any who go down into silence.
18   But we will bless the LORD
          from this time forth and forevermore.
      Praise the LORD!

∽

What is idolatry? You see it here in the psalm as the powerlessness of idols is reflected on at length (vv. 4–8). But what is an idol? Many of us might associate idolatry with worship, and that is right so far as it goes. An idol is something we falsely worship. But what does that really mean?

Notice the language of this psalm. Here the psalmist uses the language not of worship but of trust. We are called not to trust in idols (v. 8) but to trust in the Lord instead (vv. 9–11). The Heidelberg Catechism of the 1560s explicitly connects idolatry to trust in its treatment of the Ten Commandments. It explains the first commandment ("You shall have no other gods before me") like this: "What is idolatry? Idolatry is having or inventing something in which one *trusts* in place of or alongside of the only true God, who has revealed himself in his Word."

Perhaps the notion of "idolatry" seems far removed from what you discern in your heart. But in what do you trust? It might be hard to see how we *worship* our reputation, but it is easy to see how we *trust* in our reputation. It is not intuitively obvious that we *worship* the idol of a swelling bank account; it is easy to see how we might we *trust* that as our deepest functional security, a stronghold of psychological refuge. But this is a refuge with a crumbly foundation. Only in Christ are we truly secure. Trust in him. Hope in him. Bank on him. Only he will never let you down.

PSALM 116

1   I love the LORD, because he has heard
        my voice and my pleas for mercy.
2   Because he inclined his ear to me,
        therefore I will call on him as long as I live.
3   The snares of death encompassed me;
        the pangs of Sheol laid hold on me;
        I suffered distress and anguish.
4   Then I called on the name of the LORD:
        "O LORD, I pray, deliver my soul!"

5   Gracious is the LORD, and righteous;
        our God is merciful.

6   The LORD preserves the simple;
        when I was brought low, he saved me.
7   Return, O my soul, to your rest;
        for the LORD has dealt bountifully with you.

8   For you have delivered my soul from death,
        my eyes from tears,
        my feet from stumbling;
9   I will walk before the LORD
        in the land of the living.

10 I believed, even when I spoke:
        "I am greatly afflicted";
11 I said in my alarm,
        "All mankind are liars."

12 What shall I render to the LORD
        for all his benefits to me?
13 I will lift up the cup of salvation
        and call on the name of the LORD,
14 I will pay my vows to the LORD
        in the presence of all his people.

15 Precious in the sight of the LORD
        is the death of his saints.
16 O LORD, I am your servant;
        I am your servant, the son of your maidservant.
        You have loosed my bonds.
17 I will offer to you the sacrifice of thanksgiving
        and call on the name of the LORD.
18 I will pay my vows to the LORD
        in the presence of all his people,

in the courts of the house of the LORD,
     in your midst, O Jerusalem.
   Praise the LORD!

∽

D oes the Bible try to lift you out of your real life, your life
     in which pain is so pervasive that at times you can think of
nothing except life's difficulties? Does the Bible try to bring you
into a softer reality than the one you are immersed in? Does the
Bible minimize or neglect adversity?

   Not at all. "I suffered distress and anguish" (v. 3); "I was brought
low" (v. 6). "Tears" (v. 8); "stumbling" (v. 8); "alarm" (v. 11). The
Bible is filled with utter realism. The Bible does not teach that
you are to get out of your pain and into God, the way some other
world religions might. The Bible teaches that God comes out of
heaven and into your pain. We do not come to God on the other
side of pain; God comes to us in our pain.

   Here is why: "Gracious is the LORD, and righteous; our God
is merciful" (v. 5). As a result, he meets us and delivers us. He
may not remove the adversity, but he will keep and comfort the
one who looks to him with a solace that transcends whatever
is happening circumstantially all around him. We will then find
ourselves wondering, "What shall I render to the LORD for all
his benefits to me?" (v. 12).

   And we today, looking back on this psalm in the twenty-
first century, will have the deepest consolation possible. We will
remember that the phrase "Gracious is the LORD" went from
abstract truth to concrete reality in the incarnation. Then God
really came out of heaven into our pain. Could he possibly have
given us more reason to trust and love him?

PSALM 117

1   Praise the L<small>ORD</small>, all nations!
       Extol him, all peoples!
2   For great is his steadfast love toward us,
       and the faithfulness of the L<small>ORD</small> endures forever.
   Praise the L<small>ORD</small>!

               ∽

This short psalm calls for the *nations* (v. 1) to rejoice in God's love for *Israel* (v. 2). How can that be? The psalmist knows that God's love is pledged to Israel for the sake of the whole world. God called Abraham and his descendants to be a channel, not a dam; to pass on, not gobble up, God's grace and mercy (Gen. 12:2–3; Ex. 19:5–6; 1 Kings 8:41–43). And the true and final descendant of Abraham, Jesus Christ, broke open God's grace for all the world once and for all (Gal. 3:7–9, 16).

Are you a follower of Jesus Christ? Enjoy God's grace. But pass it on. To hoard God's grace is to demonstrate you do not yourself understand it. If grace is as promised, then it is free—open to all, indiscriminately. Who in your life needs to hear of this grace? If grace is truly gracious, then you are permanently forgiven, liberated, rinsed clean. Let your delight in this freedom bubble over into telling others of what they too might enjoy.

PSALM 118

1   Oh give thanks to the LORD, for he is good;
        for his steadfast love endures forever!

2   Let Israel say,
        "His steadfast love endures forever."
3   Let the house of Aaron say,
        "His steadfast love endures forever."
4   Let those who fear the LORD say,
        "His steadfast love endures forever."

5   Out of my distress I called on the LORD;
        the LORD answered me and set me free.
6   The LORD is on my side; I will not fear.
        What can man do to me?
7   The LORD is on my side as my helper;
        I shall look in triumph on those who hate me.

8   It is better to take refuge in the LORD
        than to trust in man.
9   It is better to take refuge in the LORD
        than to trust in princes.

10   All nations surrounded me;
        in the name of the LORD I cut them off!
11   They surrounded me, surrounded me on every side;
        in the name of the LORD I cut them off!

12   They surrounded me like bees;
            they went out like a fire among thorns;
            in the name of the LORD I cut them off!
13   I was pushed hard, so that I was falling,
            but the LORD helped me.

14   The LORD is my strength and my song;
            he has become my salvation.
15   Glad songs of salvation
            are in the tents of the righteous:
    "The right hand of the LORD does valiantly,
16   the right hand of the LORD exalts,
        the right hand of the LORD does valiantly!"

17   I shall not die, but I shall live,
            and recount the deeds of the LORD.
18   The LORD has disciplined me severely,
            but he has not given me over to death.

19   Open to me the gates of righteousness,
            that I may enter through them
            and give thanks to the LORD.
20   This is the gate of the LORD;
            the righteous shall enter through it.
21   I thank you that you have answered me
            and have become my salvation.
22   The stone that the builders rejected
            has become the cornerstone.
23   This is the LORD's doing;
            it is marvelous in our eyes.
24   This is the day that the LORD has made;
            let us rejoice and be glad in it.

25   Save us, we pray, O LORD!
        O LORD, we pray, give us success!

26   Blessed is he who comes in the name of the LORD!
        We bless you from the house of the LORD.
27   The LORD is God,
        and he has made his light to shine upon us.
    Bind the festal sacrifice with cords,
        up to the horns of the altar!

28   You are my God, and I will give thanks to you;
        you are my God; I will extol you.
29   Oh give thanks to the LORD, for he is good;
        for his steadfast love endures forever!

S

This psalm is saturated with joy. Ponder the language. Note the exclamations and exultations. Out of deep "distress" (v. 5) the Lord has met and delivered the psalmist. It seemed as if the whole world was set against him (vv. 10–13). But God himself was the psalmist's "strength" and "song" (v. 14).

Not only has God rescued the psalmist out of deadly peril, he also has worked a remarkable reversal so that such peril has been transformed into triumph; the valley has become the mountaintop. This is what the psalmist means when he declares, "Glad songs of salvation are in the tents of the righteous" (v. 15). God has worked "valiantly" (vv. 15–16). This is also what is meant in verse 22: "The stone that the builders rejected has become the cornerstone." The stone thrown onto the rubble heap as useless has now become the most important building block of all, the very cornerstone.

This is how God works. He comes near to us in all of our distress, taking what the world rejects and dignifying us with eternal significance. It is not our doing in any way. It is all of grace: "This is the LORD's doing" (v. 23). And we marvel at this grace. Most of all, we stand in awe of the supreme instance of his taking what the world rejected and turning it into an occasion for eternal significance—Jesus Christ, rejected by the religious elite, has become the cornerstone of the true and final temple, the church, of which each of us believers is a fellow stone (Matt. 21:42; Eph. 2:19–20).

Have you been rejected, today, by someone who ought to have accepted you? You are in good company. Take heart. God draws near to you in his rejected, crucified Son.

PSALM 119

ALEPH

1 Blessed are those whose way is blameless,
   who walk in the law of the LORD!
2 Blessed are those who keep his testimonies,
   who seek him with their whole heart,
3 who also do no wrong,
   but walk in his ways!
4 You have commanded your precepts
   to be kept diligently.
5 Oh that my ways may be steadfast
   in keeping your statutes!

6   Then I shall not be put to shame,
          having my eyes fixed on all your commandments.
7   I will praise you with an upright heart,
          when I learn your righteous rules.
8   I will keep your statutes;
          do not utterly forsake me!

BETH

9   How can a young man keep his way pure?
          By guarding it according to your word.
10   With my whole heart I seek you;
          let me not wander from your commandments!
11   I have stored up your word in my heart,
          that I might not sin against you.
12   Blessed are you, O LORD;
          teach me your statutes!
13   With my lips I declare
          all the rules of your mouth.
14   In the way of your testimonies I delight
          as much as in all riches.
15   I will meditate on your precepts
          and fix my eyes on your ways.
16   I will delight in your statutes;
          I will not forget your word.

GIMEL

17   Deal bountifully with your servant,
          that I may live and keep your word.
18   Open my eyes, that I may behold
          wondrous things out of your law.
19   I am a sojourner on the earth;
          hide not your commandments from me!

20   My soul is consumed with longing
        for your rules at all times.
21   You rebuke the insolent, accursed ones,
        who wander from your commandments.
22   Take away from me scorn and contempt,
        for I have kept your testimonies.
23   Even though princes sit plotting against me,
        your servant will meditate on your statutes.
24   Your testimonies are my delight;
        they are my counselors.

DALETH

25   My soul clings to the dust;
        give me life according to your word!
26   When I told of my ways, you answered me;
        teach me your statutes!
27   Make me understand the way of your precepts,
        and I will meditate on your wondrous works.
28   My soul melts away for sorrow;
        strengthen me according to your word!
29   Put false ways far from me
        and graciously teach me your law!
30   I have chosen the way of faithfulness;
        I set your rules before me.
31   I cling to your testimonies, O LORD;
        let me not be put to shame!
32   I will run in the way of your commandments
        when you enlarge my heart!

HE

33   Teach me, O LORD, the way of your statutes;
        and I will keep it to the end.

34   Give me understanding, that I may keep your law
          and observe it with my whole heart.
35   Lead me in the path of your commandments,
          for I delight in it.
36   Incline my heart to your testimonies,
          and not to selfish gain!
37   Turn my eyes from looking at worthless things;
          and give me life in your ways.
38   Confirm to your servant your promise,
          that you may be feared.
39   Turn away the reproach that I dread,
          for your rules are good.
40   Behold, I long for your precepts;
          in your righteousness give me life!

Waw

41   Let your steadfast love come to me, O Lord,
          your salvation according to your promise;
42   then shall I have an answer for him who taunts me,
          for I trust in your word.
43   And take not the word of truth utterly out of my
              mouth,
          for my hope is in your rules.
44   I will keep your law continually,
          forever and ever,
45   and I shall walk in a wide place,
          for I have sought your precepts.
46   I will also speak of your testimonies before kings
          and shall not be put to shame,
47   for I find my delight in your commandments,
          which I love.

48 I will lift up my hands toward your commandments,
which I love,
and I will meditate on your statutes.

Zayin

49 Remember your word to your servant,
in which you have made me hope.
50 This is my comfort in my affliction,
that your promise gives me life.
51 The insolent utterly deride me,
but I do not turn away from your law.
52 When I think of your rules from of old,
I take comfort, O Lord.
53 Hot indignation seizes me because of the wicked,
who forsake your law.
54 Your statutes have been my songs
in the house of my sojourning.
55 I remember your name in the night, O Lord,
and keep your law.
56 This blessing has fallen to me,
that I have kept your precepts.

Heth

57 The Lord is my portion;
I promise to keep your words.
58 I entreat your favor with all my heart;
be gracious to me according to your promise.
59 When I think on my ways,
I turn my feet to your testimonies;
60 I hasten and do not delay
to keep your commandments.

61 Though the cords of the wicked ensnare me,
   I do not forget your law.
62 At midnight I rise to praise you,
   because of your righteous rules.
63 I am a companion of all who fear you,
   of those who keep your precepts.
64 The earth, O LORD, is full of your steadfast love;
   teach me your statutes!

TETH

65 You have dealt well with your servant,
   O LORD, according to your word.
66 Teach me good judgment and knowledge,
   for I believe in your commandments.
67 Before I was afflicted I went astray,
   but now I keep your word.
68 You are good and do good;
   teach me your statutes.
69 The insolent smear me with lies,
   but with my whole heart I keep your precepts;
70 their heart is unfeeling like fat,
   but I delight in your law.
71 It is good for me that I was afflicted,
   that I might learn your statutes.
72 The law of your mouth is better to me
   than thousands of gold and silver pieces.

YODH

73 Your hands have made and fashioned me;
   give me understanding that I may learn your
      commandments.

74 Those who fear you shall see me and rejoice,
  because I have hoped in your word.
75 I know, O LORD, that your rules are righteous,
  and that in faithfulness you have afflicted me.
76 Let your steadfast love comfort me
  according to your promise to your servant.
77 Let your mercy come to me, that I may live;
  for your law is my delight.
78 Let the insolent be put to shame,
  because they have wronged me with falsehood;
  as for me, I will meditate on your precepts.
79 Let those who fear you turn to me,
  that they may know your testimonies.
80 May my heart be blameless in your statutes,
  that I may not be put to shame!

KAPH

81 My soul longs for your salvation;
  I hope in your word.
82 My eyes long for your promise;
  I ask, "When will you comfort me?"
83 For I have become like a wineskin in the smoke,
  yet I have not forgotten your statutes.
84 How long must your servant endure?
  When will you judge those who persecute me?
85 The insolent have dug pitfalls for me;
  they do not live according to your law.
86 All your commandments are sure;
  they persecute me with falsehood; help me!
87 They have almost made an end of me on earth,
  but I have not forsaken your precepts.

88 In your steadfast love give me life,
    that I may keep the testimonies of your mouth.

Lamedh

89 Forever, O Lord, your word
    is firmly fixed in the heavens.
90 Your faithfulness endures to all generations;
    you have established the earth, and it stands fast.
91 By your appointment they stand this day,
    for all things are your servants.
92 If your law had not been my delight,
    I would have perished in my affliction.
93 I will never forget your precepts,
    for by them you have given me life.
94 I am yours; save me,
    for I have sought your precepts.
95 The wicked lie in wait to destroy me,
    but I consider your testimonies.
96 I have seen a limit to all perfection,
    but your commandment is exceedingly broad.

Mem

97 Oh how I love your law!
    It is my meditation all the day.
98 Your commandment makes me wiser than my enemies,
    for it is ever with me.
99 I have more understanding than all my teachers,
    for your testimonies are my meditation.
100 I understand more than the aged,
    for I keep your precepts.
101 I hold back my feet from every evil way,
    in order to keep your word.

102 I do not turn aside from your rules,
     for you have taught me.
103 How sweet are your words to my taste,
     sweeter than honey to my mouth!
104 Through your precepts I get understanding;
     therefore I hate every false way.

Nun

105 Your word is a lamp to my feet
     and a light to my path.
106 I have sworn an oath and confirmed it,
     to keep your righteous rules.
107 I am severely afflicted;
     give me life, O Lord, according to your word!
108 Accept my freewill offerings of praise, O Lord,
     and teach me your rules.
109 I hold my life in my hand continually,
     but I do not forget your law.
110 The wicked have laid a snare for me,
     but I do not stray from your precepts.
111 Your testimonies are my heritage forever,
     for they are the joy of my heart.
112 I incline my heart to perform your statutes
     forever, to the end.

Samekh

113 I hate the double-minded,
     but I love your law.
114 You are my hiding place and my shield;
     I hope in your word.
115 Depart from me, you evildoers,
     that I may keep the commandments of my God.

116   Uphold me according to your promise, that I may live,
           and let me not be put to shame in my hope!
117   Hold me up, that I may be safe
           and have regard for your statutes continually!
118   You spurn all who go astray from your statutes,
           for their cunning is in vain.
119   All the wicked of the earth you discard like dross,
           therefore I love your testimonies.
120   My flesh trembles for fear of you,
           and I am afraid of your judgments.

AYIN

121   I have done what is just and right;
           do not leave me to my oppressors.
122   Give your servant a pledge of good;
           let not the insolent oppress me.
123   My eyes long for your salvation
           and for the fulfillment of your righteous promise.
124   Deal with your servant according to your steadfast love,
           and teach me your statutes.
125   I am your servant; give me understanding,
           that I may know your testimonies!
126   It is time for the LORD to act,
           for your law has been broken.
127   Therefore I love your commandments
           above gold, above fine gold.
128   Therefore I consider all your precepts to be right;
           I hate every false way.

PE

129   Your testimonies are wonderful;
           therefore my soul keeps them.

130 The unfolding of your words gives light;
    it imparts understanding to the simple.
131 I open my mouth and pant,
    because I long for your commandments.
132 Turn to me and be gracious to me,
    as is your way with those who love your name.
133 Keep steady my steps according to your promise,
    and let no iniquity get dominion over me.
134 Redeem me from man's oppression,
    that I may keep your precepts.
135 Make your face shine upon your servant,
    and teach me your statutes.
136 My eyes shed streams of tears,
    because people do not keep your law.

Tsadhe

137 Righteous are you, O Lord,
    and right are your rules.
138 You have appointed your testimonies in righteousness
    and in all faithfulness.
139 My zeal consumes me,
    because my foes forget your words.
140 Your promise is well tried,
    and your servant loves it.
141 I am small and despised,
    yet I do not forget your precepts.
142 Your righteousness is righteous forever,
    and your law is true.
143 Trouble and anguish have found me out,
    but your commandments are my delight.
144 Your testimonies are righteous forever;
    give me understanding that I may live.

Qoph

145 With my whole heart I cry; answer me, O Lord!
  I will keep your statutes.

146 I call to you; save me,
  that I may observe your testimonies.

147 I rise before dawn and cry for help;
  I hope in your words.

148 My eyes are awake before the watches of the night,
  that I may meditate on your promise.

149 Hear my voice according to your steadfast love;
  O Lord, according to your justice give me life.

150 They draw near who persecute me with evil purpose;
  they are far from your law.

151 But you are near, O Lord,
  and all your commandments are true.

152 Long have I known from your testimonies
  that you have founded them forever.

Resh

153 Look on my affliction and deliver me,
  for I do not forget your law.

154 Plead my cause and redeem me;
  give me life according to your promise!

155 Salvation is far from the wicked,
  for they do not seek your statutes.

156 Great is your mercy, O Lord;
  give me life according to your rules.

157 Many are my persecutors and my adversaries,
  but I do not swerve from your testimonies.

158 I look at the faithless with disgust,
  because they do not keep your commands.

159 Consider how I love your precepts!
        Give me life according to your steadfast love.
160 The sum of your word is truth,
        and every one of your righteous rules endures
            forever.

Sin and Shin

161 Princes persecute me without cause,
        but my heart stands in awe of your words.
162 I rejoice at your word
        like one who finds great spoil.
163 I hate and abhor falsehood,
        but I love your law.
164 Seven times a day I praise you
        for your righteous rules.
165 Great peace have those who love your law;
        nothing can make them stumble.
166 I hope for your salvation, O Lord,
        and I do your commandments.
167 My soul keeps your testimonies;
        I love them exceedingly.
168 I keep your precepts and testimonies,
        for all my ways are before you.

Taw

169 Let my cry come before you, O Lord;
        give me understanding according to your word!
170 Let my plea come before you;
        deliver me according to your word.
171 My lips will pour forth praise,
        for you teach me your statutes.

172   My tongue will sing of your word,
            for all your commandments are right.

173   Let your hand be ready to help me,
            for I have chosen your precepts.

174   I long for your salvation, O Lord,
            and your law is my delight.

175   Let my soul live and praise you,
            and let your rules help me.

176   I have gone astray like a lost sheep; seek your servant,
            for I do not forget your commandments.

᷉

This psalm celebrates the gift of God's law, his Torah, his covenant instruction for his people. Having redeemed his people and brought us through grace into relationship with him, God now lovingly instructs us in the way to enjoy fullness of life.

Although no one keeps God's law perfectly, and in fact we abuse it through legalism and works righteousness, the psalmist reminds us throughout this lengthy psalm of the delight that the law should be for the child of God. The psalm uses different words to describe the law, such as *statutes*, *rules*, *commandment*, *law*, *word*, and other similar terms; this reflects the richness of the Torah and the flourishing life into which it brings us.

We tend to view God's law as inhibiting human flourishing. C. S. Lewis helps us in his words to a friend in a 1933 letter: "God not only understands but shares the desire which is at the root of all my evil—the desire for complete and ecstatic happiness. He made me for no other purpose than to enjoy it. But He knows, and I do not, how such happiness can be really and permanently attained." This is why God has given us his law—to guide us into full happiness as we trust and follow him. Lewis goes on to say:

I think we may be quite rid of the old haunting suspicion (it raises its head in every temptation) that there is something else than God—some other country into which He forbids us to trespass—some kind of delight which He "doesn't appreciate" or just chooses to forbid, but which would be real delight if only we were allowed to get it. The thing just isn't there. Whatever we desire is either what God is trying to give us as quickly as He can, or else a false picture of what He is trying to give us—a false picture which would not attract us for a moment if we saw the real thing.

PSALM 120

A Song of Ascents.

1   In my distress I called to the LORD,
     and he answered me.
2   Deliver me, O LORD,
     from lying lips,
     from a deceitful tongue.

3   What shall be given to you,
     and what more shall be done to you,
     you deceitful tongue?
4   A warrior's sharp arrows,
     with glowing coals of the broom tree!

<blockquote>

5   Woe to me, that I sojourn in Meshech,
        that I dwell among the tents of Kedar!

6   Too long have I had my dwelling
        among those who hate peace.

7   I am for peace,
        but when I speak, they are for war!

</blockquote>

∽

"Woe to me, that I sojourn in Meshech, that I dwell among the tents of Kedar!" (v. 5). These locations are not household names for us, so it is easy to read over them without feeling the full weight of what the psalmist is lamenting. Meschech and Kedar are two places far from one another and far from Israel: they are two places to which God's people were dispersed throughout the centuries, especially in times of exile. The point is that these two places represent the world without God, as the hostile enemies of God's people surround the redeemed.

And so the psalmist is in "distress" (v. 1), living among "lying lips" and a "deceitful tongue" (v. 2), those who hate peace (v. 7). This is more than homesickness or the anxiety of traveling in a foreign land. The psalmist is drowning in the injustice and godlessness of a hostile world. The New Testament picks up this theme and uses these categories to explain the Christian's place in the world today. We are "sojourners and exiles" (1 Pet. 2:11); this world as it now stands is not our home, and we "desire a better country" (Heb. 11:16). Like our Savior, who left his true home in heaven to come to earth and sojourn among us, we sojourn among a foreign land that will one day be returned fully and openly to its rightful ruler. Until then, we trust in the Lord and, led by the psalmist, pray for deliverance.

PSALM 121

A Song of Ascents.

1   I lift up my eyes to the hills.
     From where does my help come?
2   My help comes from the LORD,
     who made heaven and earth.

3   He will not let your foot be moved;
     he who keeps you will not slumber.
4   Behold, he who keeps Israel
     will neither slumber nor sleep.

5   The LORD is your keeper;
     the LORD is your shade on your right hand.
6   The sun shall not strike you by day,
     nor the moon by night.

7   The LORD will keep you from all evil;
     he will keep your life.
8   The LORD will keep
     your going out and your coming in
     from this time forth and forevermore.

5

It is easy to go through life feeling vulnerable. Vulnerable to financial collapse, to physical illness, to relational rejection, to emotional meltdown. We naturally and easily feel small, weak, and defenseless.

What does it mean to be part of the people of God? Among a hundred other things, it means that the God who created the universe never ceases to watch over and actively protect you. It means he never takes a nap on you, never is distracted, never turns away. "He who keeps you will not slumber" (v. 3).

But how can we really know? Where is the proof?

The proof is there on a hill called Calvary. There Jesus died. Jesus Christ became truly vulnerable, truly defenseless, exposed not simply to adverse circumstances but to the forces of hell, receiving the judgment we deserved. He was overcome so that we could walk through life with the certain knowledge that we are God's children and that he is ever watching over us.

PSALM 122

A Song of Ascents. Of David.

1 I was glad when they said to me,
    "Let us go to the house of the LORD!"
2 Our feet have been standing
    within your gates, O Jerusalem!

3 Jerusalem—built as a city
    that is bound firmly together,
4 to which the tribes go up,
    the tribes of the LORD,
as was decreed for Israel,
    to give thanks to the name of the LORD.
5 There thrones for judgment were set,
    the thrones of the house of David.

6 Pray for the peace of Jerusalem!
    "May they be secure who love you!
7 Peace be within your walls
    and security within your towers!"
8 For my brothers and companions' sake
    I will say, "Peace be within you!"
9 For the sake of the house of the LORD our God,
    I will seek your good.

W hy is the psalmist so exuberant about arriving in the house of the Lord, the temple (v. 1)? Because *this is the point of all of human history*.

The deepest meaning of this psalm is not just that we should enjoy going to church. Gathered worship is certainly a key theme of this psalm, but what *is* gathered worship? It is fellowship with the Triune God, through the gospel. It is the restoring of that for which we were made. It is to become human again. It is to live.

But isn't this text simply about temple worship in Jerusalem? Yes—but what is the point of the temple in the midst of Jerusalem, according to the whole Bible? The temple is the recovery of Eden, in a limited locale, for a limited time. The same words that described what Adam was to do in Eden ("work it" and "keep it"; Gen. 2:15) are used to describe the priest's tasks in the temple throughout the Old Testament.

When the temple was destroyed 400 years before Christ, Ezekiel envisioned a more glorious temple to be built (Ezekiel 40–48). When Jesus came, he called himself the temple (John 2:19–22), and when sinners are united to him, they become part of that spiritual temple as well (Eph. 2:19–22). In Jesus, we become our true selves. We are given back our humanity. We taste Eden. And in the new earth, we will enjoy unhindered fellowship with God once more, not in a limited locale but unlimited, not for a limited time but for eternity (Rev. 21:22).

In Christ, it can truly and finally be said of us: "Peace be within your walls" (Ps. 122:7).

PSALM 123

A Song of Ascents.

1   To you I lift up my eyes,
      O you who are enthroned in the heavens!
2   Behold, as the eyes of servants
      look to the hand of their master,
  as the eyes of a maidservant
      to the hand of her mistress,
  so our eyes look to the Lord our God,
      till he has mercy upon us.

3   Have mercy upon us, O Lord, have mercy upon us,
      for we have had more than enough of contempt.
4   Our soul has had more than enough
      of the scorn of those who are at ease,
      of the contempt of the proud.

∽

The psalmist is in solidarity with those who feel scorned by the comfortable, mocked by the arrogant, ridiculed by those whose circumstances are smooth.

Consider how the psalmist handles the sting of this contempt and scorn. He does not engage his enemies. Nor does he trot out reasons this scorn is undeserved. Rather, he prays, "Have mercy upon us, O Lord, have mercy upon us" (v. 3). He takes this pain vertical. He cries out for mercy from God. And notice the way the psalmist explains exactly what he means by this request for mercy—he gives us a picture of the kind of plea he has in mind: "As the eyes of servants look to the hand of their master . . . so our eyes look to the LORD our God, till he has mercy upon us" (v. 2). The psalmist sees the Lord graciously overseeing all that washes into his life. The Lord is not distant, removed, aloof. The psalmist appeals to the close oversight of the Lord, the covenant compassion of "the LORD" (God's covenant name, "Yahweh").

Do you feel the sting of rejection? Are you ridiculed? Take heart. The mercy of the Lord is yours for the taking. Draw near to him, and he will draw near to you. In the embrace of God is a comfort and consolation no human scorning can threaten.

PSALM 124

A Song of Ascents. Of David.

1   If it had not been the LORD who was on our side—
        let Israel now say—
2   if it had not been the LORD who was on our side
        when people rose up against us,
3   then they would have swallowed us up alive,
        when their anger was kindled against us;
4   then the flood would have swept us away,
        the torrent would have gone over us;
5   then over us would have gone
        the raging waters.

6   Blessed be the LORD,
        who has not given us
        as prey to their teeth!
7   We have escaped like a bird
        from the snare of the fowlers;
    the snare is broken,
        and we have escaped!

8   Our help is in the name of the LORD,
        who made heaven and earth.

∽

As we move through this fallen world, conflict inevitably arises. Conflict with parents. Conflict with siblings. Conflict with children. With coworkers. With neighbors. With church members. Sparks, dysfunction, resentment, hurt. This is normal life in this fallen world.

We experience conflict at the invisible level, too, and it is no less real—conflict with the spiritual forces of hell. Temptation, accusation, dark thoughts of God—these are often the manifestation of conflict with the devil's friends.

We even feel conflict within ourselves. We say something and immediately regret it. We lose our temper and wonder what got into us. We capitulate to a temptation and suffer remorse. We love a family member and yet at the very same time battle thoughts of bitterness toward him or her.

One remedy the Bible gives us (among many) is that the Lord is on our side (vv. 1–2). What does this mean? Does it mean we are always in the right in any given conflict? Certainly not. But it does mean he is always with us. His deepest impulse is to help us, not to scold us. His heart reaches out to us. He is a never-failing friend. He is our wise counselor who never kicks us out of his office. The Father sent his own Son so that amid all our ups and downs in life, we are guaranteed a steady companion who loves us and is for us. He is on our side. "Our help is in the name of the LORD" (v. 8).

PSALM 125

A Song of Ascents.

1 Those who trust in the LORD are like Mount Zion,
    which cannot be moved, but abides forever.
2 As the mountains surround Jerusalem,
    so the LORD surrounds his people,
    from this time forth and forevermore.
3 For the scepter of wickedness shall not rest
    on the land allotted to the righteous,
    lest the righteous stretch out
    their hands to do wrong.
4 Do good, O LORD, to those who are good,
    and to those who are upright in their hearts!
5 But those who turn aside to their crooked ways
    the LORD will lead away with evildoers!
    Peace be upon Israel!

5

As we journey through this fallen world we are frequently tempted to ask of our walk with God, is it worth it? Is it worth the rejection? The ridicule? The contempt? The intellectual condescension? The resistance to our feeble efforts in evangelism? The emotional drain in service to our neighbors and at our churches? Is it all worth it?

The "scepter of wickedness" often holds sway—that is, godlessness often reigns in places of power (v. 3). But it will not be so forever: "The scepter of wickedness shall not rest on the land allotted to the righteous" (v. 3). God will fulfill his covenant promises to his people to place them securely in the land. In the context of Psalm 125, this refers immediately to Israel and the Promised Land. For believers today this promise will ultimately be fulfilled when God's people from every nation and tribe and tongue reign in the new earth.

And how does one survive in the meantime, amid wickedness? "Those who trust in the LORD are like Mount Zion, which cannot be moved" (v. 1). Whatever assault you feel yourself to be under today as you walk with Christ, the answer is not to respond to insults with insults, nor to hope ultimately in political or economic leadership, but to rely on the Lord. To trust him. Yield to him. Think about him. Draw strength from him. You can do so right now, by reading and praying Psalm 125.

PSALM 126

A Song of Ascents.

1   When the L ORD restored the fortunes of Zion,
        we were like those who dream.
2   Then our mouth was filled with laughter,
        and our tongue with shouts of joy;
    then they said among the nations,
        "The L ORD has done great things for them."
3   The L ORD has done great things for us;
        we are glad.

4   Restore our fortunes, O L ORD,
        like streams in the Negeb!
5   Those who sow in tears
        shall reap with shouts of joy!
6   He who goes out weeping,
        bearing the seed for sowing,
    shall come home with shouts of joy,
        bringing his sheaves with him.

∽

What comes into most people's minds when they hear the word *Christianity*? Perhaps they associate it with rules or moralism or going to church or narrow-mindedness. What comes into most people's minds when they hear the word *party*? Perhaps celebration, good times, fun, laughter, shouting.

Consider this psalm. Consider what Christianity actually is. It is the turning from every hollow pleasure of this world to real joy. As C. S. Lewis famously put it in his essay "The Weight of Glory," "We are half-hearted creatures, fooling about with drink and sex and ambition when infinite joy is offered us, like an ignorant child who wants to go on making mud pies in a slum because he cannot imagine what is meant by the offer of a holiday at the sea." This is life with God. Solid joy, not empty excitement. The kind of deep happiness that makes us truly human, which we long for and stumble around seeking to find but often miss.

This does not mean life with God is pain free. This very psalm is a community lament, reflecting on a past season of divine mercy (vv. 1–3) with a plea for renewed mercy (v. 4). But the psalmist sees through the veil of sorrows. He sees that on the other side of weeping is joy. He sees that the night of sorrow will one day turn to the morning of gladness. This is the rhythm of Christianity. Christ himself went through this—the weeping of the cross to the joy of the resurrection.

In the Lord's restorative work in Christ is true "laughter" and "shouts of joy" (vv. 2, 5, 6). Life in Christ is a celebration—not shallow merriment but a deep, pain-acknowledging celebration. For the best is yet to come.

PSALM 127

A Song of Ascents. Of Solomon.

1   Unless the LORD builds the house,
    those who build it labor in vain.
  Unless the LORD watches over the city,
    the watchman stays awake in vain.
2   It is in vain that you rise up early
    and go late to rest,
  eating the bread of anxious toil;
    for he gives to his beloved sleep.

3   Behold, children are a heritage from the LORD,
    the fruit of the womb a reward.
4   Like arrows in the hand of a warrior
    are the children of one's youth.
5   Blessed is the man
    who fills his quiver with them!
  He shall not be put to shame
    when he speaks with his enemies in the gate.

෴

This psalm lifts our vision to see the grand reality behind every human endeavor and accomplishment. Over and above all that happens on the earth is the sovereign rule of heaven. God's own people are especially dependent on the Lord's blessing in all they attempt.

But what does this really mean? It means that great churches can be built, crowds gathered, discipleship attempted, books written, evangelism conducted, significance sought, but if these things lack God's own hand of favor, they will prove themselves to be only transient or ephemeral. Solid and lasting significance comes not through impressive human ingenuity and cleverness but from the favor of God mediated through prayerful human weakness.

This is deeply encouraging for our little, everyday Christian lives. As we go through life, we are constantly tempted to latch on to worldly strategies and ambitions in our God-given quest for eternal significance. But God's recipe for significance is to get low, not high; to commit our plans to the Lord in prayer, not to move ahead without a sense of his blessing and guidance.

Build into your life self-conscious, moment-by-moment mindfulness of the Lord. Appeal to him constantly. Invite him into your thoughts and dreams and plans. He will give you a life of eternal significance beyond what you could comprehend.

PSALM 128

A Song of Ascents.

1   Blessed is everyone who fears the LORD,
        who walks in his ways!
2   You shall eat the fruit of the labor of your hands;
        you shall be blessed, and it shall be well with you.

3   Your wife will be like a fruitful vine
        within your house;
    your children will be like olive shoots
        around your table.
4   Behold, thus shall the man be blessed
        who fears the LORD.

5   The LORD bless you from Zion!
        May you see the prosperity of Jerusalem
        all the days of your life!
6   May you see your children's children!
        Peace be upon Israel!

§

"Blessed is everyone who fears the LORD!" (v. 1).
What does it mean to be "blessed"? To be blessed is to move through life with a settled depth of happiness that comes from walking with God and enjoying his fatherly favor. To be blessed means to live the human life the way it was meant to be lived. It is to enjoy a taste of Eden restored. Note the everyday

way this psalm unfolds divine blessing—it is a matter of eating and drinking, of enjoying one's spouse and children (vv. 3–4). To be blessed is to become *ourselves*, enjoying God in alignment with the way he created us to be as creatures on this globe.

What does it mean to "fear the LORD"? To fear the Lord means to live as if God exists and is who he says he is. It is to walk through life bowing to his kingship and remembering his gracious redemption. To fear the Lord means to yield to his will and seek to walk in his ways as our gracious deliverer.

And this blessing is for "everyone" who fears the Lord (v. 1). Anyone can get in on this. It is not for the elite, for those born into good families. It is for all those who are willing simply to humble themselves in the fear of the Lord—which for us today means humbling ourselves into the gospel, taking Christ's accomplishment as our own and allowing him to take our iniquities as his own.

PSALM 129

A Song of Ascents.

1   " Greatly have they afflicted me from my youth"—
        let Israel now say—
2   "Greatly have they afflicted me from my youth,
        yet they have not prevailed against me.
3   The plowers plowed upon my back;
        they made long their furrows."

4   The LORD is righteous;
         he has cut the cords of the wicked.
5   May all who hate Zion
         be put to shame and turned backward!
6   Let them be like the grass on the housetops,
         which withers before it grows up,
7   with which the reaper does not fill his hand
         nor the binder of sheaves his arms,
8   nor do those who pass by say,
         "The blessing of the LORD be upon you!
         We bless you in the name of the LORD!"

∽

Some of us have grown up amid affliction and torment even from a young age. We have never known a time when we did not live in tension and anxiety. Perhaps we were not cared for by our parents. Maybe other family members acted in cruel ways toward us. Perhaps we were born with an embarrassing feature or a frustrating disability or something else that others poked fun at.

The psalmist is speaking specifically of corporate affliction of Israel and hostility toward the people of God at that time, but God has given this psalm to all of his people, at all times. Many of us know just what it means to pray, "Greatly have they afflicted me from my youth" (vv. 1, 2).

Here is the promise of Scripture: Those who afflict you will one day wither and be carried away to eternal insignificance in the same way that dead grass flies away on a soft breeze (vv. 4–7). But if you are in Christ—if you are one of those on whom the blessing of the Lord rests (v. 8)—then, like your Savior before you, your pains will one day be transformed into glory, turned inside out into marks of beauty.

PSALM 130

A Song of Ascents.

1   Out of the depths I cry to you, O Lord!
2   O Lord, hear my voice!
     Let your ears be attentive
       to the voice of my pleas for mercy!

3   If you, O Lord, should mark iniquities,
       O Lord, who could stand?
4   But with you there is forgiveness,
       that you may be feared.

5   I wait for the Lord, my soul waits,
       and in his word I hope;
6   my soul waits for the Lord
       more than watchmen for the morning,
       more than watchmen for the morning.

7   O Israel, hope in the Lord!
       For with the Lord there is steadfast love,
       and with him is plentiful redemption.
8   And he will redeem Israel
       from all his iniquities.

John Owen was a renowned seventeenth-century English theologian, and this psalm played a special role in his life. In *John Owen on the Christian Life*, Sinclair Ferguson recounts an episode in which a younger minister named Richard Davis had come to Owen for spiritual counsel. In talking with Davis, Owen reflected on his own journey:

> I myself preached Christ some years, when I had but very little, if any, experimental acquaintance with access to God through Christ; until the Lord was pleased to visit me with sore affliction, whereby I was brought to the mouth of the grave, and under which my soul was oppressed with horror and darkness; but God graciously relieved my spirit through a powerful application of Psalm 130:4, "But there is forgiveness with thee that thou mayest be feared," from whence I received special instruction, peace, and comfort, in drawing near to God through the Mediator, and preached thereupon immediately after my recovery.

Is the gospel mere theory to you? Do you feel loved by the heart of heaven? Are you disgusted with your sins? Pray Psalm 130. Massage its truths down into your soul. With the Lord there is forgiveness (v. 4). Unfailing love (v. 7). "Plentiful redemption" (v. 7). God proved this in Jesus and at the cross. If you are a believer, God's love has brought you to Jesus Christ. You are safe. Your sins can darken your *awareness* of God's love, but they cannot darken the *reality* of that love. God does not redeem his people from *some* of their iniquities; rather, "he will redeem Israel from *all* his iniquities" (v. 8).

PSALM 131

A Song of Ascents. Of David.

1   O LORD, my heart is not lifted up;
      my eyes are not raised too high;
   I do not occupy myself with things
      too great and too marvelous for me.
2   But I have calmed and quieted my soul,
      like a weaned child with its mother;
      like a weaned child is my soul within me.

3   O Israel, hope in the LORD
      from this time forth and forevermore.

᷎

Blessed smallness! The safety of humility!
    The psalmist here reflects honestly on his refusal to give in to pride or anxiety. He is not dreaming about how to become famous or powerful or renowned. His attitude is marked instead by humble sanity: "My heart is not lifted up; my eyes are not raised too high; I do not occupy myself with things too great and too marvelous for me" (v. 1). Instead, he has "calmed and quieted [his] soul," like a small child secure and docile and silent in the care of his mother (v. 2).

This is true security. The Bible is replete with assurances that it is those who embrace this healthy quietness of soul to whom God draws near. After all, what does such a posture communicate? It declares to the Lord that one is trusting in him, not in one's own plans or cleverness or ambitions. As the psalm concludes, to bear such an attitude is to "hope in the Lord" (v. 3).

What in your life is pulling you away from saying, "I have calmed and quieted my soul" (v. 2)? Repent. Be restored. Return to the Lord. Hope in him once more.

PSALM 132

A Song of Ascents.

1   Remember, O Lord, in David's favor,
     all the hardships he endured,
2   how he swore to the Lord
     and vowed to the Mighty One of Jacob,
3   "I will not enter my house
     or get into my bed,
4   I will not give sleep to my eyes
     or slumber to my eyelids,
5   until I find a place for the Lord,
     a dwelling place for the Mighty One of Jacob."

6   Behold, we heard of it in Ephrathah;
     we found it in the fields of Jaar.
7   "Let us go to his dwelling place;
     let us worship at his footstool!"

8   Arise, O Lord, and go to your resting place,
     you and the ark of your might.

9   Let your priests be clothed with righteousness,
         and let your saints shout for joy.
10   For the sake of your servant David,
         do not turn away the face of your anointed one.

11   The LORD swore to David a sure oath
         from which he will not turn back:
    "One of the sons of your body
         I will set on your throne.
12   If your sons keep my covenant
         and my testimonies that I shall teach them,
    their sons also forever
         shall sit on your throne."

13   For the LORD has chosen Zion;
         he has desired it for his dwelling place:
14   "This is my resting place forever;
         here I will dwell, for I have desired it.
15   I will abundantly bless her provisions;
         I will satisfy her poor with bread.
16   Her priests I will clothe with salvation,
         and her saints will shout for joy.
17   There I will make a horn to sprout for David;
         I have prepared a lamp for my anointed.
18   His enemies I will clothe with shame,
         but on him his crown will shine."

∽

This psalm is a plea for God to fulfill his ancient covenant promises to his people, particularly the twin promises forming the center of the covenant: promises of God's presence and of God's king. God's presence is captured in the temple language permeating this psalm, and his chosen king is reflected in the words concerning David and his sons.

Perhaps such promises seem irrelevant to your life. But consider what they might mean for you.

God was present in Eden yet withdrew his presence when mankind fell. Ever since then he has been working to restore his presence—an insurmountable task if left to us sinners. But God himself provided a tabernacle, and then a temple, and then his own Son. In each case he was working toward the restoration and expansion of Eden, bringing the light of his presence into this sad and dark world. And now we—you and I—are the very temple of God, in which he dwells. God's presence means you have God. He is with you. He is, by virtue of your union with Christ and the indwelling Spirit, *in* you. You are never alone. You have an ever-present Friend.

And because God took it upon himself to fulfill the promise of a Davidic king, this abiding presence will never leave us. Throughout the Old Testament, God called on David and his heirs to follow and obey God (e.g., v. 12). But they were infected with the same problem the rest of humanity is plagued by: sin. Yet God sent a king who was not only a son of David but also God's own Son. He sent Jesus to love you, to lead you. Who rules over your life? Who will determine the final state of the world? Who gets the last say? Jesus Christ—not your boss, not your parents, not your political leadership. Trust him, and be at peace.

PSALM 133

A Song of Ascents. Of David.

1   Behold, how good and pleasant it is
        when brothers dwell in unity!
2   It is like the precious oil on the head,
        running down on the beard,
    on the beard of Aaron,
        running down on the collar of his robes!
3   It is like the dew of Hermon,
        which falls on the mountains of Zion!
    For there the LORD has commanded the blessing,
        life forevermore.

§

Few human joys run deeper than real unity. To know and to be known by others, to enjoy a shared heart in some endeavor, to sense the deep resonance of oneness that comes from loving and being loved—this is a foretaste of the new heavens and the new earth, when all divisiveness, strife, and harsh disagreement will melt away. To be in meaningful unity with others is in fact a reflection of the Triune God himself, who has dwelled eternally in perfect unity, Father, Son, and Spirit. Truly, "How good and pleasant it is when brothers dwell in unity!" (v. 1).

How do we find such unity? The whole Bible gives us the answer, hinted at in this psalm: unity comes where "the LORD has commanded the blessing" (v. 3). Unity comes from the Lord—that is, not from pursuing unity itself but from pursuing God. In his book *The Pursuit of God*, A. W. Tozer explains:

> Has it ever occurred to you that one hundred pianos all tuned to the same fork are automatically tuned to each other? They are of one accord by being tuned, not to each other, but to another standard to which each one must individually bow. So one hundred worshipers met together, each one looking away to Christ, are in heart nearer to each other than they could possibly be were they to become "unity" conscious and turn their eyes away from God to strive for closer fellowship.

Walk with God. Seek him. As you do, you will find relational avenues opening up that will take you into a fellowship deeper than what could otherwise be possible.

PSALM 134

A Song of Ascents.

1   Come, bless the LORD, all you servants of the LORD,
      who stand by night in the house of the LORD!
2   Lift up your hands to the holy place
      and bless the LORD!

3   May the LORD bless you from Zion,
      he who made heaven and earth!

"Bless the LORD" (v. 1).

This is such a simple instruction. But consider the life-giving wisdom that is found in carrying out this simple directive.

What is actually happening in the mind of a believer as he seeks to "bless the LORD"? To do so is to find the fundamental posture and joy that every believer should possess. To bless the Lord is to lift one's eyes to heaven, to look to God, to celebrate who he is, to count on him for all things, to acknowledge life as a gift from him. It is to thank him. At a base level, it is to *notice* him. To see him, and to rejoice in him while doing so. "Bless the LORD."

Supremely, we bless the Lord as we look up to him because of the way he has blessed us by looking down at us (v. 3). We bless because he blessed us; in sending Jesus to deliver us and the Spirit to empower us, he proved that his deepest heart is to bless us, help us, strengthen us, restore us, secure us, and finally to bring us to himself once again.

PSALM 135

1   Praise the LORD!
     Praise the name of the LORD,
          give praise, O servants of the LORD,
2   who stand in the house of the LORD,
          in the courts of the house of our God!

3   Praise the LORD, for the LORD is good;
         sing to his name, for it is pleasant!
4   For the LORD has chosen Jacob for himself,
         Israel as his own possession.

5   For I know that the LORD is great,
         and that our Lord is above all gods.
6   Whatever the LORD pleases, he does,
         in heaven and on earth,
         in the seas and all deeps.
7   He it is who makes the clouds rise at the end of the
               earth,
         who makes lightnings for the rain
         and brings forth the wind from his storehouses.

8   He it was who struck down the firstborn of Egypt,
         both of man and of beast;
9   who in your midst, O Egypt,
         sent signs and wonders
         against Pharaoh and all his servants;
10   who struck down many nations
         and killed mighty kings,
11   Sihon, king of the Amorites,
         and Og, king of Bashan,
         and all the kingdoms of Canaan,
12   and gave their land as a heritage,
         a heritage to his people Israel.

13   Your name, O LORD, endures forever,
         your renown, O LORD, throughout all ages.
14   For the LORD will vindicate his people
         and have compassion on his servants.

15	The idols of the nations are silver and gold,
	the work of human hands.
16	They have mouths, but do not speak;
	they have eyes, but do not see;
17	they have ears, but do not hear,
	nor is there any breath in their mouths.
18	Those who make them become like them,
	so do all who trust in them.

19	O house of Israel, bless the LORD!
	O house of Aaron, bless the LORD!
20	O house of Levi, bless the LORD!
	You who fear the LORD, bless the LORD!
21	Blessed be the LORD from Zion,
	he who dwells in Jerusalem!
	Praise the LORD!

∽

Ringing through the Psalms is the call to praise the Lord. And what does it mean to praise the Lord? Many angles could be taken in answering this question, but notice what this particular psalm sets up as the opposite of praising the Lord: idolatry.

What is idolatry? Idolatry is the folly of expecting a gift to be a giver. The good things of this life are not meant to generate joy in and of themselves. Rather, they are to be gratefully received as they bring our eyes up to our greatest treasure, the one who provides all things and seeks our deepest joy, the Triune God. Idolatry always disappoints. God never does.

The psalmist is calling God's people to praise him rather than committing idolatry. And why? Because "those who make them become like them" (v. 18). Idolatry dehumanizes us. Imperceptibly, perhaps, over time those who trust in anything other than God begin to take on the characteristics of that less-than-God thing into which their deepest hopes are being funneled. If we trust most deeply in money, in reputation, in our own morality, in ease and comfort, in a political party, or in anything else other than God, we begin over time to take on the worst characteristics of such things. We were made to image God in all his fullness, but instead we begin to image forth created things in all their emptiness.

Those who yield to and trust in Jesus Christ, God's perfect image, begin to take on his characteristics, like gentleness, love, and justice. We become truly human.

PSALM 136

1 Give thanks to the LORD, for he is good,
  for his steadfast love endures forever.
2 Give thanks to the God of gods,
  for his steadfast love endures forever.
3 Give thanks to the Lord of lords,
  for his steadfast love endures forever;

4 to him who alone does great wonders,
  for his steadfast love endures forever;
5 to him who by understanding made the heavens,
  for his steadfast love endures forever;
6 to him who spread out the earth above the waters,
  for his steadfast love endures forever;

7   to him who made the great lights,
    for his steadfast love endures forever;
8   the sun to rule over the day,
    for his steadfast love endures forever;
9   the moon and stars to rule over the night,
    for his steadfast love endures forever;

10 to him who struck down the firstborn of Egypt,
    for his steadfast love endures forever;
11 and brought Israel out from among them,
    for his steadfast love endures forever;
12 with a strong hand and an outstretched arm,
    for his steadfast love endures forever;
13 to him who divided the Red Sea in two,
    for his steadfast love endures forever;
14 and made Israel pass through the midst of it,
    for his steadfast love endures forever;
15 but overthrew Pharaoh and his host in the Red Sea,
    for his steadfast love endures forever;
16 to him who led his people through the wilderness,
    for his steadfast love endures forever;

17 to him who struck down great kings,
    for his steadfast love endures forever;
18 and killed mighty kings,
    for his steadfast love endures forever;
19 Sihon, king of the Amorites,
    for his steadfast love endures forever;
20 and Og, king of Bashan,
    for his steadfast love endures forever;
21 and gave their land as a heritage,
    for his steadfast love endures forever;

22   a heritage to Israel his servant,
        for his steadfast love endures forever.

23   It is he who remembered us in our low estate,
        for his steadfast love endures forever;
24   and rescued us from our foes,
        for his steadfast love endures forever;
25   he who gives food to all flesh,
        for his steadfast love endures forever.

26   Give thanks to the God of heaven,
        for his steadfast love endures forever.

∽

The resounding theme of this psalm is not hard to see: "His steadfast love endures forever." All 26 verses conclude this way. Why does this psalm display such apparent redundancy?

Because everything in us is hardwired to believe that his love could come to an end at any time. That it is not steadfast but faltering. That he is like us.

Throughout the psalm, therefore, we are reminded of God's repeated acts of deliverance for his people down through history. And each time we are told why the Lord rescued his people: "*for his steadfast love endures forever.*" He does not deliver because his people deserve it. He does not save us because we impress him. He delivers because this is who he is toward wayward sinners. Do you feel like you have "used up" God's reserve of love for you? Do you not realize that the more you need of his love, the more his heart gives it? "His steadfast love endures forever." There is no ceiling to it. No end of the line. He gives himself, all of himself, to you, all of you. The eighteenth-century theologian Jonathan Edwards preached:

> His essence being love, he is as it were an infinite ocean of love without shores and bottom, yea, and without a surface. Those that God is pleased to make the objects of his love, let them be who they will, or what they will—never so mean, never so great sinners—they are the objects of a love that is infinitely full and sufficient.

"His love endures forever." Beyond our failures. Beyond our resentments. Beyond our disgust with ourselves. Beyond the love of any friend. Jesus Christ came for us and died for us; he secured the permanence and demonstrated the depths of God's heart of love for sinners. Jesus proved it: "His steadfast love endures forever."

PSALM 137

1   By the waters of Babylon,
        there we sat down and wept,
        when we remembered Zion.
2   On the willows there
        we hung up our lyres.
3   For there our captors
        required of us songs,
    and our tormentors, mirth, saying,
      "Sing us one of the songs of Zion!"

4   How shall we sing the LORD's song
       in a foreign land?
5   If I forget you, O Jerusalem,
       let my right hand forget its skill!
6   Let my tongue stick to the roof of my mouth,
       if I do not remember you,
    if I do not set Jerusalem
       above my highest joy!

7   Remember, O LORD, against the Edomites
       the day of Jerusalem,
    how they said, "Lay it bare, lay it bare,
       down to its foundations!"
8   O daughter of Babylon, doomed to be destroyed,
       blessed shall he be who repays you
       with what you have done to us!
9   Blessed shall he be who takes your little ones
       and dashes them against the rock!

℘

As they sang the words of this psalm, the ancient people of God lamented their past sufferings at the hand of Babylon. They celebrated their loyalty to Jerusalem, the city that represented the promises of God to give his people their own land and to dwell among them.

One of the remarkable virtues of the Bible is its earthy realism. Consider that the Bible talks about physical *tears*: "We sat down and wept" (v. 1). The Bible does not summon you to a super-spiritual existence, asking you to wade stoically through life above the reach of pain and weeping. The Bible rather gives us categories and language by which to speak and pray our tears to God.

How does this psalm do that? Rather shockingly, by praying for even the destruction of the babies of Israel's enemies (v. 9)! By demanding that the pain these enemies sought for other nations would befall them instead. This does not sound like the teaching of a gentle Jesus, we might say. But this is actually deeply consoling. We are reminded that God does not look the other way when his people are afflicted. He defends them. Justice will prevail. Rights will be wronged. In a 1959 letter C. S. Lewis wrote of the modern notion of a mild and gentle Jesus domesticated into softness and spinelessness:

> "Gentle Jesus" my elbow! The most striking thing about Our Lord is the union of great ferocity with extreme tenderness. . . . So go on! You are on the right track now: getting to the real Man behind all the plaster dolls that have been substituted for Him. This is the appearance in Human form of the God who made the Tiger and the Lamb, the avalanche and the rose. He'll frighten and puzzle you: but the real Christ can be loved and admired as the doll can't.

The Bible is a real book about a real God who sent a real Son to rescue real sinners from real evil. It is not a fairy book. The Bible is a book you can trust, for it reveals to us a God we can trust.

PSALM 138

Of David.

1   I give you thanks, O LORD, with my whole heart;
      before the gods I sing your praise;
2   I bow down toward your holy temple
      and give thanks to your name for your steadfast love
        and your faithfulness,
      for you have exalted above all things
      your name and your word.
3   On the day I called, you answered me;
      my strength of soul you increased.

4   All the kings of the earth shall give you thanks, O LORD,
      for they have heard the words of your mouth,
5   and they shall sing of the ways of the LORD,
      for great is the glory of the LORD.
6   For though the LORD is high, he regards the lowly,
      but the haughty he knows from afar.

7   Though I walk in the midst of trouble,
      you preserve my life;
    you stretch out your hand against the wrath of my
        enemies,
      and your right hand delivers me.
8   The LORD will fulfill his purpose for me;
      your steadfast love, O LORD, endures forever.
    Do not forsake the work of your hands.

5

"Great is the glory of the LORD. For though the LORD is high, he regards the lowly, but the haughty he knows from afar" (vv. 5–6).

Where is God's glory seen? In his greatness, to be sure: his omnipotence, his infinitude, his eternality. Even more, however, the glory of God is seen in his goodness in light of that greatness. In all his immensity, he delights to shower his wayward creatures with grace upon grace. God is not glorious merely because he is great (although he is!) but because in that great immensity he is also merciful when he has every reason to turn the shoulder and vaporize us.

In a letter to a woman whose son had died, Jonathan Edwards wrote: "Especially are the beams of Christ's glory infinitely softened and sweetened by his love to men, the love that passeth knowledge. The glory of his person consists, preeminently, in that infinite goodness and grace, of which he made so wonderful a manifestation in his love to us." The great French reformer John Calvin agreed: "There is no honoring of God unless his mercy be acknowledged, upon which alone it is founded and established."

Do you want to glorify God? Here is one major way to do it: Let him love you. Receive his grace, drink it down, without adding one drop of your own goodness to it. Your very purpose in life and eternity is to be "to the praise of his glorious grace" (Eph. 1:6).

PSALM 139

To the choirmaster. A Psalm of David.

1   O Lᴏʀᴅ, you have searched me and known me!
2   You know when I sit down and when I rise up;
       you discern my thoughts from afar.
3   You search out my path and my lying down
       and are acquainted with all my ways.
4   Even before a word is on my tongue,
       behold, O Lᴏʀᴅ, you know it altogether.
5   You hem me in, behind and before,
       and lay your hand upon me.
6   Such knowledge is too wonderful for me;
       it is high; I cannot attain it.

7   Where shall I go from your Spirit?
       Or where shall I flee from your presence?
8   If I ascend to heaven, you are there!
       If I make my bed in Sheol, you are there!
9   If I take the wings of the morning
       and dwell in the uttermost parts of the sea,
10   even there your hand shall lead me,
       and your right hand shall hold me.
11   If I say, "Surely the darkness shall cover me,
       and the light about me be night,"
12   even the darkness is not dark to you;
       the night is bright as the day,
       for darkness is as light with you.

13   For you formed my inward parts;
        you knitted me together in my mother's womb.
14   I praise you, for I am fearfully and wonderfully made.
        Wonderful are your works;
           my soul knows it very well.
15   My frame was not hidden from you,
        when I was being made in secret,
           intricately woven in the depths of the earth.
16   Your eyes saw my unformed substance;
        in your book were written, every one of them,
           the days that were formed for me,
           when as yet there was none of them.

17   How precious to me are your thoughts, O God!
        How vast is the sum of them!
18   If I would count them, they are more than the sand.
        I awake, and I am still with you.

19   Oh that you would slay the wicked, O God!
        O men of blood, depart from me!
20   They speak against you with malicious intent;
        your enemies take your name in vain.
21   Do I not hate those who hate you, O Lord?
        And do I not loathe those who rise up against you?
22   I hate them with complete hatred;
        I count them my enemies.

23   Search me, O God, and know my heart!
        Try me and know my thoughts!
24   And see if there be any grievous way in me,
        and lead me in the way everlasting!

5

"But now that you have come to know God, or rather to be known by God . . ." (Gal. 4:9). In the New Testament letter to the Galatians, Paul seems almost to correct himself midthought, as if saying, "But now that you Galatians have come to know God—no, wait, the deeper truth is that *God* has come to know *you*." That blessed reality of being known by God is the sustained theme of Psalm 139.

Do you know God? Knowing God is a true and useful category for understanding your Christian experience. It is one the Bible itself uses, repeatedly; the purpose of life, after all, is "that we may *know him* who is true" (1 John 5:20). But our own human capacities do not exhaust what it means to be a child of God. "Such knowledge is too wonderful for me; it is high; I cannot attain it" (Ps. 139:6). The broader, deeper, wraparound category of life as the people of God is that we are known *by* him. Not only now, in our present, but way back when we were being formed in the womb, God knew us (v. 15). And he knows our future as well—every day of it (v. 16).

Do you feel alone? Unknown? Forgotten? Neglected? Sidelined? Marginalized? Remember who you are. If you are in Christ, the deepest reality of your existence is that God knows you. He knows every nook and cranny of your heart. He knows every failure, every fear. He understands you. He does not merely know *about* you. He knows *you*. He has pressed you into the inner recesses of his heart. Forgiven and adopted into his family by grace, you are loved by the Lord Jesus Christ with the very love with which the Father loves him (John 15:9).

PSALM 140

To the choirmaster. A Psalm of David.

1 Deliver me, O LORD, from evil men;
   preserve me from violent men,
2 who plan evil things in their heart
   and stir up wars continually.
3 They make their tongue sharp as a serpent's,
   and under their lips is the venom of asps.   *Selah*

4 Guard me, O LORD, from the hands of the wicked;
   preserve me from violent men,
   who have planned to trip up my feet.
5 The arrogant have hidden a trap for me,
   and with cords they have spread a net;
   beside the way they have set snares for me.   *Selah*

6 I say to the LORD, You are my God;
   give ear to the voice of my pleas for mercy, O LORD!
7 O LORD, my Lord, the strength of my salvation,
   you have covered my head in the day of battle.
8 Grant not, O LORD, the desires of the wicked;
   do not further their evil plot, or they will be exalted!
   Selah

9 As for the head of those who surround me,
   let the mischief of their lips overwhelm them!

10   Let burning coals fall upon them!
          Let them be cast into fire,
          into miry pits, no more to rise!
11   Let not the slanderer be established in the land;
          let evil hunt down the violent man speedily!

12   I know that the LORD will maintain the cause of the
          afflicted,
          and will execute justice for the needy.
13   Surely the righteous shall give thanks to your name;
          the upright shall dwell in your presence.

ॐ

Some of the Psalms can be quite difficult to reconcile with the teaching of Scripture to be kind to all and to love our enemies. How can the psalmist call for burning coals to fall upon the head of his adversary (v. 10)?

The key is to understand that the psalmist is not calling for unrighteous revenge as the boiling over of sheer emotional rage. The psalmist is rather calling for God to "execute justice" (v. 12). Most of this psalm recounts the unjust attacks of David's enemies. He is being wronged, and so he asks God to settle the score in due time. Notice also that David is asking *God* to settle the score. David is not taking matters into his own hands. In other words, he is living by faith.

How about you? How have you been wronged in your life? What memories pull at you, tempting you to slide into resentment, even now? Pray, with David, for the exacting of justice by God. Do not take matters into your own hands. Let God sort everything out at the end of time. He will settle accounts. Resist the urge to lash out in an attempt to even the score. Trust him instead.

After all, Jesus himself was sinned against unjustly. But he did not lash out. He was silent before his accusers (1 Pet. 2:23). It is our sacred privilege to follow in our Savior's footsteps.

PSALM 141

A Psalm of David.

1 O LORD, I call upon you; hasten to me!
     Give ear to my voice when I call to you!
2 Let my prayer be counted as incense before you,
     and the lifting up of my hands as the evening
          sacrifice!

3 Set a guard, O LORD, over my mouth;
     keep watch over the door of my lips!
4 Do not let my heart incline to any evil,
     to busy myself with wicked deeds
  in company with men who work iniquity,
     and let me not eat of their delicacies!

5 Let a righteous man strike me—it is a kindness;
     let him rebuke me—it is oil for my head;
     let my head not refuse it.
  Yet my prayer is continually against their evil deeds.
6 When their judges are thrown over the cliff,
     then they shall hear my words, for they are pleasant.

7   As when one plows and breaks up the earth,
        so shall our bones be scattered at the mouth of Sheol.

8   But my eyes are toward you, O God, my Lord;
        in you I seek refuge; leave me not defenseless!
9   Keep me from the trap that they have laid for me
        and from the snares of evildoers!
10 Let the wicked fall into their own nets,
        while I pass by safely.

∽

Surrounded by evil and enemies, David prays in this psalm that he would not compromise himself and fall into the very sins of which he is a victim. David asks God to sustain him and keep his own tongue from falling into the vicious speech of his adversaries (vv. 3–4).

We know the tug David is feeling. When slandered, when attacked, it feels natural to respond in kind—not only natural, but *right*. The urge to lock horns with our adversaries, even in subtle or underhanded ways, is strong. It feels impossible merely to overlook an insult, a misunderstanding, an accusation.

Left to ourselves, it is impossible. Only one healthy way forward exists: "My eyes are toward you, O God, my Lord; in you I seek refuge" (v. 8). David pulls his attention off of his accusers and puts them on the Lord. But what does this mean? It means to trust God himself to vindicate us in his own good way and time. We can either seek to justify ourselves now, intensifying the strife, or we can let God do so at the end of time, easing the strife in the present as we trust God in his rightful role as Judge.

We can look to God only to the degree that we remember that we ourselves deserve God's punishment and judgment—far more than our enemies realize! But Jesus Christ absorbed that punishment in our place. Liberated by this gospel of grace, we are free to look to God in our present interpersonal strife, even when we know ourselves to be wronged.

PSALM 142

A Maskil of David, when he was in the cave. A Prayer.

1   With my voice I cry out to the LORD;
      with my voice I plead for mercy to the LORD.
2   I pour out my complaint before him;
      I tell my trouble before him.

3   When my spirit faints within me,
      you know my way!
   In the path where I walk
      they have hidden a trap for me.
4   Look to the right and see:
      there is none who takes notice of me;
   no refuge remains to me;
      no one cares for my soul.

5   I cry to you, O LORD;
      I say, "You are my refuge,
      my portion in the land of the living."
6   Attend to my cry,
      for I am brought very low!

Deliver me from my persecutors,
  for they are too strong for me!
7 Bring me out of prison,
    that I may give thanks to your name!
The righteous will surround me,
  for you will deal bountifully with me.

∽

There is an artificial smileyness that can infect the church, in which honest complaints of the pains of life are not given room to be voiced before the Lord. We can easily paste over the hurts and challenges within us and placard before others an image of serenity that we know is not our actual lived reality. We can even feel guilty for expressing to the Lord our frustrations or hurts, as if we are not exercising enough faith.

The Bible knows of no such artificialities. While we do want to trust in the Lord's goodness and to praise him at all times, this does not mean pretending our life is tranquil when it is not. David said earlier in the Psalms, "I will bless the Lord at all times; his praise shall continually be in my mouth" (Ps. 34:1). But here in Psalm 142 the same man says, "I pour out my complaint before him; I tell my trouble before him" (v. 2). The book of Job is one book-long example of this single verse. The Bible encourages us to be honest with God.

When you feel like you are in "prison" (v. 7), take your anguish to the Lord. He can take it. He is not put off by it. His own Son Jesus Christ walked this earth and tasted deep anguish. The Bible tells us that Jesus was "made like his brothers in every respect" (Heb. 2:17) and can "sympathize with our weaknesses" because he "in every respect has been tempted as we are, yet without sin"

(Heb. 4:15). Go to God through the mediator, Jesus, who knows your anguish and has known even deeper anguish himself.

PSALM 143

A Psalm of David.

1   Hear my prayer, O Lord;
       give ear to my pleas for mercy!
       In your faithfulness answer me, in your righteousness!

2   Enter not into judgment with your servant,
       for no one living is righteous before you.

3   For the enemy has pursued my soul;
       he has crushed my life to the ground;
       he has made me sit in darkness like those long dead.

4   Therefore my spirit faints within me;
       my heart within me is appalled.

5   I remember the days of old;
       I meditate on all that you have done;
       I ponder the work of your hands.

6   I stretch out my hands to you;
       my soul thirsts for you like a parched land.   *Selah*

7   Answer me quickly, O Lord!
       My spirit fails!

Hide not your face from me,
    lest I be like those who go down to the pit.
8   Let me hear in the morning of your steadfast love,
       for in you I trust.
    Make me know the way I should go,
       for to you I lift up my soul.

9   Deliver me from my enemies, O LORD!
       I have fled to you for refuge.
10   Teach me to do your will,
       for you are my God!
    Let your good Spirit lead me
       on level ground!

11   For your name's sake, O LORD, preserve my life!
       In your righteousness bring my soul out of trouble!
12   And in your steadfast love you will cut off my enemies,
       and you will destroy all the adversaries of my soul,
       for I am your servant.

§

The German reformer Martin Luther wrote, "To those who believe in Christ, there are no works so bad as to accuse and condemn us, but again, there are no works so good that they could save and defend us." One of the central battles of the Christian life is to believe this. As we move through life, aware of our many frailties and failures, the message of the gospel insists that God delights to cover all of this weakness. And as we detect within ourselves the constant temptation to seek to strengthen our standing before God through virtue and obedience, we equally remember the gospel and its insistence that nothing good in us could aid our status before God.

This psalm is written out of profound understanding of the human heart and the deep need each of us has for the grace of God. "Enter not into judgment with your servant," we pray with the psalmist, "for no one living is righteous before you" (v. 2). The world is not divided between the righteous and the unrighteous. *No one* is righteous. Rather, the world is divided between those who know they are unrighteous and those who do not. For those who know it, hope exists: a righteousness from God. The psalmist reflects on God's "steadfast love" (vv. 8, 12). He trusts in the Lord to deliver him from the "adversaries of [his] soul" (v. 12).

Although the psalmist saw only shadows, we see the true substance of how God answers such prayers from those who know they are not righteous: he does so in Jesus Christ, the righteous one, who lived the life we should have lived and died the death we deserved to die, to bring us to God (1 Pet. 3:18). In Christ, we are righteous with a status earned and given to us irrespective of what we bring to the table (2 Cor. 5:21). All we need to offer is our need.

PSALM 144

Of David.

1   Blessed be the Lᴏʀᴅ, my rock,
     who trains my hands for war,
     and my fingers for battle;
2   he is my steadfast love and my fortress,
     my stronghold and my deliverer,
   my shield and he in whom I take refuge,
     who subdues peoples under me.

3   O Lᴏʀᴅ, what is man that you regard him,
     or the son of man that you think of him?
4   Man is like a breath;
     his days are like a passing shadow.

5   Bow your heavens, O Lᴏʀᴅ, and come down!
     Touch the mountains so that they smoke!
6   Flash forth the lightning and scatter them;
     send out your arrows and rout them!
7   Stretch out your hand from on high;
     rescue me and deliver me from the many waters,
     from the hand of foreigners,
8   whose mouths speak lies
     and whose right hand is a right hand of falsehood.

9   I will sing a new song to you, O God;
     upon a ten-stringed harp I will play to you,

10	who gives victory to kings,
	who rescues David his servant from the cruel sword.
11	Rescue me and deliver me
	from the hand of foreigners,
	whose mouths speak lies
	and whose right hand is a right hand of falsehood.

12	May our sons in their youth
	be like plants full grown,
	our daughters like corner pillars
	cut for the structure of a palace;
13	may our granaries be full,
	providing all kinds of produce;
	may our sheep bring forth thousands
	and ten thousands in our fields;
14	may our cattle be heavy with young,
	suffering no mishap or failure in bearing;
	may there be no cry of distress in our streets!
15	Blessed are the people to whom such blessings fall!
	Blessed are the people whose God is the Lord!

℘

The prayer of Psalm 144 expresses what it looks like to take refuge in God. He is our "fortress," our "stronghold," our "deliverer," our "shield" (v. 2). The rest of the psalm goes on to exult in God and his sovereign care of his beloved people as they face enemies (vv. 3–11) and raise families (vv. 12–15).

What does all of this mean? Many times the Psalms describe God as a "refuge." Consider this image—what is it saying about the Lord? That he is our deepest trust, our true security, our impenetrable place of safety. As we journey through this fallen world, we often feel deeply vulnerable. Friendships dissolve. Finances evaporate. Marriages sour. Children rebel. Work frustrates. Our bodies break down. Enemies accuse.

This psalm insists that life with God does not mean merely believing on paper various doctrines while at the same time channeling all of our old hopes and dreams into the things of this world. Nothing in this vacillating world can be a final refuge for us. Rather, our only safety is to channel our deepest trust into God himself—to make him our refuge, our stronghold, our shield.

And in Jesus we see that God has done so by his own initiative. For we are righteous in Christ. All it takes for God to be our fortress is for us to let him be so. To trust him. To turn, once more, to him. To humble ourselves and let him deliver us.

PSALM 145

A Song of Praise. Of David.

1   I will extol you, my God and King,
        and bless your name forever and ever.
2   Every day I will bless you
        and praise your name forever and ever.
3   Great is the LORD, and greatly to be praised,
        and his greatness is unsearchable.

4   One generation shall commend your works to another,
        and shall declare your mighty acts.

5   On the glorious splendor of your majesty,
        and on your wondrous works, I will meditate.
6   They shall speak of the might of your awesome deeds,
        and I will declare your greatness.
7   They shall pour forth the fame of your abundant
          goodness
        and shall sing aloud of your righteousness.

8   The LORD is gracious and merciful,
        slow to anger and abounding in steadfast love.
9   The LORD is good to all,
        and his mercy is over all that he has made.

10   All your works shall give thanks to you, O LORD,
        and all your saints shall bless you!
11   They shall speak of the glory of your kingdom
        and tell of your power,
12   to make known to the children of man your mighty
          deeds,
        and the glorious splendor of your kingdom.
13   Your kingdom is an everlasting kingdom,
        and your dominion endures throughout all
          generations.

     [The LORD is faithful in all his words
        and kind in all his works.]
14   The LORD upholds all who are falling
        and raises up all who are bowed down.
15   The eyes of all look to you,
        and you give them their food in due season.
16   You open your hand;
        you satisfy the desire of every living thing.

17   The LORD is righteous in all his ways
         and kind in all his works.
18   The LORD is near to all who call on him,
         to all who call on him in truth.
19   He fulfills the desire of those who fear him;
         he also hears their cry and saves them.
20   The LORD preserves all who love him,
         but all the wicked he will destroy.

21   My mouth will speak the praise of the LORD,
         and let all flesh bless his holy name forever and ever.

$\backsim$

Consider the great variety of words this psalm uses for praising God—"extol" (v. 1), "bless" (v. 1), "praise" (v. 2), "commend" (v. 4), "speak of" (v. 6), "pour forth" (v. 7), "sing aloud" (v. 7), "give thanks" (v. 10), "make known" (v. 12). As the psalmist ponders the Lord's lavish goodness, praise pours out. He cannot hold it in.

Praise of God is not meant to be something we drag ourselves to do. It is not a mechanical exercise done to fulfill a duty. It is rather the natural response to a glimpse of God. "The LORD is gracious and merciful" (v. 8). "The LORD upholds all who are falling and raises up all who are bowed down" (v. 14). Do you flinch at these statements, certain that your life is too difficult, too far beyond the reach of God's kindness? Reconsider. Ponder the proof God has given us.

The grace of God that this psalm extols burst into human history in the form of a man two thousand years ago. This man went to a cross and rose again. He secured God's mercy for *you*, despite the fact that he had every reason not to be good to you.

The ministry of Jesus on behalf of sinners and sufferers means you are safe. In Christ, you cannot lose. Even your pain will ultimately be transformed into your own glory and triumph (Rom. 8:18–21).

Let his goodness wash afresh into your heart. Let your lips praise him accordingly.

PSALM 146

1   Praise the LORD!
     Praise the LORD, O my soul!
2   I will praise the LORD as long as I live;
       I will sing praises to my God while I have my being.

3   Put not your trust in princes,
       in a son of man, in whom there is no salvation.
4   When his breath departs, he returns to the earth;
       on that very day his plans perish.

5   Blessed is he whose help is the God of Jacob,
       whose hope is in the LORD his God,
6   who made heaven and earth,
       the sea, and all that is in them,
   who keeps faith forever;
7   who executes justice for the oppressed,
       who gives food to the hungry.

The LORD sets the prisoners free;
8   the LORD opens the eyes of the blind.
    The LORD lifts up those who are bowed down;
        the LORD loves the righteous.
9   The LORD watches over the sojourners;
        he upholds the widow and the fatherless,
        but the way of the wicked he brings to ruin.

10   The LORD will reign forever,
        your God, O Zion, to all generations.
    Praise the LORD!

∽

The comfort of this psalm is in its contrast between human transience and divine power. Do not trust in earthly leaders, the psalmist says (v. 3), because they will soon pass away into the oblivion of human history (v. 4). The Lord, on the other hand, is the one "who made heaven and earth, the sea, and all that is in them" (v. 6).

But it is more than raw power that the psalmist reminds us of. It is also the Lord's heart for the weak and weary: "The LORD sets the prisoners free; the LORD opens the eyes of the blind. The LORD lifts up those who are bowed down. . . . He upholds the widow and the fatherless" (vv. 7–9).

When perfect power meets perfect compassion, we are free to fall into the arms of the Lord in quiet trust. He is powerful, and thus *able* to deliver us; he is loving, and thus *wants* to. This is the best of all possible worlds. This is a God who can be counted on unflinchingly. And we know for certain that this is who God is—both omnipotent and omni-compassionate—because of the incarnation. In Jesus we see God the Son triumphing over sin and death and hell with utter triumph and power, yet equally we see matchless love pouring out of heaven's heart.

Are you in distress? Are you overwhelmed? Marinate your heart in the power and love of the Savior.

PSALM 147

1 Praise the LORD!
For it is good to sing praises to our God;
    for it is pleasant, and a song of praise is fitting.
2 The LORD builds up Jerusalem;
    he gathers the outcasts of Israel.
3 He heals the brokenhearted
    and binds up their wounds.
4 He determines the number of the stars;
    he gives to all of them their names.
5 Great is our Lord, and abundant in power;
    his understanding is beyond measure.
6 The LORD lifts up the humble;
    he casts the wicked to the ground.

7 Sing to the LORD with thanksgiving;
    make melody to our God on the lyre!
8 He covers the heavens with clouds;
    he prepares rain for the earth;
    he makes grass grow on the hills.

9   He gives to the beasts their food,
       and to the young ravens that cry.
10   His delight is not in the strength of the horse,
       nor his pleasure in the legs of a man,
11   but the LORD takes pleasure in those who fear him,
       in those who hope in his steadfast love.

12   Praise the LORD, O Jerusalem!
       Praise your God, O Zion!
13   For he strengthens the bars of your gates;
       he blesses your children within you.
14   He makes peace in your borders;
       he fills you with the finest of the wheat.
15   He sends out his command to the earth;
       his word runs swiftly.
16   He gives snow like wool;
       he scatters frost like ashes.
17   He hurls down his crystals of ice like crumbs;
       who can stand before his cold?
18   He sends out his word, and melts them;
       he makes his wind blow and the waters flow.
19   He declares his word to Jacob,
       his statutes and rules to Israel.
20   He has not dealt thus with any other nation;
       they do not know his rules.
       Praise the LORD!

⸎

This psalm beckons to us to praise the Lord for his wide-ranging care for all of creation, especially his people. Consider just one strand of this psalm—God's concern for and attention to the downcast. "He gathers the outcasts of Israel. He heals the brokenhearted and binds up their wounds" (vv. 2–3); "the LORD lifts up the humble" (v. 6). The "humble" here are the afflicted, those who have been laid low by difficult circumstances.

The God of the Bible is not a God who delights to give us orders and then stands back waiting for us to execute, like a scrutinizing athletic coach. The God of the Bible finds his deepest delight in meeting the needs of those in desperate straits. Elsewhere in Scripture we are told that God dwells way up high in heaven, and also way down low with the destitute (Isa. 57:15; cf. 66:1–2). To whom does God draw near? The brokenhearted. To whom is the Lord most strongly, irresistibly pulled? The outcasts. The losers. Those rejected by the world. Those of apparent insignificance by the world's standards.

After all, when God himself came to earth in human form, he himself "had no form or majesty that we should look at him, and no beauty that we should desire him" (Isa. 53:2). This is God's way. The world runs after strength, slickness, outward appearance, impressiveness. God runs to the brokenhearted.

PSALM 148

1   Praise the LORD!
Praise the LORD from the heavens;
    praise him in the heights!
2   Praise him, all his angels;
    praise him, all his hosts!

3   Praise him, sun and moon,
    praise him, all you shining stars!
4   Praise him, you highest heavens,
    and you waters above the heavens!

5   Let them praise the name of the LORD!
    For he commanded and they were created.
6   And he established them forever and ever;
    he gave a decree, and it shall not pass away.

7   Praise the LORD from the earth,
    you great sea creatures and all deeps,
8   fire and hail, snow and mist,
    stormy wind fulfilling his word!

9   Mountains and all hills,
    fruit trees and all cedars!
10   Beasts and all livestock,
    creeping things and flying birds!

11	Kings of the earth and all peoples,
	princes and all rulers of the earth!
12	Young men and maidens together,
	old men and children!

13	Let them praise the name of the LORD,
	for his name alone is exalted;
	his majesty is above earth and heaven.
14	He has raised up a horn for his people,
	praise for all his saints,
	for the people of Israel who are near to him.
	Praise the LORD!

∽

As the book of Psalms (also called the "Psalter") nears its end, a resounding note of triumphant praise to God is swelling. More and more, the final psalms lift our hearts to praise the Lord, adoring him and giving him thanks.

Psalm 148 is striking in that it calls the universe itself into this chorus of praise. Not only are the angelic beings to worship him (v. 2), but also the "sun and moon" (v. 3), the "shining stars" (v. 3), the "highest heavens" and upper stratosphere (v. 4), the "great sea creatures" (v. 7), the "fire and hail, snow and mist" (v. 8), the mountains and hills (v. 9), the animals and birds (v. 10)—all these are to praise the Lord.

How? How does a blue whale praise God? How does a cardinal praise him? Falling snow? The moon at night? Here is how: *by being themselves.* By doing what God created them to do (v. 6). A dolphin praises the Lord by swimming, leaping, frolicking, hunting, eating—by being a dolphin.

The world in which we live is filled with inexhaustible detail and glory and beauty and diversity. Who would think that the same Being could have thought up the lion *and* the flamingo? The snowflake *and* the sun? Such creations honor their Creator by doing what he decreed them to do.

PSALM 149

1 Praise the LORD!
  Sing to the LORD a new song,
     his praise in the assembly of the godly!
2 Let Israel be glad in his Maker;
     let the children of Zion rejoice in their King!
3 Let them praise his name with dancing,
     making melody to him with tambourine and lyre!
4 For the LORD takes pleasure in his people;
     he adorns the humble with salvation.
5 Let the godly exult in glory;
     let them sing for joy on their beds.
6 Let the high praises of God be in their throats
     and two-edged swords in their hands,
7 to execute vengeance on the nations
     and punishments on the peoples,
8 to bind their kings with chains
     and their nobles with fetters of iron,

9   to execute on them the judgment written!
        This is honor for all his godly ones.
    Praise the LORD!

∽

The previous psalm spoke of creation's role in praising God and executing his decrees. This psalm now turns to speak of his *people's* role in praising him and executing his decrees.

The arresting reminder of this psalm is of how low God's people have been and often are, combined with how high a role God has destined for them. On the one hand, "The LORD takes pleasure in his people; he adorns the humble [that is, the lowly] with salvation" (v. 4). God loves helping the helpless. He delights to draw near to the destitute. It is who he is.

On the other hand, consider the lofty calling he has ultimately laid on his people: "to execute vengeance on the nations and punishments on the peoples, to bind their kings with chains and their nobles with fetters of iron, to execute on them the judgment written!" (vv. 7–9). Truly, as the next line reads, "This is honor for all his godly ones" (v. 9).

As Christians, we often speak of God's judgment at the end of time, and so we should. But God does not execute this judgment on his own; he summons his people into that judgment. The New Testament even says that we will judge not only the world but also the angels (1 Cor. 6:1–3). Consider who God is in light of this astonishing reality: God takes what is low and ignored by the world and, as they despair of themselves and cast themselves on Christ for mercy, uses them to judge the cosmos, executing judgment on the kings and rulers of this world. "Praise the LORD!" (Ps. 149:9).

PSALM 150

1   Praise the LORD!
Praise God in his sanctuary;
    praise him in his mighty heavens!
2   Praise him for his mighty deeds;
    praise him according to his excellent greatness!

3   Praise him with trumpet sound;
    praise him with lute and harp!
4   Praise him with tambourine and dance;
    praise him with strings and pipe!
5   Praise him with sounding cymbals;
    praise him with loud clashing cymbals!
6   Let everything that has breath praise the LORD!
Praise the LORD!

∽

The Psalter ends on a triumphant note of praise: "Let everything that has breath praise the LORD!" (v. 6). The picture given by this psalm is one of complete celebration of who the Lord is and what he does. Instruments are played and the psalmist even calls for dancing (v. 4). As the Psalter comes to an end, we are being led as the readers of Scripture to ponder the character of God and the extent of his great grace toward his people, as reflected throughout the entire Psalter.

Given the God who is portrayed throughout the Psalms—a God who is merciful and gracious, a God who will not ignore the needy or helpless, a God who hates wickedness and will execute perfect justice one day, a God who heals the brokenhearted, a God who is a refuge and shelter for his troubled people, a God who understands his people's internal highs and lows of living in this fallen world—what can we do but offer our lives and hearts unreservedly to him? He is our Shepherd, our Friend, our Deliverer.

And in his Son Jesus Christ, he has proven himself as tangibly and certainly as possible to be our Shepherd, Friend, and Deliverer. The God of the Psalms—the God who meets the desperate, the God who hears the distraught—took on flesh and blood. He came for us. He came for you. This is who he is.

Praise the Lord.